# Sport and the
# Neoliberal University

## The American Campus

*Harold S. Wechsler, Series Editor*

The books in the American Campus series explore recent developments and public-policy issues in higher education in the United States. Topics of interest include access to college, and college affordability; college retention, tenure, and academic freedom; campus labor; the expansion and evolution of administrative posts and salaries; the crisis in the humanities and the arts; the corporate university and for-profit colleges; online education; controversy in sport programs; and gender, ethnic, racial, religious, and class dynamics and diversity. Books feature scholarship from a variety of disciplines in the humanities and social sciences.

Vicki L. Baker, Laura G. Lunsford, and Meghan J. Pifer, *Developing Faculty in Liberal Arts Colleges: Aligning Individual Needs and Organizational Goals*

W. Carson Byrd, *Poison in the Ivy: Race Relations and the Reproduction of Inequality on Elite College Campuses*

Jillian M. Duquaine-Watson, *Mothering by Degrees: Single Mothers and the Pursuit of Postsecondary Education*

Scott Frickel, Mathieu Albert, and Barbara Prainsack, eds., *Investigating Interdisciplinary Collaboration: Theory and Practice across Disciplines*

Gordon Hutner and Feisal G. Mohamed, eds., *A New Deal for the Humanities: Liberal Arts and the Future of Public Higher Education*

Adrianna Kezar and Daniel Maxey, eds., *Envisioning the Faculty for the Twenty-First Century: Moving to a Mission-Oriented and Learner-Centered Model*

Ryan King-White, ed., *Sport and the Neoliberal University: Profit, Politics, and Pedagogy.*

Dana M. Malone, *From Single to Serious: Relationships, Gender, and Sexuality on American Evangelical Campuses*

# Sport and the Neoliberal University

## Profit, Politics, and Pedagogy

### EDITED BY RYAN KING-WHITE

RUTGERS UNIVERSITY PRESS

NEW BRUNSWICK, CAMDEN, AND NEWARK, NEW JERSEY, AND LONDON

Library of Congress Cataloging-in-Publication Data

Names: King-White, Ryan, 1979– editor.
Title: Sport and the neoliberal university : profit, politics, and pedagogy / Edited by
    Ryan King-White.
Description: New Brunswick, New Jersey : Rutgers University Press, 2018. | Series:
    The American campus | Includes bibliographical references and index.
Identifiers: LCCN 2017015406| ISBN 9780813587714 (hardback) | ISBN 9780813587707
    (paperback) | ISBN 9780813587721 (ebook (epub)) | ISBN 9780813587738
    (ebook (web PDF))
Subjects: LCSH: College sports—Economic aspects—United States. | College sports—
    Moral and ethical aspects—United States. | Neoliberalism—United States. | National
    Collegiate Athletic Association. | Universities and colleges—United States—Finance.
    | Education, Higher—Aims and objectives—United States. | BISAC: EDUCATION /
    Higher. | SPORTS & RECREATION / Sociology of Sports. | BUSINESS & ECONOMICS /
    Nonprofit Organizations & Charities. | POLITICAL SCIENCE / Public Policy /
    Economic Policy.
Classification: LCC GV351 .S68 2018 | DDC 796.04/3—dc23
LC record available at https://lccn.loc.gov/2017015406

A British Cataloging-in-Publication record for this book is available
from the British Library.

⊗ The paper used in this publication meets the requirements
of the American National Standard for Information Sciences—
Permanence of Paper for Printed Library Materials, ANSI Z39.48–1992.

www.rutgersuniversitypress.org
Manufactured in the United States of America

I dedicate this book to my patient and loving wife Meghan,
as well as our three children, Colin, Meredith, and Evelyn.

# CONTENTS

## PART II
## Emerging Concerns

# Sport and the
# Neoliberal University

# Introduction

## Contexts and Constraints in Contemporary Intercollegiate Athletics

RYAN KING-WHITE

On November 23, 1984, Boston College Eagles (BC) dueled with the University of Miami–Florida Hurricanes (UM) in a highly competitive and entertaining football game. Down 45 to 41 with 6 seconds remaining on the clock, Doug Flutie—star quarterback for BC—completed a last-second "Hail Mary" touchdown pass to Gerard Phelan that gave their team a memorable 47–45 victory. The oft-celebrated play helped catapult BC's football team to a 10–2 season record, and a #5 national ranking as tabulated by the Associated Press. Flutie—whose popularity skyrocketed nationally—received the Heisman Memorial Trophy, an award that "annually recognizes the outstanding college football player whose performance best exhibits the pursuit of excellence with integrity" (Heisman.com, 2016, ¶1). Coincidentally, it was also during Flutie's last two years on campus that freshman applications to BC increased by 16% (1984) and 12% (1985), respectively.

Seventeen years later, *USA Today* reported that it had become "widely known in admissions circles, (that) the Flutie Factor refers to a surge in applications to Boston College after its quarterback, Doug Flutie, made his fabled touchdown pass to beat Miami in 1984" (Marklein, 2001, ¶2). This relative explosion in applicants is an administrator's dream, because with more students to choose from the admissions department presumably can accept students more selectively (read: admit applicants with better standardized test scores to secure a higher national academic rating). Doug Chung (2013) conducted research on the "Flutie Factor," and concluded that major on-field improvement (three more wins than the past season in football) leads to significantly more applicants in the following year. Chung also asserts that administrators should "treat athletic success and its cumulative performance as a stock of goodwill that decays over time, but augments with current performance" (2013, p. 680). Thus, to follow this line of thinking to its seemingly logical conclusion, a good athletics program, team, and high-profile player can and do lead to a more prestigious academic profile for an institution (see DeLuca and Maddox, Chapter 3 of this text).

Since the inception of the "Flutie Effect" phenomenon, many administrators have proclaimed that intercollegiate athletics are key areas that help an institution improve its academic mission. Administrators do so by assuming that because such a response "happened" at BC—and is supplemented by careless reading of research such as Chung's (who very clearly writes about the short-lived nature of potential benefits of the Flutie Effect)—then *if* high-level success and award-winning performance in football and men's basketball took place at *their* institution, then the response from potential applicants would be similar or better. This value system has been used as justification for (athletic) administrators to spend billions of publicly and privately financed dollars on massive upgrades to stadia (Robinett, 2014); salaries and homes for high-profile coaches (Scarborough, 2014); majestic workout facilities with video-game consoles, barber shops, dedicated athletic training, hot and cold tubs in locker rooms (Uthman, 2013); athletics-only dormitories; tutoring; and private jets for traveling to visit recruits (Norlander, 2014)—all with the hope that this would be *the year* for each university making these purchases to finally receive its return on investment.

In an interview about his research, Chung states that the "Flutie Miracle" was the first American football game he had ever watched. "I saw this game live on TV with my father when I was growing up in Kansas," he says, "and have been a big fan ever since" (Silverthorne, 2013, ¶13). Similarly, although I had been exposed to American football prior to the BC–UM matchup, this was the first game that I had the attention span to watch from start to finish with my father. I rooted for the Hurricanes that day, in part enamored by the bold orange and green color scheme making up their uniforms, the "smoke screen" that their players ran through during pre-game introductions, their exciting and brash style of play, and—perhaps mostly—because my dad was rooting for BC. Tears streamed down my five-year-old cheeks after the incredible throw and catch were followed by ad nauseam replays on our television into the night (my dad taped the replay on our Betamax). What for many is an iconic play for the ages, for me was one of the worst sport-spectating moments of my youth.

Interestingly then, a formative moment for Chung leading him to study intercollegiate athletic success as positive for an institution, might have served as a similar impetus for me to seek alternative questions. For example, although the team fell short that day, UM then won four national titles over an 18-year span, and BC never again reached the year-end ranking heights achieved under Flutie. Seeing matters from this long-term view provides a different perspective. Rather than take the "Flutie Effect" at face value, I am inclined to ask the question: What actually did happen at BC after the "Flutie Effect"?

Tracing statistics through BC's self-published annual fact books reveals quite interesting results regarding the number of applications submitted to the school over time. Indeed, applications increased from 12,414 to 14,398 to 16,163 while Flutie was on campus, then did not again reach those numbers until 1995—the year after its football team went 7–4-1 (down from 9 to 3 the year prior) and the men's basketball record was a paltry 9–19 (*Boston College Fact Book* 1989–1990, 1995–1996, 2004–2005). Over the next 20 years (1996–2016), application numbers ranged from 16,501 (1996) a year after the football team struggled to a 4–8 record and men's basketball was 19–11 to 34,061 (2012) after football was again 4–8 and men's basketball fell to 9–22 (*Boston College Fact Book* 2004–2005, 2014–2015). A reasonable person could look at these numbers and conclude that attributing a significant application increase or decrease to intercollegiate athletic success or lack thereof makes little more than correlative sense. It would be more logical to suggest that—given these data points—the increase in applicants to BC during the time that Doug Flutie was on campus could be attributed to mere happenstance, because similar application increases at BC happened following mediocre athletic performances.

What's more is the fact that—even if the "Flutie Effect" was real—college athletics is a zero-sum game, whereby hundreds of universities compete for finite resources (including high-quality athletes, wins, year-end awards, and championships). As such, directing additional funding to athletics to attempt to enhance institutional reputation is simply gambling. Worse, the long-term maintenance prospects for success are even more unlikely, and it is altogether unclear whether an institution's academic reputation is positively or negatively affected by athletic performance. Witness the fact that "big-time" schools such as Alabama, Ohio State, Michigan, North Carolina, Tennessee, Notre Dame, Florida State, Texas, Oklahoma, and Nebraska were unexceptional for long stretches on the field and basketball court over the past few decades. Yet, they continued to serve as prominent institutions for high school students to apply to during both their strong and fallow athletic years. Conversely, schools such as George Mason University, Wichita State University, Butler University, Davidson College, Florida Gulf Coast University, Northern Illinois University, Boise State University, and the University of Central Florida have experienced great on-court and on-field success, but do not appear to have turned into flagship institutions academically.

Why then, would any administrator (admissions, athletic, or other) want to chase the "Flutie Effect"? One key answer is that despite it being fairly easy to dismiss the "Flutie Effect" as a coincidence, the concept still exists as a *public truth* with (athletic) administrators, admissions personnel, and the general public. For example, chair of the Knight Commission and former University System of Maryland Chancellor Brit Kirwan suggests that, although he has been a part of the college athletics "machine," he is uneasy about the fact that "higher education presidents, governing boards, and institutions have lost control of intercollegiate athletics" (Woodhouse, 2015, ¶11). Thus, it is an endeavor of mine to ask questions about *core assumptions* and *public truths* as they pertain to how intercollegiate athletics "benefit" campuses around the country. In so doing I hope to add to, alter, and reframe current public knowledge in ways that are transformative, hopeful, and socially just. This book is a start.

## A Note on Neoliberalism

Throughout the book, a term that the reader constantly encounters is "neoliberalism." Although the word exists on the fringe in popular media, its use is prevalent in academia. My stated aim for this book is for it to supplement current understanding, and to point to areas for academic research on sport and physical culture as it pertains to the university—and for the book to still be appealing to a readership that does not often encounter such language. Thus, although some might label the term "neoliberalism" as being "jargon" germane to academic writing, this section helps to clarify what neoliberalism is in such a way as to provide reasoning for why the authors have chosen to use it.

Put simply, neoliberalism is the dominant economic, social, and political ideology found in the United States and throughout much of the developed and developing world for the past few decades. Following David Harvey (2005), neoliberalism emerged in response to a "global phase of stagflation that lasted through much of the 1970s" (Harvey, 2005, at 12) resulting from the slow breakdown of *embedded liberalism* (a post-depression free-market economy with heavy social-welfare provisions aimed to protect the public from wild market swings). Essentially, the United States was economically prosperous in the post–World War II era while two chief global economic rivals—Germany and Japan—were busy rebuilding from the conflict. By the 1970s, the two countries could effectively challenge the United States (and other developed countries) in the global marketplace, and this—coupled with skyrocketing oil prices, rising unemployment, and inflation—led to an economic crisis that posed no easy answers. Thus, the social-contract policies (social security, welfare, heavily regulated industries, and labor protection) that dominated most political discourse and decision making in the United States during the *embedded liberalism* era (from FDR to Richard Nixon) were struggling mightily in rapidly globalizing times.

American political and corporate leaders as well as other economic elites were left seeking a new way forward for the country. For these policy makers: "[Arguments] ranged behind social democracy and central planning on the one hand . . . and the interests of all those concerned with liberating corporate and business power and re-establishing market freedoms on the other. By the mid-1970s, the interests of the latter group came to the fore." (Harvey, 2005, at 13)

Thus, under the presidential direction of Jimmy Carter and, especially, Ronald Reagan through Barack Obama, a new form of liberal democracy ("neoliberalism") became the new normal. It was *common sense* in the United States for national policies to support free trade and those with an "entrepreneurial spirit" via a decline in tax rates on the rich, opening global markets, crushing labor unions, seeking to cut and demonize those using social-welfare provisions, and diminishing funding to public spaces and programming (such as park and recreation programs).

The paradigm shift has created an atmosphere of policy making that continues to move away from the state providing safety nets and public programming for the many in the United States, and instead shifting toward corporations and economic elites as a means to allow the free market to solve the problems posed by stagflation. Inspired by the belief that laissez-faire capitalism provides individual rights and freedoms, American political leaders (particularly conservatives and libertarians, but also some contemporary liberals) have put in place policies, practices, and laws that have undercut social contracts between the state and its people and given rise to the *radical individual*. The usual understanding here is that the individual will operate solely in her or his own self-interest and therefore will succeed or fail based on her or his own merits. Though there exist countless critiques about the devastating effects born from this ideology, beyond the simple notion that most humans are inherently *social* beings—thus not at all radically individual—neoliberalism still has an incredible influence on the ways we experience late capitalism in the United States (e.g., Giroux, 2003, 2007, 2012; Grossberg, 2005; Harvey, 2005 among many others).

Shifting to this corporate-friendly logic has also radically changed the ways Americans imagine solutions to these social ills. Henry Giroux argues:

> neoliberalism's contempt for the social is now matched by an utter disdain for the common good. Public spheres that once encouraged progressive ideas, enlightened social policies, democratic values, critical dialogue and exchange have been replaced by corporate entities whose ultimate fidelity is to increasing profit margins and producing a vast commercial culture. (2015, ¶3)

Thus, taking massive risks with public funding on things such as "revenue-producing" intercollegiate sport; sport stadia financing; and cities agreeing to low-cost, low-, and no-tax deals that have a history of not paying off with corporations and entrepreneurs, has become the norm in American society—and to question its ability to turn a profit or serve as a public "good" is tantamount to being un-American (*see* Wiest & King-White, 2013).

Politicians, city leaders, businesspeople, and citizens wedding themselves to neoliberalism has resulted in a growing divide between those who have access to basic social provisions such as food, physical activity, educational, and—by extension—occupational opportunities (Navarro, 2007). Although this reality runs counter to neoliberalism's stated purpose that it allows for the radical individual to rise and fall based on his or her own merits, it does not stop prevailing discourses from blaming the individual for systemic problems. Neoliberalism's confounding beauty is that if it is always the individual's fault, then there exists no need to improve upon the system. Will Leitch (2015) has suggested that this neoliberal reality means we have moved into the post-truth era where empty promises outweigh any actual substance to claims of economic prosperity.

This does not mean that neoliberalism has never run into some limits. As Newman and Giardina (2011) foretold, the business-friendly climate allowed for global expansion that was too rapid for any nation-state to keep up with. Millions of outsourced jobs have decimated domestic labor, the push for capital accumulation and a declining tax base have wrecked American cities—to say nothing of suburban and rural municipalities where people are now left jobless with outdated skill-sets, and no hope for a way out or up. Neoliberalism's great failure has paved the way for something far more sinister. For, once again, the public is at an impasse about how to proceed.

On one hand, the people of America could stay the course and continue down the path laid out by neoliberalism; conversely, they could seek an alternative. As the recent presidential election results indicate, desperate for a magical change in fortunes, the United States citizenry has turned to a reality-television star—or as actor/comedian David Chappelle says, "an Internet troll"—Donald Trump to lead us forward. In this new era of Brexit-like isolationism, proto-fascism, authoritarianism, and post-truth (Davies, 2016) Trump's unbelievable policies—because they are, in fact, impossible to achieve—serve as a logical extension to the worst that neoliberalism has to offer. There literally is no way to "drain the swamp," further deregulate markets, reduce taxes, build a $30-billion wall between the United States and Mexico, invest in infrastructure (such as roads, bridges, and schools) and the military, increase good-paying blue-collar jobs, deport Muslims and other (illegal) immigrants, and eradicate the national debt as Trump has promised to do.

The situation is even more ghastly than "politics as usual." Trump is a "politician" that garnered votes by pandering to liberals and conservatives in ways that are fantastically mutually exclusive. False narratives, disillusionment, and despair are what characterize contemporary America. To fix our country's problems, we now have turned to a person and a cabinet that have abused neoliberalism to their own ends. What the future has in store is indeed cloudy, and it is up to the American people to begin to demand a turn back to reality.

## So What Did—and Does—This Mean for the American University and the Role of Sport within It?

Higher education in the United States, particularly at public institutions, often is thought of as one of the last bastions of free-flowing information, transparent leadership, and democratic power structure. In actuality, however, this too is a myth.

The emergence of neoliberalism as a political-economic governing formation—one that has developed over the last 45 years and transformed the social realties of most developed nation-states—has not left the university untouched. Rather, it has created an educational environment and administrative structure that more closely represents a private enterprise—one dominated by a focus on account-ability, efficiency, strategic planning, and managerialism (*see* Shore, 2008). The primary result of this transformation is that students have come to be regarded as customers, academic researchers are thought of as entrepreneurs compet-ing for external grant funding, and the university itself more closely resembles a business model than an institute of higher learning (*see* Giroux, 2011). Scholars ranging from Bok (2003) to Twitchell (2004) have argued that, because of this turn, the primary function of the university—education—has taken a backseat to growing enrollment by focusing on amenities such as luxury housing options, recreation spaces, online course offerings, and, for purposes in this book, erect-ing or hosting private and corporately sponsored multimillion-dollar sport sta-dia, buildings, and events. Universities thus have become veritable all-inclusive enclaves for 18- to 22-year-olds to congregate and have "experiences" rather than participate in the never-ending critical search for knowledge. In particular, Gaye Tuchman's *Wannabe U* (2005), and Jennifer Washburn's *University Inc.: The Corpo-rate Corruption of Higher Education* (2005), have pointed out the increasing need for universities to "look the part" rather than meet educational ends.

This book adds to this growing conversation on the corporatization and commercialization of intercollegiate athletics, a conversation that is inherently conflicted due to the social location of college sports in the national imagina-tion. There exists a legion of (athletic) administrators, fans, alumni, and fac-ulty who wax poetic about the "benefits" that having numerous athletic teams brings to colleges and universities. Conversely, there exists a small but growing element in the United States that has come to question the efficacy of state-ments such as athletics serving as the "front porch" to the university, that ath-letes are provided educational opportunities, and that athletes serve to enhance institutional prestige (*see, e.g.,* Bass, Schaeperkoetter & Bunds, 2015; Duderstadt, 2000; Flowers, 2009; Peterson-Horner & Eckstein, 2015; Ridpath, 2012). This lat-ter group of critics points out that not all publicity earned through sport is posi-tive, that not every team can win, and that pouring funding into athletics does not always translate to more wins, donations, or increased exposure for the uni-versity and its educational enterprise. They further argue that the goals of inter-collegiate athletics departments at Division I public universities often can run counter to the (educational) goals of the institution (i.e., shutting down campus for weekday football games; providing "paper" classes intended to raise athlete GPAs so student-athletes can participate on the field; heavy practice schedules preventing student-athletes from enrolling in coursework that they would find useful to their future employment).

Moreover, at many Division I schools every student is required to pay hundreds or even thousands of dollars during their time enrolled in the university to subsidize sport through athletics and construction fees (Ridpath, 2012)—whether they are interested in sport or not. Worse yet, some students work as interns in their athletic departments, thereby subsidizing the teams and the buildings housing the teams, and paying for college credit—all the while working as unpaid laborers doing things that the university normally would have to compensate someone for. Different still, at Division III liberal arts colleges and universities, schools are turning a profit and increasing male enrollment by offering football programming to students-athletes who do not receive athletic scholarships (Demirel, 2013; Eifling, 2013).

It is safe to say then, that intercollegiate athletics is a contested terrain of public and private interests—interests that are underpinned by economic realities, public views on the place of the university in everyday life, and the growing influence athletic departments have on the operation of the university. To this end, contributors to this book examine college sport from economic, social, legal, and cultural perspectives to cut through popular liberal and conservative "mythologies" regarding intercollegiate athletics; and, rather than making unrealistic calls for reform, instead advocate for increased clarity about what is actually going on at a variety of campuses with regard to athletics.

Contributors, to different extents, are motivated by the following questions.

1. What are the overarching contexts and prevailing logics (social, economic, and ethical) driving governance in the contemporary university?
2. How is "common sense" regarding athletics in the modern university manufactured, replicated, and made into "truth" to the consuming public? Who benefits from these truths and how?
3. How and to what ends is Title IX mobilized by (athletic) administrators in the university structure? Who has benefitted from its use and how?
4. Who are the key stakeholders in the university structure regarding athletics? Which stakeholders hold the most and least import on university decisions, and who bears the brunt of these decisions?
5. How do university finances work with regard to the athletics department? Where and to whom or what does the money go?
6. What are some actual achievable areas of reform? What steps can be taken to challenge "common sense" myths and misunderstandings about college athletics?

These overarching questions will serve to radically contextualize the contemporary socio-political conjuncture and outline the dialectic (two-way) relationships that university athletics has with broader social formations.

In so doing, it is my hope that this book will serve to undercut widely held "common sense" understandings held by the general public and academics alike: that most universities use sport to fund educational needs; that almost every football and men's basketball team actually loses money for the university; that student-athletes are provided a free education; that student-athletes are in need of surveillance; that the marketing power of a successful college athletics team is unrivaled; and that Title IX is meant to hurt male sports when teams are cut from athletic rosters. Contributors also engage with emergent moral and ethical concerns arising from the increasingly corporatized recruiting schemes for young athletes to be seen by coaches, or consultant firms serving to help hire administrators (who then turn to the consultant firm for help in their new position), and athletic administrators whose sole role is to protect the university "brand."

The contributors are themselves located in a multitude of different colleges and university contexts, including state flagships, teaching schools, and private institutions. They hail from a range of disciplines (e.g., sport management, journalism, history, law; critical pedagogy; English; cultural studies), and utilize a variety of research methods (e.g., ethnography; critical media literacy; participant-observation; law review, archival research) to inform their chapters. As such, the contributors present in toto a multifaceted critique of intercollegiate athletics in the United States. More specifically, they examine intercollegiate sport as a key site whereby neoliberalism's destructive nature is operationalized and underpinned in ways that critical research literature on academia and college sport largely have failed to account. Given that—at its highest levels—intercollegiate athletics is a multi-billion-dollar empire that is used to fund the entire athletic department and (rarely) academic buildings and programming and, alternatively, in other college and university contexts students are required to subsidize athletics programming and buildings at rates that outpace inflation by alarming sums, contributors argue that a blanket call for reform is too simple a solution.

More to the point, pressing issues at major research universities such as Florida State University, Penn State University, University of Maryland, University of North Carolina, University of Wisconsin, and Texas A&M University— where students, alumni, and the local region expect athletic success and are often centered around fielding a winning team "at all costs"—academics, the law, and the integrity of academia be damned are relatively unique to about 50 to 75 schools. At these institutions, it is not unusual to see $300-million stadium renovations, $100-million indoor practice facilities, and grand weight rooms outfitted with videogame consoles and big-screen televisions, among other massive expenditures for schools to maintain their nonprofit status and to serve as an excuse to prevent the payment of student-athletes (Schwarz, 2014). Worse, local government officials and university administrators often undercut the academic mission of these large public universities by slashing budgets for schools and reallocating those monies to private interests, and instituting punishing research- and grant-seeking requirements upon faculty that tears away at the ability for a culture of seeking higher truths to take place (see for example: Korman, 2015; see also Ternes & Giardina, this volume).

Conversely, at aspirant colleges, universities, and sister-schools to flagship universities—such as James Madison University, University of North Carolina—Wilmington, George Mason University, Virginia Military Institute, University of Alabama–Birmingham, and Towson University—there is a perceived need to constantly be prepared to change conferences to increase visibility for the university despite the lack of financial support and interest for big-time athletics teams on campus and in the broader community. In these settings, students are charged athletics and construction fees as part of tuition for teams that they generally do not actively support as fans. At these institutions, it is not uncommon for students to be charged around $2,000 per year to subsidize the athletics department and for the schools to construct $60- to $100-million stadia for relatively unpopular sport programming. Thus, the relevant issues and solutions in these contexts (which are the majority of schools in the United States) are qualitatively different than at "big-time" sports schools.

Calls for reforming the system have come from many in the media and administrative collectives such as the Drake Group, in addition to a growing set of faculty (particularly in sports studies, sport management, sport economics, and sport communications) who have been critically trained to question what the NCAA, the media, (sport) administrators, and even the general public espouse as unmitigated truth. Reformers, often wed to their immediate contexts, however, hold narrow views for how change should work for all schools without understanding that reform cannot be uniform. Put differently, although all schools have been shaped by neoliberalism and late capitalism they have each taken a unique path to the present, and to offer one solution is far too simplistic. Title IX compliance, paying student-athletes, curbing coaching salaries, preventing the bloat of athletic administration, and policing consultation companies at Towson University cannot be addressed in the same manner as at Notre Dame.

Rather than providing a blanket critique and calling for "reform" that all schools need to follow, contributors to this collection demonstrate the complex nature of these issues. Simple solutions might work in theory, but in practice there are far too many people in power with a stake in intercollegiate athletics maintaining the status quo to let those solutions come to pass.

## The Chapters

*Sport in the Neoliberal University* is organized into two thematic sections: *Ongoing Issues* and *Emerging Concerns*. Each of the 10 chapters that follow speak to various controversies that campus communities have contended with regarding intercollegiate programming and the competing/coinciding interests of (athletic) administrators, politicians, students, student-athletes, parents, fans, and other powerful stakeholders in university life (Gross & Godwin, 2005). Chapters can be read individually or out of order, because they speak to specific instances of injustice and corruption in particular settings. When read in full, however, the book collectively provides a more complete picture of how complex the issues plaguing American intercollegiate athletics are. In other words, although each chapter provides compelling stories, I would argue that they are best understood as smaller pictures of a larger whole.

In the first section, *Ongoing Issues*, authors provide an in-depth look at issues that many in the academia and the general public have been critiquing for some time. Each author (or authors) analyzes how the same socio-political context underpinning contemporary college life has yielded varying outcomes in institutional settings based on the school's historical relationship with athletics, those in power in various political settings, and the wants and needs of (perceived) major donors to these institutions. Oftentimes, but not always, this comes at the cost of having to engage in or endure some morally and ethically unsavory behavior.

In the first chapter "Truth for Sale," Henry Giroux, Susan Searls Giroux, and I outline how over-privileging the football program in Penn State created a culture in Happy Valley that put its success above and beyond reproach. We further assert that, given this context, it was a logical conclusion that the monstrous acts committed by child rapist, Jerry Sandusky (former defensive coordinator of the football team), were covered up by the head football coach (Joe Paterno) and university administrators. In an addendum to the original article, we suggest that, rather than learning a valuable lesson, Penn State administration has effectively doubled-down on this atmosphere by being in league with Terry Pegula. Pegula, the owner of the NFL's Buffalo Bills and NHL's Buffalo Sabres, made his fortune in hydro-fracking, and donated $102 million to Penn State to fund a men's and a women's hockey team and to erect Pegula Ice Arena (Leeson, 2014), while funding pro-fracking research studies throughout the state system of higher education (*c.f.* Brasch, 2014, 2015).

In Chapter 2, "A Common Sense, Fiscally Conservative Approach," Neal Ternes and Michael Giardina describe how political interests in the state of Wisconsin have led to quite different—yet similarly troubling—issues. Yes, success in football and men's basketball at the university are important to many people in the state, but so is supporting professional sport. More specifically, governor and (former) presidential hopeful, Scott Walker, slashed more than $300 million in funding for the University of Wisconsin system, and suggested that "professors and graduate assistants learn to teach more classes and do more work" (Ollstein, 2015). While making these arguments for increased efficiency from public institutions, Walker's budgetary plan shifted the "savings" provided by educational cuts to help fund a new arena for the NBA's Milwaukee Bucks basketball team. Thus, the Wisconsin and American population must quite literally face the fact that professional sport is more important than education in that state.

In Chapter 3, "Fixing the Front Porch," Jaime DeLuca and Callie Batts tackle the notion that athletics is the "front porch" of an institution, and how this has affected the University of Maryland's decision to leave the ACC and join the Big Ten. University President Wallace Loh often repeats this sentiment in interviews and social media (Loh, 2015; Walker, 2012), but there exists a relative dearth of academic research to support this contention. In fact, there has been a more consistent and compelling argument suggesting that college athletics are an ancillary concern for university stakeholders, but that the "front porch" mantra has been repeated so often that it is has become an *assumed truth* (c.f. Bass, Schaeperkoetter & Bunds, 2015; Peterson-Horner & Eckstein, 2015).

In Chapter 4, "Football, Rape Culture, and the Neoliberal University (as) Brand," Matt Hawzen, Lauren Andersen, and Joshua Newman critically evaluate the ways and reasons why former Florida State University football star, Jameis Winston, was protected from law enforcement with regard to his alleged rape of an undergraduate student. Though not all student-athletes receive preferential treatment from law enforcement it appears that the Heisman Trophy winner and national championship–winning quarterback was the beneficiary of (at least) lackadaisical police work and organizational indifference on the part of administrators at FSU. They posit that, in so doing, "real" harm is meted out on (alleged) victims of crime on campus—and that it is often addressed later by increased funding to, and the development of, new administrative policies and positions that instead serve to protect the institution.

In Chapter 5, "College Athletes as Employees and the Politics of Title IX," Ellen Staurowsky traces through a series of myths held as public truth regarding Title IX. Throughout the chapter Staurowsky provides a powerful argument that the ways men's and women's sport has been organized and to what ends renders them different. In so doing, Staurowsky provides sound reasoning for why college athletes should be paid, and demonstrates that the funds to do so already exist. To continue not paying athletes requires a complex web of rhetoric and mental gymnastics that—when held up to critical reflection—does not make logical sense.

In the second section, *Emerging Concerns*, authors discuss a number of controversial issues that have been relatively underexamined in academia. This ranges from the NCAA rebranding its mission to perpetuate the belief that college athletes are students first, to an institution voluntarily leaving the NCAA, to the ethical issues that arise when developing international athletes for American universities. Authors in this section also outline the variety of parasitic entities that have capitalized on the lack of funding for intercollegiate athletics in sports where a majority of the student-athletes come from affluent homes, as

well as the rise of consultancy firms for coaching hires and administrative decision making. Thus, this section adds to the debate that intercollegiate athletes
are unpaid (though not wholly uncompensated) professionals, and that NCAA
institutions actively seek to undermine the education and autonomy of student-
athletes while propagating the notion that the institutions are providing those
very things.

In Chapter 6, "The National Collegiate Athletic Association's 'Nothing Short
of Remarkable' Rebranding of Academic Success," Richard Southall and Crystal Southall describe the myriad ways that student-athletes have been used by
institutions to promote a narrative of their on-field and in-class achievement.
Through a two-pronged promotional effort, the NCAA has proffered the notion
that student-athletes are both "just like other students on campus," and are
more successful than traditional students as a result of the extensive tutoring
and guidance they receive from the university. To provide statistical evidence in
support of this effort, the NCAA created the Academic Progress Program (APP)
measuring student success over a 6-year time frame that consistently inflates
success numbers when compared to more traditional measures. Southall and
Southall's analysis serves to critically analyze and ultimately undercut this initiative as merely the use of numbers to mask "the myth of the student-athlete."

Oliver Rick in Chapter 7, "Is This the Beginning of the End," takes a different
tack in his examination of Spelman College. The all-women HBCU (historically
black colleges and universities) liberal arts school in Atlanta withdrew from the
NCAA in 2012 to focus on overall campus health (Grasgreen, 2012). Citing the
fiscal hardship with poor return on investment by remaining in the NCAA, Spelman reallocated its athletics budget to a wellness program for its students. In
so doing, the aim was to address health issues plaguing the female African-
American population (e.g., high blood pressure, diabetes, obesity), participation skyrocketed and the maneuver was celebrated in academia. Throughout
his chapter, Rick evaluates the possibilities and likelihood that other schools
could follow suit.

In Chapter 8, "Confessions of a Human Trafficker," Adam Beissel compli-
cates matters further with his discussion of international student-athletes (ISA).
Citing the facts of globalization, innovative recruiting methods, and ISA interest
in American intercollegiate athletic sports, Beissel notes how the ISA population
on U.S. campuses has tripled over the past 25 years (*see also* Pierce, Kaburakis &
Fielding, 2010) and provides a compelling case for why the phenomenon requires
further examination. Using an ethnographic approach to gridiron football players in American Samoa, Beissel demonstrates that the myopic application of U.S.
amateurism and educational standards to ISA without the attendant protections
and support afforded to U.S. players has led to their problematic treatment.

In Chapter 9, "Welcome to the Factory," Jake Bustad and Ron Mower delve
into the relatively under-theorized rise of outsourced and privatized recruiting

agencies that prey upon families who would like to support their child's intercollegiate sport participation dreams. Companies such as Factory Athletics offer
to evaluate, record, and compile a highlight video to be distributed for review
by coaches throughout the college sporting landscape. Taking advantage of the
fact that "non-revenue" sports have extremely limited recruiting budgets, these
programs entice parents and guardians to part with a significant amount of
capital to have their daughters and sons seen by the *right* coaches—those who
will ask these student-athletes to come play for their school in hopes of receiving an athletic scholarship.

Chapter 10, "Some Kind of Joke," closes the volume. In this chapter I
describe the development and realities of intercollegiate-athletics consulting firms, specifically Carr Sports Inc. In recent years, Carr Sports was the firm
behind the proposed cuts to: Towson University Baseball and Men's Soccer; four
programs at the University of North Carolina–Willmington; and football, men's
rifle, and men's bowling at the University of Alabama–Birmingham. The firm's
work was scrutinized and exposed for its poor accountancy and logic, and ultimately the decisions were overturned (Schwarz, 2015). I argue, however, that in
each situation the university was in a position where—aside from some negative
publicity—there was no "losing" financially. Either the team's get cut and the
university saves or reallocates funds to other teams, or—as was the case in each
of the instances noted above—supporters for each team embark on the biggest
fund-raising campaigns these programs have ever realized.

## By Way of a Conclusion

As noted above, I believe that each of these chapters contributes to a broader
understanding about the variety of people who have a stake in maintaining the
status quo. Playing on the nation's collective apathy toward and lack of knowledge about the various unjust realities plaguing intercollegiate athletics, it is
easy for savvy entrepreneurial administrators and businesspeople to profit from
ignorance. Thus, there is very little impetus for nuanced and progressive change
within university athletics. In the proem, I briefly trace through this with regard
to the "Flutie Effect," but that is just one small example.

Although this book is by no means exhaustive, as the inequities brought
about by neoliberalism and intercollegiate athletics constantly bubble to the
surface, I hope that it serves as a launching point for further critique and activism toward progressive social change in our universities. Institutional cover-
ups, misspent public funds, adhering to academically devoid public knowledge,
a growing public understanding about rape culture, athlete privilege and exploitation, and the proliferation of privatization with little reward for the many are
just a few symptoms of the disease. There are more to attend to (the politics
of cutting non-revenue programs, administrative bloat, engaging in privatized

branding deals that are detrimental to the university, and alcohol sales, to name a few), and most can be traced back to logics derived from neoliberalism. This reality leads me to return to Leitch's (2015) argument about moving further into an era of post-truth.

> It makes you wonder what the point of saying anything is. If no one is listening, if the nature of communication is just give but never to receive, if the camera is always pointing selfie, why wade into anything? Maybe you're right, maybe you're wrong, none of that matters, not really. You can have every fact at your disposal and still be wrong if enough people believe you are wrong. You can make up whatever fact you want, but if you say it to the correct people, you can still be right. You can avoid any contradictory information whatsoever. What is truth? What is correct? What is a fact? It is all debatable, in a world where everyone wants to talk, but no one wants to debate.
>
> So truth then becomes a direction, rather than a destination. It is wind, the way traffic happens to be headed or stopped up at that particular day; attempting to change it is like changing the direction a stream flows. You can stand in the way of traffic, you can go along with traffic, but you can't *alter* traffic. You can become a lone voice screaming at everyone that they're going the wrong way. Or you can just merge into their lanes and go where they're going, wherever that is. (¶16–17)

This project seeks to be an answer to post-truth, to offer peer-reviewed understandings to contemporary university athletic issues, to ask questions, and hopefully, one day, to change the direction of traffic.

It is imperative that we look at ways to improve upon the conditions underpinned by neoliberalism. We must search for more collective answers to concerns that have been privatized for far too long. The university is supposed to be the beacon for such socially just thought and progressive change. There is no time like the present to make improvements in the contemporary structure of intercollegiate sport and, by extension, of society. Our collective futures depend on it.

REFERENCES

Bass, J., Schaeperkoetter, C. & Bunds, K. (2015). The "front porch": Examining the increasing intersection of university and athletic department funding. *ASHE Higher Education Report 41*(5), 1–128.

Bok, D. (2003). *Universities in the marketplace: The Commercialization of higher education.* Princeton, NJ: Princeton University Press.

*Boston College Fact Book* (1989–1990). "Institutional, planning, research, and assessment. Retrieved November 11, 2016, from http://www.bc.edu/publications/factbook.html

*Boston College Fact Book* (1995–1996). Institutional, planning, research, and assessment. Retrieved November 11, 2016, from http://www.bc.edu/publications/factbook.html

*Boston College Fact Book* (2004–2005). Institutional, planning, research, and assessment. Retrieved November 11, 2016, from http://www.bc.edu/publications/factbook.html

*Boston College Fact Book* (2014–2015). Institutional, planning, research, and assessment. Retrieved November 11, 2016, from http://www.bc.edu/publications/factbook.html

Brasch, W. (2014). The other scandal at Penn State: Fracking. *Truthout*. Retrieved October 12, 2016, from http://www.truth-out.org/buzzflash/commentary/the-other-scandal-at -penn-state-fracking

Brasch, W. (2015). At Penn State—reading is fracking. Retrieved October 12, 2016, from https://frackorporation.wordpress.com/2015/09/03/at-penn-state-reading-is-fracking/

Chung, D. (2013). The dynamic advertising effect of college athletics. *Marketing Science* 32(5), 679–698.

Davies, W. (2016). The age of post-truth politics. *The New York Times*. Retrieved October 12, 2016, from http://www.nytimes.com/2016/08/24/opinion/campaign-stops/the-age-of -post-truth-politics.html

Demirel, E. (2013). The DIII revolution: How America's most violent game may be saving liberal arts colleges. *SBNation*. Retrieved June 14, 2016, from http://www.sbnation.com /longform/2013/10/1/4786810/diii-football-revolution

Duderstadt, J. (2000). *Intercollegiate athletics and the American university: A university president's perspective*. Ann Arbor, MI: University of Michigan Press.

Eifling, S. (2013). How Division-III colleges profit from football no one watches. *Deadspin*. Retrieved June 14, 2016, from http://deadspin.com/how-division-iii-colleges-profit -from-football-no-one-w-1440369611

Flowers, R. (2009). Institutionalized hypocrisy: The myth of intercollegiate athletics. *American Education History Journal 36*(2), 343–360.

Giroux, H. (2004). *The abandoned generation: Democracy beyond the culture of fear*. London: Palgrave Macmillan.

Giroux, H (2007). *The university in chains: Confronting the military-industrial-academic complex*. Boulder, CO: Paradigm.

Giroux, H. (2011). The politics of ignorance: Casino capitalism and higher education. *Counterpunch*. Retrieved November 29, 2016, from http://www.counterpunch.org/2011/10 /31/casino-capitalism-and-higher-education/

Giroux, H. (2012). The scorched earth politics of America's fundamentalisms. *Policy Futures in Education 10*(6), 720–727.

Giroux, H. (2015). Youth in authoritarian times: Challenging neoliberalism's politics of disposability. *Truthout*. Retrieved October 13, 2016, from http://www.truth-out.org/news /item/33312-youth-in-authoritarian-times-challenging-neoliberalism-s-politics-of -disposability

Grasgreen, A. (November 1, 2012). Beyond sports. Retrieved June 9, 2017, from https://www .insidehighered.com/news/2012/11/01/spelman-eliminates-athletics-favor-campus -wide-wellness-initiative

Gross, K. & Godwin, P. (2005). Education's many stakeholders. *University Business*. Retrieved November 11, 2016, from https://www.universitybusiness.com/article/educations -many-stakeholders

Grossberg, L. (2005). *Caught in the crossfire: Kids, politics, and America's future*. London: Paradigm Press.

Harvey, D. (2005). *A Brief history of neoliberalism*. Oxford: Oxford University Press.

Heisman.com (2016). Heisman Trust mission statement. Retrieved November 29, 2016, from http://heisman.com/sports/2014/9/15/gen_0915145605.aspx

Leitch, W. (2015). Nobody cares if you lie. *Deadspin*. Retrieved December 31, 2015, from http://deadspin.com/nobody-cares-if-you-lie-1750284878

Leeson, D. (December 5, 2014). Meet the Pegulas: Parents of Penn State hockey. *Onward State*. Retrieved October 12, 2016, from http://onwardstate.com/2014/12/05/meet-the -pegulas-parents-of-penn-state-hockey/.

Loh, W. (2015). Athletics is the "front porch" of a university. These 500 @umterps student-athletes make us proud. #GoTerps. Retrieved November 12, 2016, from https://twitter .com/presidentloh/status/638531623647059968

Marklein, M. (2001). College sport success is not a major draw. *USA Today*. Retrieved October 14, 2016, from http://usatoday30.usatoday.com/life/2001-03-20-college-sports.htm

Navarro, V. (2007). Neoliberalism as a class ideology: Or, the political causes of the growth of inequalities. *International Journal of Health Services 37*(1), 47–62.

Newman, J. & Giardina, M. (2011). Neoliberalism's last lap: NASCAR nation and the cultural politics of sport. *American Behavioral Scientist 53*(10), 1511–1529.

Norlander, M. (2014). Report: Kentucky racked up nearly $450k in private jet costs last year. *CBS Sports*. Retrieved November 11, 2016, from http://www.cbssports.com /collegebasketball/eye-on-college-basketball/24640320/report-kentucky-racked-up -nearly-450k-in-private-jet-costs-last-year

Ollstein, A. (2015). Scott Walker to cut $300 million from universities, spend $500 million on a pro basketball stadium. *Think Progress*. Retrieved April 23, 2016, from https:// thinkprogress.org/scott-walker-to-cut-300-million-from-universities-spend-500 -million-on-a-pro-basketball-stadium-3ae657182b9a#.qlpah1wo7

Peterson-Horner, E. & Eckstein, R. (2015). Challenging the "Flutie Factor": Intercollegiate sports, undergraduate enrollments, and the neoliberal university. *Humanity & Society 39*(1), 64–85.

Pierce, D., Kaburakis, A. & Fielding, L. (2010). International student athletes and NCAA amateurism: Setting an equitable standard for eligibility after Proposal 2009–22. *Vanderbilt Journal of Transnational Law 46*, 659–692.

Ridpath, D. (2012). *Tainted glory: Marshall University, the NCAA, and one man's fight for justice.* Iuniverse Press.

Robinett, K. (2014). College football: Facility upgrades the rule in Big 12. *The Kansas City Star*. Retrieved October 12, 2016, from http://www.ndinsider.com/college-football-facility -upgrades-the-rule-in-big/article_af4e6f22-f41a-5df0-b71b-540f8809043a.html

Scarborough, A. (2014). "Bama boosters pay off Saban's home." *ESPN.com*. Retrieved October 12, 2016, from http://www.espn.com/college-football/story/_/id/11772033/alabama -crimson-tide-boosters-pay-coach-nick-saban-home?ex_cid=espnapi_public

Schwarz, A. (2014a). How athletic departments (and the media) fudge the cost of scholarships. *Deadspin*. Retrieved May 1, 2016, from http://regressing.deadspin.com/how -athletic-departments-and-the-media-fudge-the-cost-1570827027

Schwarz, A. (2015). UAB's tangled web of numbers doesn't add up. *Vice Sports*. Retrieved June 7, 2016, from https://sports.vice.com/en_us/article/uabs-tangled-web-of -numbers-doesnt-add-up

Shore, C. (2008). Audit culture and illiberal governance: Universities and the politics of accountability. *Anthropological Theory 8*(3), 278–298.

Silverthorne, S. (2013). The Flutie Effect: How athletic success boosts college application. *Forbes*. Retrieved October 12, 2015, from http://www.forbes.com/sites/hbsworking knowledge/2013/04/29/the-flutie-effect-how-athletic-success-boosts-college -applications/#e0d222a6ac9c

Tuchman, G. (2005). *Wannabe U: Inside the corporate university.* Chicago: University of Chicago Press.

Twitchell, J. (2004). *Branded nation: The marketing of megachurch, College Inc., and Museum-world.* New York: Simon & Schuster.

Uthman, D. (2013). Stunning amenities in Oregon's new football facility. *USA Today*. Retrieved November 12, 2016, from http://www.usatoday.com/story/sports/ncaaf/2013/08/01/outrageously-unique-amenities-in-oregons-new-football-facility-hatfield-dowlin-complex/2606223/

Walker, C. (2012, November 20). Move to Big Ten a defining one for University of Maryland president Wallace Loh. *The Baltimore Sun*. Retrieved July 2, 2016, from http://www.baltimoresun.com/sports/terps/bs-sp-big-ten-maryland-loh-1121-20121120-story.html

Washburn, J. (2005). *University, Inc.: The corporate corruption of higher education*. New York: Basic Books.

Wiest, A. & King-White, R. (2013). Selling out (in) sport management: Practically evaluating the state of the American (sporting) union. *Sport Education & Society 18*(2), 200–221.

Woodhouse, K. (2015). Higher ed's incurable sports problem. *Inside Higher Ed*. Retrieved November 8, 2016, from https://www.insidehighered.com/news/2015/07/14/brit-kirwan-troubling-transformation-college-athletics

# PART ONE

## Ongoing Issues

# 1

---

# Truth for Sale

## Penn State, (Joe) Paterno, and (Terry) Pegula

HENRY GIROUX, SUSAN SEARLS GIROUX, AND RYAN KING-WHITE

$B$y now, most people are aware of the deeply disturbing Penn State rape scandal, and the events that took place over the better part of 30 years at the institution. News story after news story has broken down the gruesome details of Jerry Sandusky using his charitable football camp—2nd Mile—to rape young boys, and thus rob them of their innocence and of a chance at the life his organization purported to support. Sandusky—who was investigated by the state in 2008—was convicted on 45 of 48 counts of sexual assault and sentenced to 60 to 442 years in jail on June 22, 2012. The entire ordeal was thoroughly considered by the national populace, scores of news sources and commentaries, powerful, heart-wrenching, and academic presentations at the 2012 *International Congress of Qualitative Inquiry*. Ultimately, it gave rise to an in-depth analysis in the August 2012 issue of *Cultural Studies–Critical Methodologies*.

Nearly concurrent to the investigation, trial, and conviction of Sandusky, Penn State found itself entangled in another curious university-athletics relationship that largely flew under the radar. Specifically, on September 18, 2010, Terry and Kim Pegula provided the funds for a men's and women's ice hockey team by "put(ting) forth an $88 million contribution for a yet to be named, state-of-the-art arena as well as scholarships for both teams and the beginning of operation costs for such an undertaking" (Vecellio 2010, ¶2). On April 20, 2012, just two months before Sandusky was sentenced, the Pegulas announced that they had increased their donation by $14 million at the "groundbreaking for Pegula Ice Arena" (Marsh 2012, ¶1). The first games were played in Fall 2013, and the arena was "available 360 days per year for public use" (Community Rink Information, 2016).

Although the Sandusky rape case is clearly a scenario whereby university officials placed the image of the school ahead of social justice, the Pegula situation is far less straightforward to critique. Indeed, the school has a new men's and women's hockey program, a space for students to take physical activity courses, and an arena that is open to the broader Happy Valley community. In what follows, however, we demonstrate that the university accepting the donation from Pegula emerges from an administrative mindset similar to that which led to the cover-up of Sandusky's heinous crimes. Finally, we argue that this administrative athletic advocacy and community culture has been to the detriment of humanity at Penn State, and speaks to broader moral and ethical issues within higher-education administration.

## Penn State as Neoliberal Institution

Too many universities are now beholden to big business, big sports, and big military contracts. Thus, it is within these contexts that we more closely examine Penn State's relationships with Jerry Sandusky and Terry Pegula. Much media attention was given to the fact that Penn State pulls in tens of millions of dollars in football revenue, but nothing has been said of the fact that it also receives millions from U.S. Department of Defense contracts and grants—ranking sixth among universities and colleges receiving funds for military research (Giroux 2007; Price 2011). Or that, as a result of considerable influence by corporate interests, the academic mission of the university now is determined less by internal criteria established by faculty researchers with the knowledge expertise and a commitment to the public good, than by external market forces concerned with achieving fiscal stability and—if possible—increasing profit margins. The excesses to which such practices have given rise have proven obscene to the point of the pornographic. One has only to look closely at the media-saturated Sandusky tragedy as compared with how the Pegula donation was largely ignored by the media in a critical sense at Penn State University to understand the potentially catastrophic consequences of this decades-long transformation in higher education for universities more generally.

The Sandusky crisis might well prove to be one of the most serious scandals in the history of college athletics and university administration. It also reinforces the claim made by Paul Krugman (2011) "that democratic values are under siege in America" (p. 23). Jerry Sandusky—who coached the Nittany Lions for more than 30 years—used his position of authority at the university as well as at his Second Mile Foundation (a foster home) to lure vulnerable minors into situations in which he preyed on them sexually, having gained unfettered access to male youths through a range of voluntary roles. On at least three occasions, extending from 1998 to 2002, Sandusky was caught abusing young boys on the Penn State campus. Despite these events, it took 14 years for the police to investigate, arrest, and convict Sandusky.

In 2016, the Associated Press reported that documents had surfaced "as part of a civil litigation case between the university and an insurance company," and indicated that Penn State "had agreed to a settlement covering abuse dating back to 1971" (Korman, 2016, ¶3). Additionally, citing a CNN story written by Sara Ganim, a Penn State graduate, it was argued that not only did Sandusky rape a boy in 1971, but that the boy "spoke to two people from Penn State who bullied him into silence" (Korman, 2016, ¶8), and that one of the individuals he spoke to was Joe Paterno.

In the most shameful of ironies, the national response to the story has similarly covered-up the violent victimization of children that lay at the story's core. The young boys who have been sexually abused have been relegated to a footnote in a larger and more glamorous story about the rise and sudden fall of the legendary Paterno—a larger-than-life athletic icon (c.f. Jenkins, 2016). The children's erasure also is evident in the equally sensational narrative about how the university attempted to hide the horrific details of Sandusky's history of sexual abuse by perpetuating a culture of silence to protect the privilege and power of the football and academic elite at Penn State. If any attention at all was paid to distraught and disillusioned youth, then it was to focus on the Penn State students who rallied around "JoePa," not on the youth who bore the weight into their adulthood of being victims of the egregious crimes of rape, molestation, and abuse. As many critics have pointed out, both dominant media narratives fail to register just how deeply this tragedy descends in terms of what it reveals about our nation's priorities about youth and our increasing unwillingness to shoulder the responsibility—as much moral and intellectual as financial—for their care and development as human beings.

As tantalizingly sensational as the media have found these events, the Sandusky scandal is about much more than a person of influence using his power to sexually assault innocent young boys. This tragic narrative is as much about the shocking lengths to which rich and powerful people and institutions will go to cover up their complicity in the most horrific crimes and to refuse responsibility for egregious violations that threaten their power, influence, and brand names. The desecration of public trust is all the more vile when the persons and institution in question have been assigned the intellectual and moral stewardship of generations of youth that they show little care for—case in point: the Pegula donation.

On the surface, Terrance "Terry" Pegula and his wife, Kim, would seem to be the personification of the "American Dream." Terry grew up in western Pennsylvania, graduated from Penn State with a "degree in petroleum and natural gas engineering" (Leeson, 2014, ¶6), and founded the oil and gas production company East Resources in 1983. An American family in western New York adopted Kim after she was found on a street corner in her home country of South Korea at the age of five. Terry and Kim became romantically involved while conducting business and worked to further develop East Resources. Twenty-five years later, East Resources purchased 650,000 net acres of land, and was drilling for petroleum on the Marcellus Shale (Filloon, 2016) utilizing a highly controversial form of extraction known as "hydrofracking" ("fracking"). This form of extraction requires drilling vertically and horizontally into rock and tight sands, which then are flooded at high pressure with a fluid composed of water, proppant, and chemicals to create small fissures in the rock to release gas (Barcelo & Bennett, 2016).

The damage that fracking for oil can cause has been widely researched. Indeed, numerous studies have found that the process generally is bad for the environment (Ahmad & John, 2015; Eaton, 2013; Hays et al., 2015), produces volatile emissions (Bunch et al., 2014; Mckenzie et al., 2012; Meng, 2015; Werner et al., 2015), poses risks to drinking water (Chen et al., 2015; Johnson et al., 2015; Lester et al., 2015; Pancras et al., 2015), and has negative effects on the shale and sand itself (Klamerth et al., 2015; Kuznetsov et al., 2015; Zhang et al., 2015; Zubot et al., 2012)—not to mention that the process utilizes several metric tons of freshwater (Barcelo & Bennett 2016). Moreover, the oft-business-friendly *Wall Street Journal* published an article outlining that "regulators repeatedly cited [East Resources] for spills or other environmental infractions, almost two for every shale well it drilled" (Gilbert & Gold 2013, ¶1). East Resources was also responsible for a toxic spill at a farm in north-central Pennsylvania that resulted in the "first livestock quarantine related to natural gas drilling" (Kusnetz, 2010 ¶2). Essentially, the Pegulas operated at the margins of the law, working in favor of raising profits for their company to the detriment of the local environment. They ultimately sold most of their company to Royal Dutch Shell for $4.7 billion in 2010 (Kovach 2014).

After peddling East Resources, the Pegulas began investing in sport and real estate development—specifically hockey, lacrosse, football, and the city of Buffalo (*c.f.* Annarelli 2015; Pignataro, 2014). As mentioned, the Pegulas donated $102 million to Penn State to help create an ice arena and men's and women's hockey between 2010 and 2012. They also purchased the NLL's Buffalo Bandits and NHL's Buffalo Sabres in a package deal for $189 million in 2011 (Inside Lacrosse, 2011; Ozanian, 2011), the AHL's Rochester American's for $5 million in 2011 (Adams, 2011), the NFL's Buffalo Bills for $1.4 billion in 2014 (Mcindoe, 2014), and have invested hundreds of millions of dollars into Buffalo's waterfront area dramatically changing the city skyline as it quickly becomes the next entrepreneurial city in the American "rust belt" (Maiorana, 2015).

To many people in Happy Valley and western New York the Pegulas are generous benefactors, creating opportunity for athletics at Penn State, keeping the Bills in Buffalo (it was rumored that John Bon Jovi or Donald Trump was going to purchase the franchise and potentially move them to nearby Toronto), and helping to "develop" the city of Buffalo by (supposedly) creating jobs and stimulating the economy along the way (Leeson 2014; Maiorana 2015). Yet, this perception is clouded by the fact that Pegula has wielded his considerable power and wealth quite dangerously and without regard for the betterment of the local and global

environment. More to the point, when Pegula made his initial $88 million dona-
tion to Penn State he was asked by a reporter for the school news website if
he had one message for students enrolled at the institution. He responded, "I
would tell students that this contribution could be just the tip of the iceberg,
the first of many such gifts, if the development of the Marcellus Shale is allowed
to proceed" (Davis 2010, ¶9). Indeed, the university not only founded the Marcellus Center for Outreach and Research (MCOR; a multi-disciplinary research
team that advocates for the proliferation of fracking despite its known environmental issues) in 2010, but it also prevented the publication of research that
revealed some dangers associated with fracking (c.f. Efsthanfiou Jr. 2012). That
the university was willing to give up what is supposed to be the never-ending
search for the "truth" via critical research dovetails quite alarmingly with its
willingness to cover for a child rapist to protect the Penn State brand image.

More to the point, Michael Bérubé rightly asserts that the rape scandal
at Penn State and the ensuing "student riots on behalf of a disgraced football
coach" should not be used to condemn the vast majority of teachers, researchers,
and students at Penn State, "none of whom had anything to do with this mess"
(Bérubé, 2011, p. A33). Equally pertinent is his observation that Penn State has a
long history of rejecting any viable notion of shared governance and that "decisions, even about academic programs, are made by the central administration
and faculty members are 'consulted' afterward" (Bérubé, 2011, p. A33). As noted,
this is particularly true when it comes to the MCOR. The American Association
of University Professors (AAUP) extended Bérubé's argument, insisting that the
lack of faculty governance has to be understood as a consequence of a university
system that favors the needs of a sports empire (be it hockey or football) over
the educational needs of students, the working conditions of faculty, and health
and safety of children and our environment (Nelson & Potts, 2011).

The call for forms of shared governance in which faculty through their
elected representatives are treated with respect and exercise power alongside
administrators signals an important question: How many university administrations operate in nontransparent and unaccountable ways that prioritize financial matters over the well-being of students and faculty? At the same time, it is
not uncommon for entrepreneurial faculty members to transgress established
strategic priorities and circumvent layers of university oversight and adjudication altogether by bringing in earmarked funding for a pet project (through
which the faculty member stands to gain), confident that no administrator can
refuse up-front cash, whatever the Faustian bargain attached to it.

Big money derived from external sources has changed the culture of universities across the United States in still other ways. For example, in 2010, Penn State
made $70,208,584 in total football revenue and $50,427,645 in profits; moreover,
it was ranked third among American universities in bringing in football revenue.
By 2015, ice hockey had become the third leading revenue sport at Penn State

(behind football and men's basketball), earning more than $2 million in ticket sales and parking alone (Gilbert, 2015). As part of the huge enterprise that is NCAA Division I sport, Penn State and other high-profile Big Ten universities not only make big money, but also engage in interlocking campus relationships with private-sector corporations. Lucrative deals that generate massive revenue are made through media contracts involving television broadcasts, video games, and Internet programming. Substantial profits flow in from merchandizing sporting goods, signing advertising contracts, and selling an endless number of commodities from toys to alcoholic beverages and fast food at the stadia, tailgating parties, and sports bars. Yet, as is outlined throughout this book, the flow of capital is not unidirectional; massive expenditures are made on sport to compensate administrators, scholarships, advertising, pre-game set up, and post-game clean up.

What should be deeply unsettling and yet remains unspoken in mainstream media analyses is that the youth have also learned these lessons *at the university*, where they have been immersed in a culture that favors entertainment over education—the more physical and destructive, the better; competition over collaboration; a worshipful stance toward iconic sports heroes over thoughtful engagement with academic leaders, who should inspire by virtue of their intellectual prowess and moral courage; and herd-like adhesion to coach and team over and against one's own capacity for informed judgment and critical analysis. The consolidation of masculine privilege in such instances enshrines patriarchal values and exhibits an astonishing indifference to the criminal behaviors associated with sport on campus.

The hardened culture of masculine privilege, big money, and sport at Penn State is reinforced as much through a corporate culture that makes a killing off the entire enterprise as it is through a retrograde culture of illiteracy—defined less in terms of an absence of knowledge about alternatives to normative gender behavior and more in terms of a willfully embraced ignorance—that is deeply woven into the fabric of campus life. Even and especially in higher education, one cannot escape the visual and visceral triumph of consumer culture, given how campuses have come to look like shopping malls, treat students as customers, confuse education with training, and hawk entertainment and commodification rather than higher learning as the organizing principles of student life. Across universities, the ascendancy of corporate values has resulted in a general decline in student investment in public service, a weakening of social bonds in favor of a survival-of-the-fittest atmosphere, and a pervasive undercutting of the traditional commitments of a liberal arts education: Critical and autonomous thinking, a concern for social justice, and a robust sense of community and global citizenship.

As academic labor is linked increasingly to securing financial grants or is downsized altogether, students often have little option than to take courses that have a narrow instrumental purpose, and those who hold powerful administrative positions increasingly spend much of their time raising money from private donors. All the while, students accrue more debt than ever before; student debt, in fact, now has surpassed the accumulated credit card debt in a nation of notoriously robust consumers. The notion that the purpose of higher education might be tied to the cultivation of an informed, critical citizenry capable of actively participating and governing in a democratic society has become cheap sloganeering on college advertising copy—losing all credibility in the age of big money, big sports, and corporate influence. Educating students to resist injustice, to refuse anti-democratic pressures, and to learn how to make authority and power accountable remains (at best) a receding horizon—despite the fact that such values are precisely why universities are pilloried as hotbeds of Marxist radicals.

The displacement of academic mission by a host of external corporate and military forces surely helps to explain the spontaneous outbreak of rioting by a segment of Penn State students once the university announced that Joe Paterno has been fired as the coach of the storied football team. Rather than holding a vigil for the minors who had been repeatedly sexually abused, students ran through State College wrecking cars, flipping a news truck, throwing toilet paper into trees, and destroying public property. J. Bryan Lowder understands this type of behavior as part of a formative culture of social indifference and illiteracy reinforced by the kind of frat-house insularity that is produced on college campuses where sports programs and iconic coaches wield too much influence. Lowder wrote:

> Building monuments to a man whose job is, at the end of the day, to teach guys how to move a ball from one place to another, is . . . inappropriate. And, worst of all, allowing the idea that anyone is infallible—be it coach, professor or cleric—to fester and infect a student body to the point that they'd sooner disrupt public order than face the truth is downright toxic to the goals of the university. . . . Blind, herd-like dedication to a coach or team or school is pernicious. Not only does it encourage the kind of wild, unthinking behavior displayed in the riot, but it also fertilizes the lurid collusion and willful ignorance that facilitated these sex crimes in the first place. But what to do? As David Haugh asked in *The Chicago Tribune*: "When will [the students] realize, after the buzz wears off and sobering reality sinks in, that they were defending the right to cover up pedophilia?" (Lowder 2011, ¶16)

Phil Rockstroh extends Lowder's analysis, rightfully connecting the political illiteracy reflected in the student rampaging at Penn State to a wider set of forces characterizing the broader society to the obvious detriment of students. Rockstroh wrote:

> Penn. State students rioted because life in the corporate state is so devoid of meaning . . . that identification with a sports team gives an empty

existence said meaning. . . . These are young people, coming of age in a time of debt-slavery and diminished job prospects, who were born and raised in and know of no existence other than life as lived in U.S. nothingvilles i.e., a public realm devoid of just that—a public realm—an atomizing center-bereft culture of strip malls, office parks, fast food eateries and the electronic ghosts wafting the air of social media. Contrived sport spectacles provisionally give an empty life meaning. . . . Take that away and a mindless rampage might ensue. . . . Anything but face the emptiness and acknowledge one's complicity therein and then direct one's fury at the creators of the stultified conditions of this culture. (Rockstroh 2011, ¶16)

The Penn State rape scandal and the development of MCOR should call attention to the crisis of moral leadership that characterizes the neoliberal managerial models that now exert a powerful influence over how university administrations function. As the investment in the public good collapses, leadership cedes to reductive forms of management—concerned less with big ideas than with appealing to the pragmatic demands of the market, such as raising capital, streamlining resources, and separating learning from any viable understanding of social change. Anything that impedes profit margins and the imperatives of instrumental rationality with its cult of measurements and efficiencies often is considered useless. Within the logic of the new corporate-driven managerialism, there is little concern for matters of justice, fairness, equity, and the general improvement of the human condition insofar as these relate to expanding and deepening the imperatives and ideals of a substantive democracy (Giroux 2008). Discourses about austerity, budget shortfalls, managing deficits, restructuring, and accountability so popular among college administrators serve largely as a cover "for a recognisably ideological assault on all forms of public provision" (Collini, 2010, ¶21).

If university administrators cannot defend the university as a public good, and instead—as in the case of Penn State—align themselves with big money, big sports, and the instrumental values of finance capital, then they will not be able to mobilize the support of the broader public and will have no way to defend themselves against the neoliberal and conservative attempts by state governments to continually defund higher education. In recent years, universities have not hesitated to place the burden of financial shortfalls onto the backs of students—even as that burden grows apace, wrought by austerity measures, by internal demands for new resources and space to keep up with record growth, and by new competition with international and online educational institutions. All this amounts to a poisonous student tax—one that has the consequence of creating an enormous debt for many students. Penn State has one of the highest tuition rates of any public college—amounting to $14,416 per year. But it is hardly alone in what has become a pitched competition to raise fees. Some public colleges (such as Florida State University) have increased tuition by 49 percent in just two years. In Chapter 2, Ternes and Giardina outline the bleak outlook for students enrolled in Wisconsin public institutions. The lesson here is that abuse of young people comes in many forms, extending from egregious acts of child rape and sexual violence against women to the creation of a generation of students burdened by massive debt and a bleak, if not quite hopeless, jobless future.

Penn State, then, is symptomatic of a much greater set of challenges—and the abuses they almost invariably invite—which are deeply interconnected and mutually informing. On one hand, Penn State symbolizes the corruption of higher education by big sports, governmental agencies, and corporate power with vested interests and deep pockets. Conversely, the tragedy surely can be seen as a part of what has been called the "war on youth." The media emphasis on the fall of Paterno and those who had the power to prevent further sexual assault serves ironically to deflect attention from the egregious sexual assault of young boys—who have carried this grievous burden into adulthood. Juxtaposed with the relative media silence about what has been described as the "other Penn State scandal: Fracking" (Brasch, 2014) that was taking place concurrently, this means that students, faculty, and administrators also pay a terrible price when a university loses its moral compass and refashions itself in the values, principles, and managerial dictates of a corporate culture.

## Conclusion

Neither the media accounts of the rise and fall of a celebrity coach, nor what many insiders like to characterize as a woeful series of administrative miscommunications tell us much about how Penn State is symptomatic of what has happened to a number of universities since at least the mid-1940s, and at a quickened pace since the 1980s. Penn State, like many of its institutional peers, has become a corporate university caught in the grip of the military-industrial complex rather than existing as a semi-autonomous institution driven by an academic mission, public values, and ethical considerations (Giroux, 2007). It is a paradigmatic example of mission drift—one marked by a fundamental shift of the university away from its role as a vital democratic public sphere toward an institutional willingness to subordinate educational values to market values. As Peter Seybold suggested, the Penn State scandals are indicative of the ongoing corruption of teaching, research, and pedagogy that has taken place in higher education (Seybold, 2008).

Beyond the classroom and the lab, evidence of ongoing corporatization abounds: Bookstores and food services are franchised; part-time labor replaces full-time faculty; classes are oversold; and online education replaces face-to-face teaching, less as a pedagogical innovation and more as a means to deal with the capacity issues now confronting those universities that pursued financial sustainability through aggressive growth (Higgs, 2011).

It gets worse. The corporate university is descending more and more into what has been called "an output fundamentalism," prioritizing market mechanisms that emphasize productivity and performance measures that make a mockery of quality scholarship and diminish effective teaching—scholarly commitments are increasingly subordinated to bringing in bigger grants to supplement operational budgets negatively impacted by the withdrawal of governmental funding.

Additionally, the student experience has hardly been untouched by these shock waves, which have further undermined the genuinely intellectual, financial, social, and democratic needs of undergraduate and graduate students alike. Young people are increasingly devalued as knowledgeable, competent, and socially responsible, despite the fact that their generation inevitably will be the leaders of tomorrow. Put bluntly, many university administrators demonstrate a notable lack of imagination, conceiving of students primarily in market terms and showing few qualms about subjecting young people to forms of education as outmoded as the factory assembly lines they emulate. Campus extracurricular activities unfold in student commons designed in the image of shopping centers and high-end entertainment complexes. Clearly, students are not perceived as worthy of the kinds of financial, intellectual, and cultural investments necessary to enhance their capacities to be critical and informed individual and social agents. Nor are they provided with the knowledge and skills necessary to understand and negotiate the complex political, economic, and social worlds in which they live and the many challenges they face now and will face in the future. Instead of being institutions that foster democracy, public engagement, and civic literacy, universities and colleges now seduce and entertain students as prospective clients, act as recruitment offices for the armed forces, and serve in the interest of big oil (Giroux, 2007; Price, 2011; Turse, 2008). In other words, students are being sold on a certain type of collegial experience that often has very little to do with the quality of education they might receive, and university leaders appear content to have the faculty provide entertainment and distraction for students in between football games.

Against the notion that the neoliberal market should organize and mediate every human activity—including how young people are educated—we must develop a new understanding of democratic politics and the institutions that make (in)formal education possible; we also must organize individually and collectively to create the formative cultures that teach students and others that "they are not fated to accept the given regime of educational degradation" (Aronowitz, 2008, p. 118) and the eclipse of civic and intellectual culture in and outside of the academy. What is crucial to recognize is that higher education might be the most viable public sphere left in which democratic principles and modes of knowledge and values can be taught, defended, and exercised. Surely, public higher education remains one of the most important institutions in which a country's commitment to young people can be made visible and concrete. The scandal(s) at Penn State illuminates a profound crisis in American life, one that demands critical reflection—by those both inside and outside the academy—on the urgent challenges facing higher education as part of the larger interconnecting crisis of youth and democracy.

Such scandal demands that we connect the dots between the degradation of higher education and those larger economic, political, cultural, and social forces that benefit from such an unjust and unethical state of affairs—and which, in the end, young people will pay for with their sense of possibility and their hope for the future. Learning from the Penn State scandal requires that faculty, parents, artists, cultural workers, and others listen to students who are mobilizing across the country and around the world as part of a broader effort to reclaim a democratic language and political vision. These insightful and motivated youth are rejecting the narrow prescriptions and heavy burdens that would be foist upon them, and instead are choosing to invent a new understanding of what it means to make substantive democracy possible. If this does not take place, we fear that no truer words will be spoken than those of victim 6's mother who—as Sandusky's sentence was being read—said, "Nobody wins. We've all lost" (Scolforo, 2012, ¶1).

## Discussion

In an era when state funds for institutions are continually dwindling how would you propose to navigate this situation at Penn State? The university essentially took a bribe in the form of a hockey arena that the community can use to produce research that has a particular slant. Is this how an institution of higher learning should operate?

### NOTE

This chapter is a significantly updated version of Henry and Susan Giroux's article, "Universities Gone Wild: Big Money, Big Sports, and Scandalous Abuse at Penn State," *Cultural Studies–Critical Methodologies 12*(4), 267–273.

### REFERENCES

Adams, T. (2011, July 8). Hockey, not cash, is top goal for new Amerks leader. *Rochester Business Journal*. Retrieved October 12, 2016, from http://www.rbj.net/print_article.asp?aID =188109

Ahmadi, M. & John, K. (2015). Statistical evaluation of impact of shale gas activities on ozone pollution in North Texas. *Science of the Total Environment 536*, 457–467.

Annarelli, S. (2015). Pegula, Shaner team up in Buffalo, NY development. *Centre Daily Times*. Retrieved October 12, 2016, from http://www.centredaily.com/news/article42927039 .html

Aronowitz, S. (2008). *Against schooling: Toward an education that matters*. Boulder: Paradigm.

Barcelo, D. & Bennett, J. (2016). Human health and environmental risks of unconventional shale. *Science of the Total Environment, 544*(15), 1139–1140.

Bérubé, M. (2011). At Penn State, a bitter reckoning. *New York Times*, November 17, A33.

Bunch, A., Perry, C., Abraham, L., Wikoff, D., Tachovsky, J., Hixon, J., Urban, J., Harris, M., & Haws, L. (2014). Evaluation of impact of shale gas operations in the Barnett Shale region on volatile organic compounds in air and potential human health risks. *Science of the Total Environment, 468–469*, 832–842.

Brasch, W. (2014). The other scandal at Penn State: Fracking. *Truthout*. Retrieved October 12, 2016, from http://www.truth-out.org/buzzflash/commentary/the-other-scandal-at -penn-state-fracking

Chen, Y., Mc Phedran, K., Perez-Estrada, L., & Gamal El-Din, M. (2015). An Omic approach for the identification of oil sands process-affected water compounds using multivari-ate statistical analysis of ultrahigh resolution mass spectrometry datasets. *Science of the Total Environment 511*, 230–237.

Collini, S. (November 4, 2010). Browne's Gamble. *London Review of Books 32*(21), 23–25.

Community Rink Information. (2016). Retrieved October 12, 2016, from http://www .gopsusports.com/pegula-ice-arena/

Davis (2010). "Pegula: Marcellus Shale development good for us." *Onward State*. Retrieved October 12, 2016, from https://onwardstate.com/2010/09/18/pegula-marcellus-shale -development-good-for-students/

Eaton, T. (2013). Science based decision making on complex issues: Marcellus Shale gas hydrofracking and New York City water supply. *Science of the Total Environment 461*, 158–169.

Efsthanfiou Jr., J. (2012). Penn State faculty snub of fracking study ends research. *Academics or Frackademics*. Retrieved October 12, 2016, from http://www.nofrackingway.us/2012 /10/03/academics-or-frackademics/

Filloon, M. (2016). Guide to oil and gas plays in North America: Marcellus. *Investopedia*. Retrieved October 12, 2016, from http://www.investopedia.com/university/guide-to -trading-oil-and-gas-north-america/marcellus.asp

Gilbert, T. (2015). Penn State hockey is third most profitable sport. *Onward State*. Retrieved October 12, 2016, from http://onwardstate.com/2015/02/17/penn-state-hockey -becomes-universitys-third-profitable-sport/

Gilbert, D. & Gold, R. (April 2, 2013). As big drillers move in, safety goes up. *Wall Street Journal*. Retrieved October 12, 2016, from http://www.wsj.com/articles /SB10001424127887324582804578346741120261384

Giroux, H. (2007). *The University in chains: Confronting the military-industrial-academic com-plex*. Boulder: Paradigm.

Giroux, H. (2008). *Against the terror of neoliberalism*. Boulder: Paradigm.

Hays, J., Finkel, M., Depledge, M., Law, A., & Shonkoff, S. (2015). Considerations for the development of shale gas in the United Kingdom. *Science of the Total Environment 512– 513*, 36–42.

Higgs, S. (November 21, 2011). The Corporatization of the American university. *Counter-Punch*. Retrieved October 12, 2016, from http://www.counterpunch.org/2011/11/21/the -corporatization-of-the-american-university/

Inside Lacrosse (2011). NLL: Buffalo Bandits sold, "for sale" Calgary Roughnecks. Retrieved October 12, 2016, from http://www.insidelacrosse.com/wire.php?id=4529

Jenkins, S. (2016, May 10). Penn State should own its role in the Sandusky Scandal. *Wash-ington Post*. Retrieved October 12, 2016, from https://www.washingtonpost.com

/sports/colleges/penn-state-should-own-its-role-in-the-sandusky-scandal/2016/05/10/41eea4ce-16b3–11e6–924d-838753295f9a_story.html

Johnson, E., Bradley, J., Inlander, E., Gallipeau, C., Evans-White, M., & Entrekin, S. (2015). Stream macroinvertebrate communities across a gradient of natural gas development in the Fayetteville Shale. *Science of the Total Environment 530–531*, 323–332.

Klamerth, N., Moreira, J., Li, C., Singh, A., McPhedran, K., Chelme-Ayala, P., Belosevic, M., & El-Din, M. (2015). Effect of ozonation on the naphthenic acids speciation and toxicity of Ph-dependent organic extracts of oil sands process-affected water. *Science of the Total Environment 506–507*, 65–75.

Korman, C. (2016, May 9). Penn State still hasn't learned anything from the Sandusky Scandal. *USA Today*. Retrieved October 12, 2016, from http://ftw.usatoday.com/2016/05/penn-state-joe-paterno-jerry-sandusky-sexual-abuse-scandal

Kovach, W. (2014, April 23). Terry Pegula a fracking billionaire. *Your Energy Blog*, April 23. Retrieved October 12, 2016, from http://www.yourenergyblog.com/terry-pegula-a-fracking-billionaire/

Krugman, P. (2011, December 12). Depression and democracy. *New York Times*, p. 23.

Kusnetz, N. (2010, July 2). A fracking first in Pennsylvania: Cattle quarantine. *ProPublica*. Retrieved from October 12, 2016, from https://www.propublica.org/article/a-fracking-first-in-pennsylvania-cattle-quarantine

Kuznetsov, P., Kuzentsova, A., Foght, J., & Siddique, T. (2015). Oil sands thickened froth treatment tailings exhibit acid rock drainage potential during evaporative drying. *Science of the Total Environment*, *505*, 1–10.

Leeson, D. (2014, December 5). Meet the Pegulas parents of Penn State hockey. *Onward State*. Retrieved October 12, 2016, from http://onwardstate.com/2014/12/05/meet-the-pegulas-parents-of-penn-state-hockey/

Lester, Y., Ferrer, I., Thurman, E., Sitterley, K., Korak, J., Aiken, G., & Linden, K. (2015). Characterization of Hydraulic Fracturing Flowback Water in Colorado: Implications for Water Treatment. *Science of the Total Environment*, *512–513*, 537–644.

Lowder, B. (2011, November 10). The danger of Joe Paterno's 'father-figure' mystique. *Slate*. Retrieved October 12, 2016, from http://www.slate.com/blogs/xx_factor/2011/11/10/the_danger_of_joe_paterno_s_father_figure_mystique.html

Maiorana, S. (2015). From orphan to NFL owner. *Democrat and Chronicle*. Retrieved October 12, 2016, from http://www.democratandchronicle.com/story/sports/2015/08/23/kim-pegula-making-difference-adopted-hometown/32166573/

Marsh, R. (2012, April 25). Pegulas increase Penn State hockey commitment to $102 million. *Penn State News*. Retrieved October 12, 2016, from http://news.psu.edu/story/149402/2012/04/25/pegulas-increase-penn-state-hockey-commitment-102-million

Mcindoe, S. (2014). Who's that guy? New Buffalo Bills owner Terry Pegula! *Grantland*. Retrieved October 12, 2016, from http://grantland.com/the-triangle/whos-that-guy-new-buffalo-bills-owner-terry-pegula/

Mckenzie, L., Witter, R., Newman, L., & Adgate, J. (2012). Human health risk assessment of air emissions from development of unconventional natural gas resource. *Science of the Total Environment*, *424*, 79–87.

Meng, Q. (2015). Spatial analysis of environment and population at risk of natural gas fracking in the state of Pennsylvania, USA. *Science of the Total Environment*, *515–516*, 198–206.

Nelson, C. & Potts, D. (2011, November 29). The dangers of a sports empire. *AAUP Newsroom*. Retrieved November 15, 2014, from http://www.aaup.org/AAUP/newsroom/prarchives/2011/psu.htm

Ozanian, M. (2011, February 2). Buffalo Sabres sold for $165 million to billionaire Terry Pegula. *Forbes.com*. Retrieved October 12, 2016, from http://www.forbes.com/sites

/mikeozanian/2011/02/02/buffalo-sabres-sold-for-165-million-to-billionaire-terry
-pegula/#3fe957753e06

Pancras, J., Norris, G., Landis, M., Kovalacik, K., McGee, J., & Kamal, A. (2015). Application of ICPO-OES for evaluating energy extraction and production wastewater discharge impacts on surface waters in western Pennsylvania. *Science of the Total Environment*, *528*, 21–29.

Pignataro, T. 2014. "Pegulas officially open HarborCenter. *The Buffalo News*. Retrieved October 12, 2016, from http://buffalonews.com/2014/11/06/pegulas-officially-open -harborcenter/

Price, D. (2011). *Weaponizing anthropology*. Oakland: AK Press.

Rockstroh, P. (2011, November 15). The police state makes its move: Retaining one's humanity in the face of tyranny. *Common Dreams*. Retrieved October 12, 2016, from http:// www.commondreams.org/views/2011/11/15/police-state-makes-its-move-retaining -ones-humanity-face-tyranny

Scolforo, M. (2012). Sandusky found guilty. Victim 6's mother states: 'Nobody wins. We've all lost'." *Janet, Jenner & Suggs, LLC*. Retrieved October 12, 2016, from http://myadvocates .com/in-the-news/sandusky-found-guilty-victim-6s-mother-states-nobody-wins-weve -all-lost

Seybold, P. (2008). The Struggle against corporate takeover of the university. *Socialism and Democracy 22*(1), 1–11.

Turse, N. (2008). *The Complex: How the military invades our everyday lives*. New York: Metropolitan.

Vecellio, D. (2010, September 18). Happy Valley is now hockey valley. *Onward State*. Retrieved October 12, 2016, from http://onwardstate.com/2010/09/18/happy-valley-is-now -hockey-valley/

Werner, A., Vink, S., Watt, K., & Jagals, P. (2015). Environmental health impacts of unconventional natural gas development: A review of the current strength of evidence. *Science of the Total Environment*, *505*, 1127–1141.

Zhang, Y., McPehdran, K., & El-Din, M. (2015). Pseudomonads biodegradation of aromatic compounds in oil sands process-affected water. *Science of the Total Environment 521– 522*, 59–67.

Zubot, W., MacKinnon, M., Chelme-Ayala, P., Smith, D., & El-Din, M. (2012). Petroleum coke adsorption as a water management option for oil sands process-affected water. *Science of the Total Environment 427–428*, 364–37.

# 2

# "A Common-Sense, Fiscally Conservative Approach"

## Sport, Politics, and the Death of Higher Education in Wisconsin

NEAL C. TERNES AND MICHAEL D. GIARDINA

### Proem

In the East Gallery of the Wisconsin Capitol sits a bust of former congress-man and governor, Robert La Follette, Sr. "Fighting Bob" was the founder of the Wisconsin Idea, which promoted the control of institutions by the people over private interests, and expanded the role of the university and academics in determining public policy. Progressive reforms stemming from the Wisconsin Idea included laws that protected injured workers, expanded conservation of waterways and forests, and the formation of cooperatives and unions (*see, e.g.* Barnett, 1907). The Wisconsin Idea was codified in the University of Wisconsin (UW) system's mission statement, which reads:

> The mission of the system is to develop human resources, to discover and disseminate knowledge, to extend knowledge and its application beyond the boundaries of its campuses and to serve and stimulate society by developing in students heightened intellectual, cultural, and humane sen-sitivities, scientific, professional and technological expertise, and a sense of purpose. Inherent in this broad mission are methods of instruction, research, extended training and public service designed to educate people and improve the human condition. Basic to every purpose of the system is the search for truth. (University of Wisconsin System Mission, n.d.)

For the better part of a century, the echoes of the Wisconsin Idea permeated the state, and the La Follette name became synonymous with democratic idealism and progressive political orientations.

On January 3, 2011, Scott Walker was sworn in at the Wisconsin statehouse in Madison. Breaking with tradition, Walker's team moved the inaugural cer-emony to the North Gallery of the statehouse, thus positioning the governor out of sight of the bust of La Follette (Barbour & Spicuzza, 2010). The optics of this arrangement have become symbolic of the Walker administration, as the guarantees of a liberal democracy promised by La Follette's work and the Wisconsin Idea have been pushed aside for a neoliberal re-envisioning of democracy, one that has inarguably had numerous crippling effects on the state. Although many of Walker's ideas are far from original—in fact, they represent similar applications of neoliberal economic doctrine in the United States including (but not limited to) the erosion of public higher–education funding, tax cuts for the wealthy, and a legislative focus on freeing markets— this chapter focuses on Walker's application of neoliberal principles, which is both particularly problematic and especially useful for demonstrating how the marketization of everyday life engages in a violent assault on the promises of liberal democracy.

Consider the following:

On January 27, 2015, Governor Walker made public comments in support of at least $220 million in public funding for a new basketball arena for the National Basketball Association's (NBA) Milwaukee Bucks. Walker and his political patrons contended that the tax revenue generated by the team—which would amount to approximately $6 million per year and thus cover the state-issued bonds needed to finance the arena construction project—was simply a "common-sense, fiscally conservative approach" (*see, e.g.,* Davidson, 2015; Johnson, 2015). The very same day, Walker's office announced a reorientation of the University of Wisconsin system, including $300 million in budget cuts. Importantly, the plans also included restrictions on faculty tenure, cutting protections of faculty rights (including extramural political speech), and shifted governance away from university faculty and the state legislature towards the governor's appointees on the Board of Regents (*see, e.g.,* Bidwell, 2015a; Heim, 2016; Strauss, 2015). The enactment of these funding cuts has led to an exodus of faculty members, and there is concern among higher-education advocates that once the two-year moratorium on tuition increases currently in place expires in 2017, the bourgeoning costs of funding cuts will be placed upon the student body in the form of increased tuition and fees. More damaging still, email correspondences within the Walker administration showed a planned attempt to rewrite the Wisconsin Idea (as it is encoded within the UW System's mission statement) to replace "the search for truth" with a commitment to filling the workforce needs of the state (Bump, 2015)—a trend witnessed in other states governed by right-wing politicians (e.g., Florida, Texas, etc.).

It is at the convergence of these twin narratives—the use of public funds for stadium financing and the assault on higher education in Wisconsin—that the structural elements of neoliberal rationality, sport, and governance emerge. Beyond the temporal linkages of each announcement, we find a re-evaluation of the outcomes and promises of democracy in a society whereby democratic values are transmuted to fit the needs of free-market fundamentalism. This chapter thus presents the twin discourses of the Walker administration's plans to publicly finance the construction of a new arena for the Milwaukee Bucks and to correlatively slash public funding for the UW System as emerging from the same neoliberal logics—logics of human capital and economic preeminence, the forces by which neoliberal political rationality dismantles and reconstructs society to redistribute global wealth upward. We see these forces of neoliberalism as reorganizing the human subject as a product of and for the production of free-market capital, through which it is made and unmade. In so doing, the state is left with an unconventional—but no less problematic—combination of public policies that combine privately held professional sport and public higher education under the auspicious calculations of "the market." A reading of these twin narratives uncovers the biopolitical ramifications for a re-imagined democracy in the historical present, whereby sport, space, and thought are brought together under market rationality.

Our reading of these narratives is largely informed by the work of Wendy Brown (*see, e.g.,* Brown, 2006; 2015), who outlines the ways in which the political bonds of neoliberalism represent an undoing of the liberal democratic state, one that originated in the work of Plato (1998) and Aristotle (1999) and was implicit within numerous forms of Western governance for nearly two millennia. Liberal democracy is primarily characterized here by the subject as *homo politicus*—Plato's (1998) political animal who is capable of self-rule. This is not democracy in its purest governmental form, of course—even Plato (1998) and Aristotle (1999) argued against a government controlled entirely by the people—but rather an ethical pact whereby the ruling class is given a moral imperative to concern itself with the betterment of all of their governed subjects and to protect their subjects' social welfare and well-being (Brown, 2015; *see also* Agamben, 1998). The commitment to a collective relationship in governance, in which all those within the governed and governing bodies are aware of the position and needs of others within the social sphere, has been the hallmark of Western democracy for centuries, inflecting a sense of consciousness—to various degrees and in different forms of government—throughout Western civilization. It is this consciousness—the awareness of all those within society, but particularly those less fortunate—that culminates in the socially conscious governing body capable of growing as a societal unit instead of as a loose collection of individual actors (Brown, 2003; 2006; 2015).

The accumulation of wealth and goods is, for *homo politicus*, only desirable insofar as such behavior can benefit the collective of society, and the excessive accumulation of wealth and goods is a direct assault on the moral foundations of the liberal democratic society. Whereas Plato (1998) argued against individual accumulation of wealth of any kind, Aristotle (1999) contended that material accumulation of wealth was possible within this ethical framework, provided that such accumulation was not done for its own sake but instead was used to better the lives of all in society. Both saw that the overt accumulation of wealth—particularly as it created large gaps in wealth—was counter to the needs of *homo politicus*, and that the needs of the political subject placed the need to work within the governing system above the need to accumulate personal fortunes. Although we can acknowledge the flaws in Western governance—imperialism, racism, classism, sexism, genderism, to name a few—this chapter contends that these issues extend from an inability to extend liberal democracy far enough, and not a more permanent flaw with the concept of liberal democracy itself. Thus, liberal democratic idealism is seen as a necessary basis to a truly just society, as justice necessitates an ability to understand those afflicted by *injustice* (Plato, 1998; Aristotle, 1999).

The implicit promises of liberal democracy—that of a moral commitment to ensuring that all members of society benefit from governance, and that the work of the polis is to improve lives for all citizens beyond the basic needs for sustaining life—are, we argue, necessarily ravaged by the reconceptualization of the human subject as what Foucault (2004) deems *homo oeconomicus*, the economic subject who is defined by rational action meant to maximize his or her own value toward the purpose of consuming itself. With rational action there can be no concern for the other, no work towards the welfare of all. There is no oxygen for liberal democracy in neoliberal spaces, and the moral imperatives that define *homo politicus* are quickly evaporated for the self-focused appropriation of *homo oeconomicus*, which does not concern itself with the survival of those beyond itself. The promise of democracy in the neoliberal sense is thus the promise of autonomy, the promise of immunization from the communitarian ethos of liberal democracy, the reduction of democracy itself to the market and its defense (*see* Esposito, 2010).

In the words of Brown (2003),

> Put simply, what liberal democracy has provided over the last two centuries is a modest ethical gap between economy and polity. Even as liberal democracy converges with many capitalist values (property rights, individualism, Hobbesian assumptions underneath all contract, etc.) the formal distinction it establishes between moral and political principles on the one hand and the economic order on the other has also served as insulation against the ghastliness of life exhaustively ordered by the market and measured by market values. It is this gap that a neo-liberal political rationality closes as it submits every aspect of political and social life to economic calculation: asking not, for example, what does liberal constitutionalism stand for, what moral or political values does it protect and preserve, but rather what efficacy or profitability does constitutionalism promote . . . or interdict? (p. 46).

This *un*-making of democracy is thus the un-making of the bonds which bind community, governance, and people together—separating them and re-engineering their relationships to maximize the efficiency of the market.

To this end, it might behoove us to view neoliberalism not as a form of economic policy but rather as "a peculiar form of reason", one that is "converting the distinctly political character, meaning, and operation of democracy's constituent elements into economic ones (Brown, 2015, p. 17). As such, we locate the Walker administration's machinations with respect to the Milwaukee Bucks arena and the University of Wisconsin system within this milieu, as images of a social exhibition in neoliberalism's reimagining of the body, the social, and governance as subservient components to a radicalized free-market. In so doing, we contend that, despite the flaws and missed opportunities of liberal democracy in the history of Western civilization, the neoliberal revolution has decayed the bonds between the governed and sacrificed justice for the sake of personal autonomy.

## The Un-Doing of Space

In May 2014, the NBA approved the sale of the Milwaukee Bucks from former U.S. Senator (D-WI) Herb Kohl for $550 million ($450 million plus a $100 million pledge by Kohl to be spent on the construction of a new arena) to a pair of billionaire hedge-fund managers, Marc Lasry (co-founder of Avenue Capital Group) and Wesley Edens (co-founder of Fortress Investment Group). The deal included a provision specifying that if a new publicly funded arena was not constructed in Milwaukee by 2017 to replace the BMO Harris Center (which was constructed in 1988, and which the Bucks share with Marquette University), then the NBA would buy back the team for $575 million and move the franchise to a different city (Associated Press, 2015). Such tactics by a major sports league or team-ownership group to acquire public funding for new arenas has been commonplace during the past decade. The Minnesota Vikings, Miami Marlins, Oakland Raiders, St. Louis Rams, and several other professional sports franchises have threatened to move if they were not given public funding for new facilities projects.[1] These maneuvers have been largely successful, with roughly $26.9 billion in accumulated taxpayer dollars being used to construct new stadiums across the United States since the early 1990s (Fischer-Baum, 2012). This is despite the fact that multiple studies and numerous economists have concluded that public financing of stadiums is generally a wasted investment, creating few if any long-term jobs and often pulling entertainment dollars away from existing local businesses rather than attracting new money from outside sources (*see, e.g.,* Kittle, 2015; Zaretsky, 2001; Zimbalist & Noll, 1997).

The Bucks had been a long-struggling franchise. Several seasons of poor performances and some of the worst attendance figures in the NBA had drawn into question whether the Milwaukee sports market—already serviced by Major League Baseball's Milwaukee Brewers, the National Football League's Green Bay Packers, the University of Wisconsin and Marquette University sports teams (among a handful of other popular small colleges), as well as a host of teams in nearby cities including Minneapolis and Chicago—was oversaturated and whether it even could continue sustaining the Bucks (Hunt, 2009). It was widely rumored that—despite the sale of the team to Lasry and Edens being confirmed by the NBA—the league was likely to offer a small transfer fee to the new owners to incentivize moving the Bucks to Seattle, Washington, where the franchise theoretically would provide more value to both the owners and the league (Gaines, 2014).

Instead, Lasry and Edens approached Gov. Walker to generate public funding for a new arena that would need to begin breaking ground at the end of 2015 to be ready by the 2017 deadline. Walker, a Republican, as well as a number of state congressional Democrats, were recipients of significant campaign contributions from the new Bucks' owners. Although not to suggest a *quid pro quo* agreement, work did begin on a funding plan for the new stadium despite bipartisan protest from a dizzying array of sources ranging from Democratic assemblymen from downtown Milwaukee's primarily African American districts to the politically connected billionaire Koch brothers and their Super PAC, which had ironically helped Walker win three previous gubernatorial elections (Olstein 2015a; Powell, 2015). Walker and others argued that publicly financing the new stadium would guarantee a long-term NBA presence in downtown Milwaukee, and would aid in the revitalization of an area that had long been home to poverty and urban decay.

When he announced the deal with the Bucks, Walker stood in front of a sign that read "Cheaper to Keep Them," a nod to his argument that the revenue generated from income tax on Bucks players and officials, along with presumed revenue from tourism, would cover the majority of the stadium construction costs and would save both the city and the state money that otherwise would be used to renovate the existing arena, which Walker noted would require $120 million (it also had $20 million in outstanding debt; Davidson, 2015). Proponents of the deal even produced an ad claiming the new arena would spur economic growth across the entire state of Wisconsin if it came to fruition. In the final budget plan that was passed, Walker had pledged $250 million in public bonds, which would likely be accompanied by an estimated $174 million in interest payments (Davidson, 2015).

Yet, the estimated $424 million price tag of the state's commitment to the new arena does not capture all of the local commitments made by the city of Milwaukee's leaders. According to *New York Times'* reporter Michael Powell,

> The gift-giving did not end. Edens and Lasry formed a development company called Front of the Herd. [Milwaukee county executive Chris] Abele,

whose office essentially controls land sales in Milwaukee County, sold 10 acres of vacant publicly owned downtown land—appraised at $8 million—to the developers for the exquisitely reasonable cost of $1. I know, Abele told me, that this looks like another favor for the wealthy. But the land had lain fallow for years. To his view, he had a rare chance to complete the renovation of downtown Milwaukee, which in too many places looked like a desert. For years, developers shied away from that site because they would have to remove a large sewer pipe at a cost of millions of dollars. As it turns out, say those close to the arena negotiations, the city will absorb the cost of removing that pipe as part of its share of the deal. Sometimes a sweet gift for a developer is truly sweet. Let's pause here: Based on state legislative estimates, and talks with negotiators, the real public cost of the Bucks arena, with interest payments and risky bond offerings tossed in, stands at about $500 million, or nearly twice what was proposed a year ago. (2015)[2]

Calculating all of the interest on the state bonds and the various side deals that have been used to keep the Bucks in Milwaukee, it appears that the state of Wisconsin is paying more for a new stadium than Lasry and Edens paid for the Bucks when they purchased the franchise in 2014.

Although the Koch brothers and other right-wing organizations have called the public financing of the Milwaukee Bucks arena "irresponsible," the irony is that the "fiscally conservative" approach championed by these critics is in no way broken by Walker's financing plan. On the contrary, it is the imperative of the neoliberal state to assert itself in the marketplace, as the market is not a natural phenomenon but rather a series of logics that must be maintained and ordered. Thus, the state—which is subject and subservient to market logics— *must also serve to create and maintain both the market and its conditions in order for them to exist* (Foucault, 2004; Brown, 2015). In this, governmentality is marketed as economized under the logics of *homo oeconomicus*, pulling the act of governing itself into a position where public and private interests are fused. Within this sphere, the seemingly corrupt fusion of politicians and private business— which form the backbone of the corporate welfare state—is normalized, turning Walker's decision to use public funds to assist private actors into a politically rationalized choice reflective of power-knowledge relationships inherent to the neoliberal state (Foucault, 2004, Brown, 2006, 2015). For Walker, his plan is the outcome of his own subjectification as *homo oeconomicus*, and the political rationalization of the free market as a governing force for relationships between the public and private sector. More broadly, however, as Brown (2015) would have it, the plan enacted by his administration is "not about the state leaving the economy alone" (p. 61). Rather, such action "activates the state on behalf of the economy, not to undertake economic functions or to intervene in economic

effects, but rather to facilitate economic competition and growth and to economize the social, or as Foucault puts it, *to regulate society by the market*" (pp. 61–
62, emphasis added).

Beyond the collaborations between a neoliberal government and the privileged few who can afford its services, this arena plan throws into stark relief how
those without economic means have become disposable fodder for the market.
In their comments after Walker's $250 million–dollar funding proposal, the new
Bucks' owners cited a "moral commitment" to the city of Milwaukee as part of their
agreement. This phrasing was meant to signify the financial investment on the
part of the NBA owners, and their goal to transform the area around the new stadium into a vibrant commercial and residential area (Gruman, 2015). From here,
we read the promises of democracy from the perspective of *homo oeconomicus*,
the rationalization of exploiting hundreds of residents during the real-estate crisis—as well as the Wisconsin government—so that others can profit off from their
success. This is the great inherent falsehood of neoliberal governmentality—that
individual prosperity breeds community success (a position trumpeted by free-
market disciples of the Chicago School since the mid-twentieth century). For Wisconsin, and for the city of Milwaukee in particular, the rhetoric seems especially
hollow. Milwaukee is responsible for roughly $100 million of the $250 million
stadium package promised by Gov. Walker. This is on top of the land incentives
and other perks that were added to the deal. Most experts agree that the likely
outcome will be escalations in property taxes and other fees for both the city and
county of Milwaukee (*see, e.g.*, Hrodey, 2015). In exchange, the new team owners
are promising jobs—both in construction of the new stadium and in the business
district they intend to construct around the stadium area.

There is no question that economic interventions are well overdue for both
the city and its outlying neighborhoods in Milwaukee County. Milwaukee is the
fifth most impoverished major city in America, with a poverty rate of nearly
29%, which is more than double the national average. Almost half (42.1%) of
all children living in the city live in poverty. The median household income is
$35,049, nearly $20,000 less than the national average (Glauber & Crowe, 2015).
These trends have particularly been felt in the African American community,
as Milwaukee has long been considered the most racially segregated city in the
country (Dale, 2016). The city's African American population—which is concentrated on the north side of town—is effectively segregated from white majorities
living in the more affluent, surrounding counties. This demographic trend is a
historical anomaly—the result of a late African American push to the city after
most of its manufacturing jobs had already been lost—and continuing public
policy, which has disadvantaged the African American community in education, mobility, housing, policing, and nearly all other facets of civic life (*see, e.g.*,
Powell, 2015, Tidmarsh, 2014, Tolan & Glaubur, 2010).

Walker himself began his career in the state legislature as a representative for the suburban Milwaukee counties, building his popularity by shooting down proposals that would have opened access for the African American city populace to move into the white suburbs (Dale, 2016). In addition to being the most segregated city, a 2013 review by University of Wisconsin–Milwaukee professor Marc Levine noted that Milwaukee was home to the country's largest disparity in employment between African Americans and whites, the highest incarceration rate for African American men, the second-highest black poverty rate, and the second-highest disparity in poverty rate between whites and African Americans (Levine, 2013).[3]

The "moral commitment" of expanded financial opportunities promised by the new team owners is highly problematic. One issue is that most of the job opportunities are non-union or temporary positions, either in construction of the new arena and downtown shopping center or working in a retail position in one of the new venues (Kittle, 2015). Another problem is there is no guarantee that even those non-temporary jobs will exist long term—particularly because there is no mechanism to keep the Bucks from uprooting to a new city shortly after their new stadium is constructed. As noted, the city asked for a guarantee that the Bucks would remain in Milwaukee throughout the life of the 30-year lease agreement with the new stadium, but the owners rejected the condition and agreed only to pay off the remaining public debt on the stadium should they decide to relocate the franchise to a different city (Davidson, 2015). One estimate shows that, under the terms of this deal, if the owners did decide to leave Milwaukee in 2025—10 years after the initial stadium deal—the team's owners only would have to pay roughly $140 million to be able to sell the team to new owners who would move the team to another location.

Given that the average purchasing cost of an NBA franchise is currently $1.1 billion, it is almost certain the current owners could sell the team to a group who sought to change cities and easily turn a hefty profit (Small, 2015). Such a move would not only mean the loss of many of the jobs promised by the team owners' "moral obligation" to the city, but would leave the residents of Milwaukee responsible for undisclosed regular maintenance fees and general upkeep of the new venue (Small, 2015). Thus, not only are the residents now committed to fund this new arena, but they have been left with very little in the way of tangible economic commitments to improve the local community and have no long-term guarantee that the team even will be around in the future to give the arena purpose. Importantly, this example does not exist in isolation. In what follows in the next section, we read it over and against the Walker administration's "common-sense, fiscally conservative" decision to dramatically slash funding from the University of Wisconsin System.

## The Un-Doing of Thought

On the same day as his comments supporting the $250 million stadium subsidy, Gov. Walker presented a new state budget meant to address an expected $2.2 billion shortfall in revenue. As part of the plan, Walker proposed cutting $300 million from the University of Wisconsin System, as well as reorganizing the university system governance structure so that the Board of Regents (whose members are appointed by the governor) would have a greater say in university policies (which traditionally had been controlled by the state legislature; Strauss, 2015). Wisconsin's university system consists of 13 four-year institutions and 13 two-year universities with a total enrollment of approximately 130,000 students and a combined budget of $6 billion, roughly $1.2 billion of which comes from state funds. The system was created in the 1970s when the University of Wisconsin and Wisconsin State systems merged under a single board of regents, with UW–Madison serving as the flagship institution (Wisconsin Board of Regents, 2014). The Walker plan was a continuation of anti-education policies and statements that had become *de rigueur* during the Walker administration, best exemplified by comments made in January of 2015 that faculty in the UW System should, "start thinking about teaching more classes and doing more work" (Bidwell, 2015b). Despite significant backlash from within the state and outside of it, the cuts were only reduced to $250 million when the final version of the budget was passed later that year (Bidwell, 2015a). The withdrawal of public support from higher education has become a national trend, as neoliberal economic and political rationality reforms colleges and universities into a conglomeration of private research labs, brand synergies, and military training centers (*see, e.g.,* Giroux, 2007; 2014; Brown, 2011a; 2011b).

In this case, however, Walker's cuts and revisions to the UW System were seemingly targeted at university faculty, intended (it would seem) to unseat some of his most vocal political critics and to ensure educator subservience to the new order of things he has been crafting in Wisconsin. Walker's cuts included a two-year moratorium on tuition increases in the UW System—increases which would have helped offset the budget cuts (Heim, 2016). If Walker's intent about where the majority of cuts to higher education should be made had not been abundantly clear, then a press release from his office—crafted in response to a no-confidence vote from faculty at UW–Milwaukee and titled "University of Wisconsin–Milwaukee Faculty Fuss Leaves Out Important Facts: 'Job For Life' Tenure Wrong for Wisconsin"—left no doubt (Walker, 2016). In the release, Walker notes that the average salary for a full professor at UW–Milwaukee was almost twice that of the average income of the average Milwaukee county resident, that faculty support hours for students had declined, and that student enrollment had declined to the point of a "2.8" to 1 student to faculty ratio. Walker is quoted as saying:

Some faculty bodies, including faculty at UW-M today, appear more interested in protecting outdated "job for life" tenure than about helping students get the best education possible. . . . The University should not be
about protecting the interests of the faculty, but about delivering value
and excellence to Wisconsin. (Walker, 2016)

According to fact checkers, the actual student-to-faculty ratio at UW–
Milwaukee is 29 to 1, with faculty including full, associate, and assistant professors, and 19 to 1 when the list of faculty is expanded to include lecturers and
adjuncts. Further, they found that the student-to-faculty ratio actually had been
growing, not shrinking as the Walker administration had claimed (Kertscher,
2016). For the flagship UW–Madison campus, the cuts seemed to have their
intended effect, as more than 400 layoffs and unfilled positions were used
to help fill the gap in the 2015 budget (Jones, 2015, University of Wisconsin–
Madison, 2016). University of Wisconsin–Eau Claire—one of the smaller institutions in the university system—also was forced to cut roughly 168 employees, or
14% of its total staff, to meet the demands of the new budget, with even more
layoffs expected (Savidge, 2015).[4]

Behind the misrepresentations and slanders against faculty members
in Wisconsin has been a clear agenda to not only defund and remove faculty
positions, but also to undermine faculty authority and control over the state's
higher-education institutions. Included in the budget proposal along with the
funding cuts was language that would strip faculty and students of shared governance rights, and transfer control over university policies such as allocation of
student fees and maintaining certain degree programs to the Board of Regents
with faculty only serving an "advisory" role. Walker himself has characterized
the changes to tenure policies and academic oversight as the "Act 10 of higher
education"—referencing legislation he passed as governor in 2011, which deeply
cut the collective bargaining rights of public sector unions (Bidwell, 2015a). Further, the new state budget removed teacher tenure from the state charter and
put the Board of Regents in charge of establishing a new tenure policy for the
university system (Olstein, 2015b).

The combined effect of these policies was that the Board of Regents—16
members of which are Walker appointees—would have the *de facto* ability to fire
faculty and destroy entire departments on a whim (Schuman, 2016). At the same
time, a number of "faculty stars" at the University of Wisconsin–Madison were
retained by the school due to the significant amount of grant money they provide to the institution (*see* Herzog, 2016); UW–Madison paid $9 million in reten-
tion salary to keep those whose research has brought in significant amounts of
grant funding (by one estimate, UW–Madison would have lost upwards of $20
million in research grants attached to professors to whom the $9 million was
apportioned).

We see in these events the creep of neoliberalism as it reimagines public education as private enterprise. More than an attack on educators and researchers in Wisconsin, the culmination of these policies constitutes a battle for knowledge and control over the dominant power–knowledge relationships in the state. Through these policies, Walker and his political appointees have fired a salvo at academics, which have been one of the largest opponents to his free-market orientation. These actions are revealing in that they demonstrate the hidden authoritarianism within neoliberal democratic promises—of an orientation in which only subjects reflective of the logics of *homo oeconomicus* can prosper. In this way, the keepers of neoliberalism must work to stamp out the ideological usurpers to ensure the survival of the free-market, creating a paradox whereby the economic system which espouses freedom and competition exists only in a space defined by a lack of both qualities (Brown, 2015). Walker's actions only are an extension of the logics necessary to ensure the survival of the neoliberal system he espouses. This extends even further beyond the job status of instructors, reaching into the very research ideas and teaching subjects which can be taught within the university.

Through the *de facto* elimination of tenure and shared governance, Walker and his allies have created an education system in which the political appointees of his office can reshape the very ideas that form the bedrock of the university. The potentials of this are terrible and far-reaching—including the elimination of departments which teach critical theory, gender studies, social justice, and other important subjects (something already threatened by Walker and the Board of Regents; see Bidwell, 2015b); cutting service programs; and even the firing of faculty based on the ideas published in their research (Olstein, 2015). Indeed, although the governor was forced to backtrack from the released documents showing that he had intended to remove the "search for truth" from the UW System's mission statement and replace it with "serve the workforce needs of the state," Walker's policies have all but guaranteed that as the outcome of the current changes to the university system (Bump, 2015).

Brown (2011b) notes that democracy is fundamentally defined through rule by the people, but that such rule also requires,

> a people who are educated, thoughtful, and democratic in sensibility. This means a people modestly knowing about these constellations and powers; a people with capacities of discernment and judgment in relation to what it reads, watches, or hears about a range of developments in its world; and a people oriented toward common concerns and governing itself. Such knowledge, discernment, and orientation is what a university liberal arts education has long promised and what is now being sacrificed on the pyre of neoliberal rationality, metrics, and imperatives in every sphere. (Brown, 2011b, p. 36)

In the end, the promise of democracy within the neoliberal order, like so many other promises made within the confines of these logics, is a hollow façade. Democracy in this context exists only in the weakest sense (though Brown would go further, and say it has been "undone" in toto).

Beyond the restrictions on the UW faculty, we see the effects of the neoliberal reorganization of the university system on every member of the university community. This perhaps is most obvious in how it has affected students, whom Gov. Walker has said he is trying to protect through these various reforms (Walker, 2016). Though a tuition freeze on the university system was been put into effect until 2017, students across the UW System have felt the effects of the budget cuts to their universities.

- Class sizes are expected to increase substantially because of faculty cuts.
- Student advising services are being cut.
- Facility maintenance has experienced a $100-million shortfall system wide.
- Competitive programs and majors are less accessible.
- Lab hours and availability are reduced.
- Access to university resources is more restricted.
- Student employment opportunities are shrinking.

Additionally, the Regents and the Walker administration threaten that system programs without direct workforce marketability could lose funding or be cut entirely (Heim, 2016; University of Wisconsin-Madison, 2016). Further, most insiders and experts agree that tuition will start to rise rapidly once the freeze ends because of the shift in control over tuition funding from the state legislature to the Board of Regents (Heim, 2016). For years, the system's tuition has been kept artificially low by the state legislature, making tuition at UW schools significantly more affordable than at institutions in neighboring states including Illinois, Iowa, Michigan, and Minnesota—which all have used tuition increases in recent years to overcome significant cuts in public funding for their public universities. To keep the UW System viable without using state funding, however, and as leaders of the UW system and the flagship campus in Madison have publicly stated, tuition rates likely will increase at substantial rates quickly after the initial freeze has ended (Rivard, 2015).

Here we see the student body as *homo oeconomicus*, transmuted into a being designed for the consumption of the elite class to become part of the market. We also see the lost promises of liberal democracy in education, the American system which was a hotbed of activism during the Cold War period—from the Civil Rights and Women's Rights movements to anti-war and anti-capitalist demonstrations—has been hollowed out by corporate actors who use its remaining shell to advance their own goals (Brown, 2011b). These changes to the UW System reflect a growing trend toward devaluing public education by restricting or eliminating goods and services, and simultaneously increasing the cost burden on the student-consumer. The same logics that facilitate the exploitation of the urban poor in Milwaukee—who are being tasked with funding an arena for billionaires—are the ones being used to justify the exploitation of UW students. Despite promises of economic opportunities through new jobs or college degrees, we inevitably find that these positions exist purely as points of exploitation for the benefit of the elite—which widen gaps in wealth and achievement (whether intended or not). In this process, undergraduate education and specialized knowledge become commodities produced by the higher-education factory at the cheapest possible cost and sold to the consumer at a high price.

Coupled with the emphasis on "faculty stars" and grant research discussed previously in this chapter, we can see the neoliberal university model for what it is: an expensive business serving the needs of major corporate actors at the expense of undergraduates, and whose cheap knowledge product is marked up exponentially to pay for the cost of research intended to benefit the private sector (Giroux, 2007). Like those living in urban Milwaukee, the students are left paying for the financial advancements of the wealthiest individuals, and have nothing but debt and a devalued education to show for it. The opportunities for social advancement promised in exchange for the working class taking on the debt of the elite continue to be empty lies; part-time work with no benefits, lack of organization and union protection, and massive personal debt continue to subjugate the workforce and bind people in an unending cycle of servitude to the wealthy few. There is no justice, no concern for the student who is left with enormous debt and a devalued education after they are bled dry by the corporate welfare state's education machine, just as there is no concern for the Milwaukee resident who is left with only temporary work and a greater tax burden when they are betrayed by their own government officials looking to satisfy the whims of a major sports franchise. There is only the cynical promise that they all one day also might have the means to exploit their way to greater wealth and riches. That is all that is left, the only promise of democracy in a society stripped of morality, justice, and empathy by the corrosive politics of the neoliberal regime.

## Conclusion: The Undoing of Hope

On January 27, 2015, Governor Walker made two bold proclamations. Fused within twin narratives of public stadium financing and cuts to public higher education, Walker both eulogized the principles of moral governance which had long governed the state, and promulgated a new regime of thought based on extreme free-marketization. Walker's pronouncements regarding the Milwaukee Bucks and the UW System reflect the calculating logics of neoliberalism and its constituencies, revealing a reimagined democratic order that promises competition and guarantees inequality (rather than freedom). Within these logical formations, the whims of billionaire sports team owners can lead to influence over government officials and the exploitation of an entire populace to achieve individualistic economic goals. Simultaneously, they have caused the dismantling of public education; the reimagining of a former bastion of liberal democratic values to commoditize educators, economize student consumers, and develop hierarchies of knowledge and thought production.

Governor Walker's twin announcements for funding of the new Milwaukee Bucks arena and the de-funding of the UW system are read as a singular edict; a death sentence for liberal democratic values that is to be carried out by the subjects of neoliberalism. American society steps to the scaffold as *homo oeconomicus* prepares its axe, and although Walker has played the part of the headsman in this telling, there is a seemingly endless supply of executioners across the present political landscape. From Kansas, to Louisiana, to Arizona, to Florida—and even within the highest reaches of the federal government— American governance is being reimagined through a neoliberal lens to the detriment to all but the most powerful among us. There can be little doubt that the continuation of these market trends translates to an inevitable conclusion, wherein the communal bonds that have brought Western society together for generations are tossed aside so that the most privileged citizens can extend themselves at our expense.

There are signs, at least, of resistance to the corporate logics that have arrested the development of the working class and the poor to subsidize welfare projects for the one percent. Though the Bucks' arena deal and cuts to the UW System were enacted by the state legislature, both were heavily denounced by a surprisingly bipartisan coalition of journalists, politicians, and citizens who found the idea of cutting into the vaunted UW System at the same time that the state was pushing to subsidize a sporting franchise run by billionaires to be a disgusting misappropriation of public finances. Whatever hope is left for the unmasking of such neoliberal schemes—in Wisconsin and around the globe— seems tied to these individuals who are willing to publicly resist such machinations in popular forums outside of the academic echo chamber. And yet, although there is at least this perception of an increased resistance to these specific implementations of neoliberal doctrine, we cannot help but concern ourselves with the underlying logics of this resistance. There are certainly those who have called for a more "fiscally responsible" approach to governance than what has been done by the Walker administration, however, we believe that such calls are anathema to the true solutions we need. Many of the critiques levied against the Walker administration's stadium financing and higher-education budgets have approached these issues from the perspective of *homo oeconomicus*, attempting to render these moves illogical by out-maneuvering them within the free market *zeitgeist*. As demonstrated in this chapter, these tactics fail to acknowledge the lack of moral consideration in governance which has been removed through neoliberal doctrine—and which cannot be replaced with a banal rereading of the same flawed logics of governance that have created these problematic circumstances in the first place. The authors of this present work are firmly in agreement with scholars such as Brown (2003, 2006, 2015), Giroux (2014), and Harvey (2005) that neoliberal governance and liberal democratic representation are mutually exclusive entities whose promises are directly opposed to one another. If we desire a moral government concerned with the welfare of all—and not just the most privileged—of its citizens, then we must favor the promises of liberal democracy over the machinations of neoliberalism.

## Discussion

In an era where state funds for institutions are continually dwindling how would you propose to navigate the situation at the University of Wisconsin? The University System has seen its budget slashed to support the construction of a NBA basketball arena, the efforts of faculty undermined by the state governor, and many research programs have been gutted—to what ends?

### NOTES

1. The Rams are the most recent team to make good on their threat, moving to Los Angeles following the conclusion of the 2015–2016 NFL season.
2. Sweetheart land deals often are at the heart of many downtown stadium and arena development projects, witnessed most notably in the construction of Staples Center in downtown Los Angeles.
3. Racial injustice in Milwaukee recently reached a boiling point with the death of Sylville Smith, who was shot in the back while fleeing from local police. His death sparked widespread public outrage in the city, including a riot. This was the second fatal police shooting of an African American man in the Milwaukee area in 2016, and the third such shooting since 2014.
4. Similar trends have been witnessed in Illinois, to the same destructive effect.

### REFERENCES

Agamben, G. (1998). *Homo sacer*. Palo Alto, CA: Stanford University Press.
Aristotle (1999). *The Politics* (B. Jowett, Trans.). Batoche Books. Retrieved May 15, 2016, from https://socserv2.socsci.mcmaster.ca/econ/ugcm/3ll3/aristotle/Politics.pdf
Associated Press (2015). Wisconsin governor announces deal for new $500 million Milwaukee Bucks arena. *The Chicago Tribune*. Retrieved March 10, 2016, from http://www.chicagotribune.com/news/nationworld/ct-milwaukee-bucks-arena-20150604-story.html
Barbour, C. & Spicuzza, M. (2010). On the capitol: No pics of Walker and 'Fighting Bob' at inauguration. *Wisconsin State Journal*. Retrieved March 10, 2016, from http://host.madison.com/wsj/news/local/govt-and-politics/on-the-capitol-no-pics-of-walker-and-fighting-bob/article_2b121594–1531–11e0-a9a7–001cc4c03286.html

Barnett, M. (1907). *The school beautiful.* Wisconsin Historical Society. Retrieved March 10, 2016, from http://content.wisconsinhistory.org/cdm/ref/collection/tp/id/46029

Bidwell, A. (2015a). Scott Walker, professors clash over tenure in Wisconsin. *US News and World Report.* Retrieved March 10, 2016, from http://www.usnews.com/news/articles/2015/06/12/scott-walker-gop-lawmakers-pitted-against-wisconsin-academics-in-tenure-battle

Bidwell, A. (2015b). Higher ed cuts: Crisis management or political ploy? *US News and World Report.* Retrieved March 10, 2016, from http://www.usnews.com/news/articles/2015/02/27/scott-walker-bobby-jindal-aim-to-slash-higher-ed-funding

Brown, W. (2003). Neo-liberalism and the end of liberal democracy. *Theory & Event,* 7:1. The Johns Hopkins University Press. Retrieved April 24, 2016, from Project MUSE database.

Brown, W. (2006). American nightmare: Neoliberalism, neoconservatism, and de-democratization. *Political Theory,* 34:6, 690–714.

Brown, W. (2011a). Neoliberalized knowledge. *History of the Present,* 1:1, 113–129.

Brown, W. (2011b). The end of educated democracy. *Representations,* 116:1, 19–41.

Brown, W. (2015). *Undoing the demos: Neoliberalism's stealth revolution.* Brooklyn, NY: Zone Books.

Brown, W. (2016). Sacrificial citizenship: Neoliberalism, human capital, and austerity politics. *Constellations,* 23:1, 3–14.

Bump. P. (2015). Walker moved to drop "search from truth" from the University of Wisconsin mission. His office claims it was an error. *The Washington Post.* Retrieved March 10, 2016, from https://www.washingtonpost.com/news/the-fix/wp/2015/02/04/scott-walker-wants-to-drop-search-for-truth-from-the-university-of-wisconsin-mission-heres-why/

Dale, D. (2016). "Back in time 60 years"; America's most segregated city. *The Toronto Star.* Retrieved August 25, 2016, from https://www.thestar.com/news/world/2016/01/25/back-in-time-60-years-americas-most-segregated-city.html

Davidson, K. A. (2015). Scott Walker's misguided stadium deal. *Bloomberg View.* Retrieved March 10, 2016, from: http://www.bloomberg.com/view/articles/2015-08-14/scott-walker-s-misguided-milwaukee-bucks-stadium-deal

Esposito, R. (2010). *Communities: The Origin and destiny of community.* Palo Alto, CA: Stanford University Press.

Fischer-Baum, R. (2012). Animated infographic: Watch as America's stadiums pile up on the backs of taxpayers through the years. *Deadspin,* Retrieved March 10, 2016, from http://deadspin.com/5964116/animated-infographic-watch-as-americas-stadiums-pile-up-on-the-backs-of-taxpayers

Foucault, M. (2004). *The birth of biopolitics: Lectures at the College de France 1978–1979* (G. Burchell, trans.). New York: Picador.

Gaines, C. (2014). NBA owners could split a $1 billion pot if they can force the Milwaukee Bucks to move to Seattle. *Business Insider.* Retrieved March 10, 2016, from http://www.businessinsider.com/nba-owners-milwaukee-bucks-move-seattle-2014-10.

Glauber, B. & Crowe, K. (2015). Poverty keeps tight grip on Milwaukee, new census figures show. *Milwaukee Journal Sentinel.* Retrieved March 10, 2016, from http://www.jsonline.com/news/milwaukee/poverty-keeps-tight-grip-on-milwaukee-new-census-figures-show-b99578039z1-327971271.html

Giroux, H. (2007). *The university in chains: Confronting the military-industrial-academic complex.* Boulder: Paradigm Publishers.

Giroux, H. (2014). *Neoliberalism's war on higher education.* Chicago: Haymarket Books.

Gruman, A. (2015). Bucks unveil $1 billion plan for new arena, entertainment district. *Fox Sports Wisconsin,* Retrieved May 13, 2016, from http://www.foxsports.com/wisconsin

/story/milwaukee-bucks-unveil-1b-plan-for-new-arena-entertainment-district
-040815

Harvey, D. (2005). *A brief history of neoliberalism*. Oxford: Oxford University Press.

Herzog, K. (2016). UW-Madison spends nearly $9 million to retain faculty stars. *Milwaukee Journal Sentinel*. Retrieved 5/13/16, from http://www.jsonline.com/news/education/uw
-spends-nearly-9-million-in-effort-to-retain-faculty-stars-b99682882z1–371376511
.html

Heim, M. (2016). UW schools face early effects of declining state support for higher education. *The Daily Cardinal*. Retrieved March 10, 2016, from http://www.dailycardinal.com
/article/2016/02/us-schools-face-early-effects-of-declining-state-support-for-higher
-education

Hrodey, M. (2015). How a new Bucks arena could raise your property taxes. *Milwaukee Magazine*. Retrieved May 13, 2016, from http://www.milwaukeemag.com/2015/04/20/how-a
-new-bucks-arena-could-raise-your-property-taxes/

Hunt, M. (2009). What's the Buck's future in Milwaukee? *Milwaukee Journal Sentinel*. Retrieved March 10, 2016, from http://www.jsonline.com/blogs/sports/38702447.html

Johnson, J. (2015). Scott Walker approves spending $250 million on Milwaukee Bucks arena. *The Washington Post*. Retrieved March 10, 2016, from https://www.washingtonpost.com
/politics/scott-walker-approves-spending-250-million-on-milwaukee-bucks-arena
/2015/08/12/5cd72d54–4055–11e5–9561–4b3dc93e3b9a_story.html

Jones, M. (2015). University of Wisconsin regents enact budget reflecting state cuts. *Milwaukee Journal Sentinel*. Retrieved March 10, 2016, from http://www.jsonline.com/news
/education/university-of-wisconsin-regents-enact-budget-reflecting-state-cuts
-b99534871z1–312964111.html

Kertscher, T. (2016). Scott Walker way off in saying University of Wisconsin-Milwaukee has 2.8 students per faculty member. *PolitiFact Wisconsin*. Retrieved May 13, 2016, from http://www.politifact.com/wisconsin/statements/2016/may/13/scott-walker/scott
-walker-way-saying-university-wisconsin-milwa/

Kittle, M. D. (2015). Taxpayer arenas don't pay: Milwaukee Bucks arena backers are bucking history. *Wisconsin Watchdog.org*, Retrieved March 10, 2016, from http://watchdog.org
/222707/taxpayer-milwaukee-bucks-arena/

Levine, M. (2013). Race and inequality in Milwaukee, 2013; A region at the crossroads. *YWCA*. Retrieved August 25, 2016, from http://www.ywcasew.org/atf/cf/%7B3F0D434D
-68FC-4740-B9B8–03B6B1B81BAE%7D/Marc%20Levine%20slides.pdf

Levine, C. (2016). UW English Chair Caroline Levine—enough with Scott Walker and the GOP, I'm leaving. *The Capital Times*. Retrieved May 15, 2016, from http://host.madison
.com/ct/opinion/column/uw-english-chair-caroline-levine-enough-with-scott-walker
-and/article_8a10b56e-86bf-588f-9a16–9689da0150bd.html

Olstein, A. (2015a). After massive contribution to Scott Walker, NBA owner will get $250 million in tax dollars for new arena. *Think Progress*. Retrieved March 10, 2016, from http://thinkprogress.org/politics/2015/08/12/3690020/scott-walker-signs-bill-to
-spend-hundreds-of-millions-of-tax-dollars-on-a-private-stadium/

Olstein, A. (2015b). Backlash against Scott Walker's war on the University of Wisconsin. *Think Progress*. Retrieved March 10, 2016, from http://thinkprogress.org/politics/2015
/06/17/3669629/backlash-scott-walkers-war-university-wisconsin/

Plato (1998). *Republic* (R. Waterfield, Trans.), New York, Oxford University Press.

Powell, M. (2015). Buck's owners win, at Wisconsin's expense. *The New York Times*. Retrieved March 10, 2016, from http://www.nytimes.com/2015/08/15/sports/bucks-new-owners
-get-house-warming-gift-of-public-money.html

Rivard, R. (2015). Deep cuts in Wisconsin. *Inside Higher Ed.* Retrieved May 13, 2016, from https://www.insidehighered.com/news/2015/01/28/wisconsin-looks-cut-higher-ed-300m-tries-give-something-return

Savidge, N. (2015). On campus: Tracking effects of UW budget cuts, work on tenure policies continues. *Wisconsin State Journal.* Retrieved March 10, 2016, from http://host.madison.com/wsj/news/local/education/university/on-campus-tracking-effects-of-uw-budget-cuts-work-on/article_375c7bf5-2422-5359-8afe-1308e631a13e.html

Schuman, R. (2016). The end of research in Wisconsin. *Slate.* Retrieved May 13, 2016, from http://www.slate.com/articles/life/education/2016/03/ university_of_wisconsin_and_the_aftermath_of_destroying_professor_tenure.html

Small, P. (2015). Will Bucks break their lease? *Urban Milwaukee.* Retrieved May 13, 2016, from http://urbanmilwaukee.com/2015/08/11/will-bucks-break-their-lease/?version=meter+at+null&module=meterLinks&pgtype=article&contentId=&mediaId=&referrer=&priority=true&action=click&contentCollection=meter-links-click

Strauss, V. (2015). Gov. Scott Walker savages Wisconsin public education in new budget. *The Washington Post.* Retrieved March 10, 2016, from https://www.washingtonpost.com/news/answer-sheet/wp/2015/07/13/gov-scott-walker-savages-wisconsin-public-education-in-new-budget/

Tidmarsh, K. (2014). Milwaukee: The most segregated and polarized place in America. *The Governing.* Retrieved August 25, 2016, from http://www.governing.com/topics/politics/gov-milwaukee-most-segregated-polarized-place.html

Tolan, T. & Glauber, B. (2010). Milwaukee area tops Brookings segregation study of census data. *Milwaukee Journal Sentinel.* Retrieved August 25, 2016, from http://archive.jsonline.com/news/milwaukee/111898689.html

University of Wisconsin Board of Regents (2014). *Fact Book.* Retrieved March 10, 2016, from https://www.wisconsin.edu/download/publications(2)/Fact-Book.pdf

University of Wisconsin–Madison (2016). UW–Madison, UW system schools detail budget cut impacts. *UW-Madison and the State Budget.* Retrieved May 13, 2016, from https://budget.wisc.edu/

University of Wisconsin System Mission [n.d.]. University of Wisconsin Board of Regents. Retrieved March 10, 2016, from https://www.wisconsin.edu/regents/policies/the-university-of-wisconsin-system-mission/

Walker, S. (2016). University of Wisconsin–Milwaukee faculty fuss leaves out important facts: "Job for life" tenure wrong for Wisconsin. Retrieved May 13, 2016, from http://walker.wi.gov/newsroom/press-release/university-wisconsin-milwaukee-faculty-fuss-leaves-out-important-facts

Zaretsky, A. M. (2001). Should cities pay for sports facilities? *Federal Reserve Bank of St. Louis.* Retrieved May 13, 2016, from https://www.stlouisfed.org/Publications/Regional-Economist/April-2001/Should-Cities-Pay-for-Sports-Facilities

Zimbalist, A. & Noil, R. G. (1997). *Sports, jobs, and taxes: The economic impact of sports teams and stadiums.* Washington D.C.: Brookings Institute Press.

# 3

---

# Fixing the Front Porch?

## Maryland's Move to the Big Ten

JAIME DELUCA AND CALLIE BATTS MADDOX

In 1953, the University of Maryland became a charter member of the Atlantic Coast Conference (ACC), an affiliation of universities competing in NCAA Division I athletics. During its time in the ACC, Maryland developed highly successful athletic programs in a variety of sports. Despite its long tenure in the ACC—and strong rivalries with conference foes rooted in campus culture—the Maryland Board of Regents approved a measure to leave the conference in 2012 and join the Big Ten after its presidents voted to accept the University of Maryland (Mihoces, 2012). The Big Ten is the oldest Division I collegiate athletic conference in the country, and includes Ohio State, Michigan, and Penn State. Prompted by a mounting athletics deficit, Maryland's move to the Big Ten also was anchored in a desire to augment the brand image of the university across the nation. Peterson-Horner and Eckstein (2015) have dubbed this investment in intercollegiate athletics to increase the brand of the university making it more visible and attractive to prospective students as the "Flutie Factor." Using this flawed logic to steer the future of the University of Maryland brand, President Wallace Loh described the university's athletic programs as the "front porch" contending, "what happens on that front porch has a big impact on what happens with the rest of the academic house" (Barker, 2010, ¶8). Forfeiting an exit fee of $31.4 million to leave the ACC, Maryland ultimately realigned in the Big Ten to buttress its "front porch," to reinforce the foundation of the athletics department to secondarily strengthen the "academic house."

This move, however, has been fraught with contradictions and a problematic blending of athletics and academics that obscures the stated mission of the University of Maryland, but nevertheless is fast becoming a hallmark of the neoliberal university. President Loh has stated that the university's two main goals are a commitment to "No. 1, academic excellence, and No. 2, athletic excellence" (Barker, 2010, ¶8). Yet, the University of Maryland's institutional decisions appear to promote a deliberate mixing of the two, in which the power and potential of athletics is exploited to enable the university to service its mission as an educational enterprise. Specifically, the University of Maryland recently eliminated seven varsity sports teams in response to fiscal concerns; entered into a corporate partnership with global sports-apparel company, Under Armour; and began construction on a new $155-million facility that features a football training center alongside an academy for entrepreneurship (Gerstner, 2012; McClure, 2015; Tracy, 2015; Wells, 2014).

These athletics-related decisions illustrate the contradictions, and perhaps corruption, that characterize the neoliberal university environment. Further, this approach echoes the ideology associated with the "Flutie Factor," and "reflects an increasingly corporatized and commercialized university that promulgates policies more concerned with marketing images and profit maximization than with the production and dissemination of knowledge" (Peterson-Horner & Eckstein, 2015, p. 65). It is within this context that we situate "athademics," a merging, blending, and blurring of the competing, and perhaps complementary, university athletic and academic agendas. Central to the successful operation of an "athademic" agenda is the neoliberal university's push for profit, increased brand exposure in the competitive marketplace of higher education, and corporate support—all of which are core elements associated with Maryland's Big Ten move. This chapter illustrates the complexities of a focus on athademics through the case of the University of Maryland's conference realignment and institutional decision making.

## Maryland Athletics: Big Money in the Big Ten

The University of Maryland is a public research university located in the city of College Park, Maryland, approximately four miles from the northeast border of Washington, DC, and 35 miles from Baltimore. Established in 1856 as the Maryland Agricultural College, it is the flagship institution of the University System of Maryland and is the largest university both in the state of Maryland and in the DC metropolitan area. The university enrolls more than 27,000 undergraduates and approximately 10,000 graduate students across 300 academic programs and 13 schools and colleges. Recent rankings place the University of Maryland at #19 among public universities (*U.S News & World Report*), #7 for "best value" (*Kiplinger's Personal Finance*), and #10 overall for undergraduate entrepreneurship programs (*The Princeton Review*). Notable alumni include Jim Henson, creator of the Muppets; Sergey Brin, co-founder of Google; Connie Chung, journalist and newscaster; Larry David, co-creator of *Seinfeld*; Boomer Esiason, former NFL quarterback; and Kevin Plank, founder and CEO of Under Armour who remains deeply involved with the university.

Athletically, Maryland found great success during its time in the ACC with men's and women's basketball, men's and women's lacrosse, men's soccer, and women's field hockey. Under the leadership of Gary Williams, the men's basketball team won the NCAA national championship in 2002. Before retiring in 2011, Williams became the third-winningest coach in ACC history, behind Dean Smith of North Carolina and Mike Krzyzewski of Duke. The women's basketball team, under head coach Brenda Frese, captured its own national championship in 2006 and has made an appearance in the NCAA postseason tournament every year since. Other athletic achievements include 8 national championships in women's field hockey, 13 national championships in women's lacrosse, and 3 national championships in men's soccer. Steeped in a rich history, the men's lacrosse team has enjoyed consistent success, winning 26 ACC championships. Although not a conference powerhouse, the football team has made appearances in 24 bowl games and regularly produces players who go on to play professionally.

Despite its athletic prowess, the financial solvency of the University of Maryland's athletic department had been problematic for some time, with expenses outpacing revenue year after year. This prompted Gaul (2015, p. 200) to refer to the institution as "a poster child for schools living beyond their means." In 2002, former Maryland Athletic Director, Debbie Yow (now at N.C. State), "embarked on an ambitious facilities upgrade that ran to more than $175 million even as the school's revenue programs sank into mediocrity" (Mandel, 2014, p. 55). Specifically, in the mid-to-late 2000s, football had a middling record, basketball missed making the NCAA tournament three of four seasons, and season-ticket holders and donations decreased (Mandel, 2014). Consequently, attendance at games dropped along with ticket revenues (Giannotto, 2012). Further, the Byrd Stadium (now named "Capital One Field at Maryland Stadium"[1]) expansion and upgrade in 2006 cost $50.8 million and the athletic department incurred $35 million of debt (Gerstner, 2012; Giannotto, 2012). In 2010, Kevin Anderson succeeded Yow, and the athletic department ran a $7.8 million deficit (Mandel, 2014).

The 2010–2011 year became a pivotal year for the University of Maryland as it faced a "dire financial situation" (Giannotto, 2012, ¶15). To facilitate spending, the athletic department was "borrowing from a reserve fund to cover its annual losses—until 2011, when it couldn't borrow any more, and the department blew up" (Gaul, 2015, p. 200). Likely this was in relation to the fact that during 2010–2011, Head Football Coach Ralph Friedgen was fired, and his contract was bought out for $2 million—despite a winning season and receipt of an ACC Coach of the Year Award (Duggan, 2014). Additionally, coaching staff spending increased 30%, from $18.7 million to $24.3 million, largely to include a hefty salary for new Head Football Coach Randy Edsall, but total revenue increased by only 15% (Clarke, 2012, June 28).

In the seven-year period from 2009 to 2015, University of Maryland financial data demonstrates that the athletic department either broke even or had

TABLE 3.1

**University of Maryland Athletics Finances, 2009–2015**

| Year | Student Fees | Total Revenues | Total Expenses | Difference |
|------|-------------|----------------|----------------|------------|
| 2009 | $8,944,228 | $62,949,159 | $62,901,837 | +47,322 |
| 2010 | $9,408,122 | $54,661,992 | $54,661,992 | 0 |
| 2011 | $9,508,278 | $61,634,829 | $61,632,000 | +2,829 |
| 2012 | $11,064,475 | $68,142,660 | $68,109,639 | +33,021 |
| 2013 | $11,181,286 | $63,714,470 | $63,367,929 | +346,541 |
| 2014 | $11,315,001 | $73,434,869 | $72,952,894 | +481,975 |
| 2015 | $11,632,008 | $92,686,128 | $92,558,535 | +127,593 |

Source: NCAA Finances, *USA Today*, http://sports.usatoday.com/ncaa/finances/

a slight surplus (*see* Table 3.1). In large part, however, that is related to various subsides—including a substantial contribution from student fees. In 2014, For example, the University of Maryland received $73,434,869 in athletics revenue, 24.7% of which was made up of subsidies (student fees, funds allocated by the school, and government support) (Wolverton et al., 2015).

The University of Maryland's financial struggles led it down the path of conference realignment, a catalyst explaining most institutional conference moves (Grasgreen, 2012). As mentioned previously in this chapter, on November 19, 2012, the University of Maryland Board of Regents agreed to accept an invitation to join the Big Ten conference and the university left its home in the ACC—an association in which it was a founding member and called home for 61 years. The Big Ten, composed of 14 member institutions, is "a national leader in intercollegiate athletics on and off the field" with a "mission of academic achievement and athletic success" ("BIG," 2016). Despite the University of Maryland's forfeiture of a $34.1 million exit fee to the ACC, University President Wallace Loh claimed the move was "to guarantee the long-term future of Maryland athletics" ("Loh Announces Maryland will join Big Ten," 2012, ¶4). Loh referred to the move as a "strategic interest" for the university, capable of "insur[ing] the financial sustainability of Maryland athletics for decades to come" (Mihoces, 2012, ¶3). Specifically, Loh explained that "[n]o future president will have to worry about cutting teams or that Maryland athletics will be at risk" ("Loh Announces Maryland will join Big Ten," 2012, ¶4). According to Loh, this conference shift would usher in an era in which the University of Maryland would develop "'a new financial paradigm for intercollegiate athletics' whereby the program supports the university and not vice versa" (Grasgreen, 2012, ¶11). In fact, Loh also indicated that "substantial funds" from the

Big Ten revenue stream would be earmarked for financial aid for the general student body (Grasgreen, 2012).

Maryland's membership in the ACC yielded an annual payout of $17 million, whereas the Big Ten contract was slated to provide $24 million annually at the time of the realignment (Grasgreen, 2012). Moreover, the Big Ten has the biggest television contract in college sports, with the conference projecting a $44.5 million revenue-sharing arrangement in 2017–2018, although the University of Maryland will not receive a full distribution until 2020–2021 (Mandel, 2014).

Conference realignments are "driven almost totally by a search for the best football TV contract. This TV money is viewed by some university leaders as a delightful balm that can soothe even the worst financial wounds" (Peterson-Horner & Eckstein, 2015, p. 79). Television revenue is thought to more than cover the spending associated with new facilities, coaching salaries, and a variety of highly paid athletics-related consultants, among other major expenses—despite the fact that the majority of intercollegiate athletics programs regularly lose large sums of money and the programs are subsidized in a variety of ways, just as the University of Maryland has been in recent years (Peterson-Horner & Eckstein, 2015).

In addition to a larger share of the revenue with the Big Ten TV contract, larger audiences and higher ratings are incentives for the University of Maryland as it aims to bolster its alumni base and increase the university's exposure across the country. Coaches and players have been happy with the Big Ten coverage via the cable channel, and the social media hits have improved for the athletics platforms, thus indicating the veracity of the Big Ten potential (Markus, 2015).

Loh has been very vocal about this type of exposure with his comments engendering the athademics ideology: "Athletics are the front porch of the University House—thousands of people who view athletics on cable television see the front porch. . . . What we are doing now is to connect the front porch between the rest of the academic house" (Silverman, 2014, ¶45). For its part, the Big Ten was keen on adding Maryland to the conference as the sports rights "package will now include 15% more league games before demographics and market forces even enter the picture" (Mandel, 2014, p. 56). Further, regionally, the University of Maryland brings the Big Ten access to the Washington D.C. and Baltimore markets, which adds 40 to 50 million viewers ("Listen to Ohio State," 2013). Recent developments also find Maryland alongside its fellow Big Ten rival, Rutgers, entering into the "Big Ten Battle in the Bronx" in a game held in Yankee Stadium in 2017, an event focused on "enhancing the Big Ten brand in the world's media capital" (Sargeant, 2016, ¶4).

## "A Democracy of Pain": The Contradictions of Elimination

Almost exactly one year prior to officially joining the Big Ten, and in response to the financial crisis of 2010–2011, the University of Maryland decided to cut 8 of the school's 27 varsity sports programs. On November 20, 2011, President Loh accepted the recommendation of an athletics commission formed to address the athletic department's mounting deficit, expected to total $4 million in 2012 and reach $17 million by 2017 (Gerstner, 2012). The commission recommended the elimination of the following programs: men's cross-country; men's indoor and outdoor track and field; men's and women's swimming and diving; men's tennis; women's water polo; and women's acrobatics and tumbling (formerly known as competitive cheer). The cuts would take effect on July 1, 2012, unless the teams could independently raise enough money to keep themselves afloat for the next 8 years. According to figures provided by the university, the funding required to save all 8 programs totaled $29 million, making the success of an independent fundraising drive over only 7 months highly unlikely (Prisbell, 2011). Additionally, for each program to survive, the University mandated the establishment of an endowment to fully finance the targeted sports and allow them to exist beyond 2020 (Gerstner, 2012).

Only one team managed to raise enough money to survive. The men's outdoor track and field team raised $888,000 out of the $940,000-mark set by the university, enough to allow the team to compete for the subsequent season (Gerstner, 2012). The other seven teams failed to meet the fundraising requirements and were officially eliminated on July 1, 2012. Upon accepting the recommendation that put the cuts into motion, Loh issued a written statement in which he acknowledged the tension between performance and opportunity:

> To continue to make deep cuts across all programs—to impose a democracy of pain—is not the path to excellence. . . . In a time of constrained resources, we have to choose: should we have fewer programs so that they can be better supported and, hence, more likely to be successful at the highest level? Or, should we keep the large number of programs that are under-supported compared to their conference peers? (quoted in Prisbell, 2011, ¶ 11)

Instead of honoring opportunity and participation, Loh chose the purported promise of "success." For Loh, the athletics department, and by extension the University of Maryland as a whole, the definition of that "success" is measured by the performance of the football and men's basketball teams—the programs that generate the most revenue and serve to enhance the branded image of the university (and pave the way for the proliferation of the athademic agenda).

In addition to denying more than 130 student-athletes annually the chance to participate in a varsity sport, the decision to eliminate the seven programs also erased important pieces of the university's athletic history and limited the natatorium to recreational use only. With the elimination of the women's acrobatics and tumbling team, the University of Maryland lost a program that had previously garnered national attention for its athletic prowess and cultural significance. In 2003, the University of Maryland was the first university to add women's competitive cheer as a varsity sport, meaning that the team was recognized as part of the athletic department, existed primarily for competition (rather than in support of other teams), and could offer athletic scholarships (Buzuvis, 2011). This separation of sideline cheerleading and competitive cheer was a pioneering move by the university, as it represented a nod to the growing popularity of competitive cheer and offered a challenge to standard definitions of sport used to comply with Title IX regulations (Clarke, 2012, April 13; Olson, 2008). Praised by many observers as "role models that did not need glitter, excessive makeup, and tiny midriff-baring tops to generate fan support, attention, and respect" (Buzuvis, 2011, p. 464), competitive cheer athletes at the University of Maryland helped to redefine notions of sport, athleticism, and femininity. As one member of Maryland's squad remarked upon learning of the team's elimination, "We can look back and say we did accomplish something and we did make a statement for women's sports" (quoted in Clarke, 2012, April 13, ¶35).

The swimming and diving and water polo teams represent three of the seven sports teams which were cut, all of which utilized the Eppley Recreation Center's (ERC) natatorium, a facility recognized as "one of the premier swimming and diving venues in the country" (Eppley Recreation Center, 2008, p. 3) and "one of the nation's most beautiful 50 m facilities" (Maryland—One Year Later, 2012, ¶5). Maryland's natatorium opened on January 31, 1998, as part of the $40 million ERC (Eppley Recreation Center, 2008). In addition to the other recreational opportunities the center provides, ERC maintains a substantial aquatics infrastructure, superior to that of most Division I programs around the country. It features an instructional pool, a competition pool, and two 1-m and two 3-m diving boards indoors, as well as a recreational pool and splash pool outdoors (Natatorium, 2016). The swimming complex—boasting seating for more than 1,000 spectators—hosted many important national and global swim meets, including, ACC Championships, FINA World Cup, YMCA Nationals, and USA Swimming Summer Long Course National Championships (Eppley Recreation Center, 2008). Today the natatorium hosts various swimming lessons programs and is utilized by the University of Maryland Aquatic Club (UMAC). The UMAC was established in 2013, founded by the ERC's aquatics director, and is sponsored by Campus Recreation Services (University of Maryland Aquatic Club, 2016).

Three years after the elimination of these aquatic sports, following the move to the Big Ten and the firing of Head Football Coach Randy Edsall, an editorial in *The Diamondback* (the student newspaper) took a strong position on the lack of varsity swimming, diving, and water polo programs at the University of Maryland:

> [This is a] very surprising circumstance, considering that the University of Maryland competes in a conference with outstanding aquatic

programs. In fact, having an aquatic program is fairly common for most universities, especially large public schools. Our failure in aquatic representation is pathetic and simply highlights the senseless decisions made by athletic department officials. (Sinha, 2015, ¶1)

To add to this lack of swimming infrastructure at the state's flagship university, is the fact that Maryland is home to some of the country's best club swimming teams and athletes, including Michael Phelps and Katie Ledecky, gold medalists who led the United States at the Rio Olympics in 2016. Maryland is the only school in the Big Ten that does not sponsor swimming and diving for women, and one of four that does not host a men's team (NCAA Sport Sponsorship, 2016). Further, based on sports that maintain an NCAA championship competition, Maryland hosts the fewest intercollegiate varsity teams in relation to their Big Ten conference peers (NCAA Sport Sponsorship, 2016) (*see* Table 3.2).

However, there is still no progress being made to bring back these seven eliminated sports though Loh and Anderson claimed they hoped some of the Big Ten money would be used to reinstate some of the teams that were cut (Grasgreen, 2012). The swimming and diving programs would cost only $11.6 million to maintain, and to fund all seven teams would have totaled less than $30 million (Sinha, 2015). In contrast, the Big Ten payout stands at $24 million annually (Grasgreen, 2012) and administration approved funding for the upcoming $155 million Cole Field House renovation (more later). Echoing Sinha (2015), a reporter for *The Diamondback*, this seems like a "pathetic" and "senseless" approach to intercollegiate athletic administration (c.f. Sinha, 2015).

## Athletics + Academics = The Cole Field House Renovation

Surprisingly, just three years after announcing the elimination of the eight programs to help balance the athletic department's budget, the University of Maryland unveiled plans for a $155-million renovation of Cole Field House, the historic former basketball arena and home to a multitude of campus offices, classroom spaces, meeting areas for university clubs, student groups, and an indoor practice facility for football. Plans for the 87,000 square-foot building were released in November 2014, construction began in late 2015, and work is expected to be complete by 2020. In announcing the renovation, President Loh—linking the academic enterprise with sporting prowess (more or less proffering the University of Maryland's attempt at the athademics paradigm), declared this to be "a signature project for our entire institution" and a "reminder of the world-class athletics, groundbreaking research and innovative academics" at the university (Maryland Athletics, 2014, ¶3). Loh placed athletics at the beginning of that list, but the new Cole Field House is supposed to be a place where athletics and academics coexist, mingle, and collaborate to showcase the strengths of the university. Only 30% of the total space, however, is slated for academic use (Kirshner, 2015), leading many to speculate that the project is a response to Maryland's move to the Big Ten as the football team attempts to keep pace with such conference stalwarts as Ohio State and Michigan. After all, the University of Maryland will be the last of the 14 Big-Ten institutions to have an indoor football complex (Stubbs, 2015).

The cornerstone of the project is the Terrapin Performance Center (TPC), which will include a regulation-size indoor football field, strength and conditioning facilities, locker rooms, offices for coaching staff, and team meeting rooms—all of which are purported to be "unmatched in Division I sports" (McClure, 2015, ¶3). These spaces are for the exclusive use of the football team, designed in response to similar facilities at other large universities such as Ohio State's Woody Hayes Athletic Center, Michigan State's Skandalaris Football Center, and the University of Oregon's Hatfield-Dowlin Complex. By investing so heavily in the football program, goes the logic employed by the university, Maryland will be able to recruit top football players, see a concomitant improvement in the team's performance in the Big Ten, and then benefit from increased national exposure and visibility. As Tom McMillen, a member of the University of Maryland Board of Regents who voted in support of the project, astutely noted, "We are in the football business. We need to make this work and be competitive" (quoted in Silverman, 2014, ¶10).

In addition to the TPC, the new Cole Field House will also feature the Center for Sports Medicine, Health & Human Performance (CSMHHP), a partnership between the University of Maryland College Park and the University of Maryland School of Medicine located in Baltimore. The center will provide medical services for all varsity athletes, as well as treatment for the rest of the student body and for members of the general public. Research conducted at the center will focus on such topics as improving human performance, understanding brain trauma, and designing injury-recovery and rehabilitation plans. Still, a key impetus for locating the center in the new Cole Field House is proximity to the athletics programs, particularly to the football team. The importance of this partnership was not lost on Athletic Director Kevin Anderson, who remarked that housing the CSMHHP alongside the football program is "a way we can make our student-athletes bigger, stronger, faster, and even more competitive than they are now" (quoted in Silverman, 2014, ¶32). The desire to create bigger, stronger, and more-competitive athletes through biomedical intervention sits alongside the supposed "need" for the TPC for the University of Maryland—specifically the football team—to perform well in the Big Ten and project a national image of success and achievement.

The final piece of the new Cole Field House is the Academy of Innovation and Entrepreneurship (AIE), a university-wide project that encourages students to design original products and start their own businesses. Launched by Loh

**Big Ten Sport Sponsorship**

| School | Baseball | Field Hockey | Football | M. Basketball | M. Cross Country | M. Fencing | M. Golf | M. Gymnastics | M. Ice Hockey | M. Lacrosse | M. Soccer | M. Swimming & Diving | M. Tennis | M. Track (Indoor) | M. Track (Outdoor) | M. Wrestling | Softball | W. Basketball | W. Cross Country | W. Fencing | W. Golf | W. Gymnastics | W. Lacrosse | W. Rowing | W. Soccer | W. Swimming & Diving | W. Tennis | W. Track (Indoor) | W. Track (Outdoor) | W. Volleyball | Grand Total |
|---|---|---|---|---|---|---|---|---|---|---|---|---|---|---|---|---|---|---|---|---|---|---|---|---|---|---|---|---|---|---|---|
| Indiana | 1 | 1 | 1 | 1 | 1 |  | 1 |  |  |  | 1 | 1 | 1 | 1 | 1 | 1 | 1 | 1 | 1 |  | 1 |  |  | 1 | 1 | 1 | 1 | 1 | 1 | 1 | 23 |
| Johns Hopkins |  |  |  |  |  |  |  |  |  | 1 |  |  |  |  |  |  |  |  |  |  |  |  | 1 |  |  |  |  |  |  |  | 2 |
| Michigan State | 1 | 1 | 1 | 1 | 1 |  | 1 |  | 1 |  | 1 | 1 | 1 | 1 | 1 | 1 | 1 | 1 | 1 |  | 1 | 1 |  | 1 | 1 | 1 | 1 | 1 | 1 | 1 | 25 |
| Northwestern | 1 | 1 | 1 | 1 |  |  | 1 |  |  |  | 1 | 1 | 1 |  |  | 1 | 1 | 1 | 1 |  | 1 |  | 1 |  | 1 | 1 | 1 | 1 | 1 | 1 | 20 |
| Penn State | 1 | 1 | 1 | 1 | 1 | 1 | 1 | 1 | 1 | 1 | 1 | 1 | 1 | 1 | 1 | 1 | 1 | 1 | 1 | 1 | 1 | 1 | 1 |  | 1 | 1 | 1 | 1 | 1 | 1 | 29 |
| Purdue | 1 |  | 1 | 1 | 1 |  | 1 |  |  |  |  | 1 | 1 | 1 | 1 | 1 | 1 | 1 | 1 |  | 1 |  |  |  | 1 | 1 | 1 | 1 | 1 | 1 | 20 |
| Rutgers | 1 | 1 | 1 | 1 | 1 |  | 1 |  |  | 1 | 1 |  |  | 1 | 1 | 1 | 1 | 1 | 1 |  | 1 | 1 | 1 | 1 | 1 | 1 | 1 | 1 | 1 | 1 | 24 |
| Ohio State | 1 | 1 | 1 | 1 | 1 |  | 1 | 1 | 1 | 1 | 1 | 1 | 1 | 1 | 1 | 1 | 1 | 1 | 1 |  | 1 | 1 | 1 | 1 | 1 | 1 | 1 | 1 | 1 | 1 | 28 |
| Illinois | 1 |  | 1 | 1 | 1 |  | 1 | 1 |  |  |  |  | 1 | 1 | 1 | 1 | 1 | 1 | 1 |  | 1 | 1 |  |  | 1 | 1 | 1 | 1 | 1 | 1 | 21 |
| Iowa | 1 | 1 | 1 | 1 | 1 |  | 1 | 1 |  |  |  | 1 | 1 | 1 | 1 | 1 | 1 | 1 | 1 |  | 1 | 1 |  | 1 | 1 | 1 | 1 | 1 | 1 | 1 | 24 |
| Maryland | 1 | 1 | 1 | 1 |  |  | 1 |  |  | 1 | 1 |  |  |  |  | 1 | 1 | 1 | 1 |  | 1 | 1 | 1 |  | 1 | 1 | 1 | 1 | 1 | 1 | 20 |
| Michigan | 1 | 1 | 1 | 1 | 1 |  | 1 | 1 | 1 | 1 | 1 | 1 | 1 | 1 | 1 | 1 | 1 | 1 | 1 |  | 1 | 1 | 1 | 1 | 1 | 1 | 1 | 1 | 1 | 1 | 28 |
| Minnesota | 1 |  | 1 | 1 | 1 |  | 1 | 1 | 1 |  |  | 1 | 1 | 1 | 1 | 1 | 1 | 1 | 1 |  | 1 | 1 |  | 1 | 1 | 1 | 1 | 1 | 1 | 1 | 24 |
| Nebraska | 1 |  | 1 | 1 | 1 |  | 1 | 1 |  |  |  |  | 1 | 1 | 1 | 1 | 1 | 1 | 1 |  | 1 | 1 |  |  | 1 | 1 | 1 | 1 | 1 | 1 | 21 |
| Wisconsin |  |  | 1 | 1 | 1 |  | 1 |  | 1 |  | 1 | 1 | 1 | 1 | 1 | 1 | 1 | 1 | 1 |  | 1 |  |  | 1 | 1 | 1 | 1 | 1 | 1 | 1 | 22 |
| Grand Total | 13 | 9 | 14 | 14 | 12 | 1 | 14 | 7 | 6 | 6 | 9 | 10 | 12 | 12 | 13 | 14 | 14 | 14 | 14 |  | 14 | 10 | 7 | 8 | 14 | 14 | 14 | 14 | 14 | 14 | 331 |

in 2013, and drawing on the "Fear the Turtle" university branding campaign, the AIE collaborates with various academic departments to offer "Fearless Ideas"—courses that focus on particular social, economic, or scientific problems and employ an experiential learning model to offer solutions through design and invention. These classes deliberately "emphasize practical experience over theoretical learning" (Wells, 2014, ¶7) and form the foundation of a wide-ranging program that aims to engage all students at the University of Maryland in entrepreneurship. Seeking to equip all students with the ability to make their own livelihood, Loh also recognizes the broader financial benefits of the AIE in remarking that "the odds are in your favor that if you educate students in entrepreneurship, they can have a big impact on the state's economy, create the next Under Armour" (quoted in Wells, 2014, ¶5). Loh's reference to the athletic apparel company started by Maryland alumnus Kevin Plank is apt, as Plank donated $25 million to the construction fund for the new Cole Field House and actively supports the mission of the AIE. In conversing with Loh, Plank told him that he wants "all 38,000 students to be exposed to innovation and entrepreneurship" and that Maryland has the opportunity to market itself as "the entrepreneurship university" (quoted in Barker, 2014, ¶30). Locating the AIE within the new Cole Field House is not without irony—the intersections of college athletics, academics, performance, business, and profit come crashing together under one athademically incestuous roof.

Accordingly, to finance this "transformative" athademic project, which, as Loh remarked, "brings together academics, research and athletics in ways that's never been done before, at least not on this campus," Plank donated $25 million and another $65 million is funded from private donations (Silverman, 2014). Just after plans for the renovation were approved, the university received authorization for $25 million ($5 million per year over five years) of state money for the project (Silverman, 2014). Revenues from the Big Ten will contribute $25 million, and the university itself will invest $5 million. The remaining amount will be covered by leasing clinical space in the CSMHHP and through academic programs (Silverman, 2014).

## The University of Under Armour and Maryland's Academic Focus

In addition to donating $25 million for the new Cole Field House project, Kevin Plank—founder and CEO of Under Armour and a former University of Maryland football player who graduated in 1996—has been intimately involved in numerous aspects of the university. Plank sits on the university's Board of Trustees, developed an endowment fund to support the AIE, and established the Cupid's Cup, an annual student entrepreneurial competition that awards $100,000 to a budding company. He also played a role in the hiring of Kevin Anderson as Maryland's athletic director in 2010. According to Anderson, Plank interviewed him as part of the hiring process (Tracy, 2015), an unusual role for the CEO of an apparel company to take on, but indicative of Plank's intense involvement in the business of the university.

Plank was also a vocal advocate for Maryland's move to the Big Ten, issuing the following statement when the move was approved.

> The ACC has been a great partner to Maryland throughout the years, however joining the Big Ten now provides new and exciting opportunities for our beloved university. The positive financial impact of this move has been well-documented; however, enhancing the experiences for all of our student-athletes and our campus as a whole is the most important consideration. I look forward to this new chapter for Maryland and I am excited for our future. (quoted in Walker, 2012, ¶17)

Ultimately Plank's involvement with Maryland has been both influential and important for the university's path forward in recent years. Yet, this also speaks to blending private and corporate interests with public education. Giroux and Giroux (2012, ¶1) warn that this practice positions "the academic mission of the university [as] less determined by internal criteria established by faculty researchers with the knowledge expertise and a commitment to the public good than by external market forces concerned with achieving fiscal stability."

Nevertheless, cementing Plank's ties to the University of Maryland, Under Armour and Maryland signed a 10-year partnership agreement in 2014 that will pay the university nearly $33 million in cash, apparel, and gear (Tracy, 2015). The company has long used the campus as a testing ground for new products, and the football players are often the first to try on the newest versions of Under Armour shoes, shirts, gloves, and other equipment. With the new Cole Field House project, this relationship between Under Armour and the university is set to expand and deepen. Not only did Plank make the keystone private donation, but he also lobbied to retain the Cole name. Speaking in reference to Plank's commitment to the new Cole Field House, President Loh stated that Plank "was the first to say, 'I want to keep the Cole name' " in order to enhance the branding of not only the new building, but the University as a whole (quoted in Barker, 2014, ¶33).

Maryland's increasing financial and leadership reliance on Plank and Under Armour echoes the recent interdependency between the University of Oregon and Nike. In fact, Anderson openly embraces the comparison and is seeking to replicate what has happened at Oregon. Reflecting on Maryland's connection with Under Armour, Anderson remarked that he "saw the beginnings of what Nike did with Oregon, and that's been our conversation from day one—that we can and do have that kind of relationship" (quoted in Tracy, 2015, p. A1). The link between Nike and Oregon has been steadily strengthening in the past decade due, in large part, to private donations from Phil Knight,

Nike's founder and an Oregon alumnus. Knight as spent more than $100 million of his own money to fund renovations of Autzen Stadium and the construction of the Hatfield-Dowlin Complex, the football team's operations and training center built at an estimated cost of $68 million and completed in 2013 (Gaul, 2015). A "testament to the college football arm's race" (Bishop, 2013, p. D1), Hatfield-Dowlin features locker rooms accessed by biometric thumbprints, a weight room decked in Brazilian hardwood, coaching offices complete with hydrotherapy pools, a Ring Room to display bowl and conference championship awards, an onsite barbershop with fixtures from Italy, and a cafeteria offering farm-to-table cuisine and espresso. Further to the notion of privatizing public space (Weaver, 2014) the behemoth locker room is only open to members of the football team and coaching staff (and occasionally the media and pro scouts).

It is this opulence that officials use to recruit talented players and lend an air of importance—however superficial—to the university as a whole. The influence of Knight and the Nike brand is so widespread across campus that the University of Oregon is regularly referred to as the "University of Nike" (Bishop, 2013; Gaul, 2015). In addition to Hatfield-Dowlin, other buildings on campus financed by Knight include the John J. Jaqua Academic Center for Student Athletes, Matthew Knight Arena, the Knight Library, and the Knight Law Center. Nike's presence on campus is inescapable, from the names on the buildings to the "Nike swooshes on some of the trash cans" (Gaul, 2015, p. 120). This interweaving of corporatization, branding, academics, and athletics demonstrates a successful, transformative athademics agenda, allowing Oregon to move "from a regional university with middling academic and athletic programs to a nationally ranked power in sports" (Gaul, 2015, p. 119), with an array of athletic infrastructure that has set the new standard for competitive programs.

In its drive to become a competitive force both within the Big Ten and nationally, Maryland is seeking to emulate Oregon, leverage its relationship with Under Armour, and ultimately ride "the largess of a multibillion-dollar apparel company to athletic prominence" (Tracy, 2015, p. A1). "Intercollegiate sports is all about branding—and monetizing the brand, especially football" (Gaul, 2015, p. 120), and is crucially important to long-term athletic and institutional success. "The glitz, glamour, and alleged profitability of high-visibility sports merge seamlessly with the growing neoliberal emphasis on branding, image, and mass consumption" (Peterson-Horner & Eckstein, 2015, p. 80). Thus, Maryland's public education merger with Under Armour's private corporation serves the university in a variety of important ways.

Further, there purported to be a positive relationship between the brand image fostered by sports, namely football, and university admissions, in that athletic success translates into higher SAT scores for incoming freshman (Mixon, Trevino & Minto, 2004). This trend has been evident at Maryland on the academic side. Data collected by the University of Maryland's Office of Institutional

TABLE 3.3

**University of Maryland New Freshman Profile**

|  | 2011 | 2012 | 2013 | 2014 | 2015 |
|---|---|---|---|---|---|
| Midpoint SAT Score | 1295 | 1300 | 1310 | 1315 | 1315 |
| High School GPA | 4.01 | 4.07 | 4.11 | 4.15 | 4.2 |

Source: Developed from annual "UMD Undergraduate Application Summary"
information prepared by the University of Maryland Office
of Institutional Research, Planning, & Assessment

Research, Planning, and Assessment, demonstrates that the academic profile of the university has increased since the announcement of the move to the Big Ten. In 2011, the midpoint SAT score for new freshman was a 1295. This steadily has increased each year, and by 2015 the midpoint was 1315. More telling than this change, perhaps, is the average high school GPA of new freshman students. In 2011 the average was 4.01, and this number also steadily has increased to 4.20 for the admitted class in 2015 (*see* Table 3.3). However, "athletic success" in the marquee revenue sports at Maryland might be overstating facts, particularly in comparison to many of their Big Ten peers. For example, from 2011 to 2015, the University of Maryland football went 23–39 and men's basketball was 88–51, with only one 20-win season in this period.

Overall, these numbers function as a barometer of student quality as measured by standardized tests and high school grade point averages. As Peterson-Horner & Eckstein (2015) argue, however,

> SAT scores are a problematic measure of academic quality because they can reflect things that have nothing to do with academic potential. Since SAT scores are standardized yearly, it is also very difficult to make comparisons except within the group taking the test in any given year. While 85 correct answers one year may receive a 660, the same number of correct answers the following year may receive a 640. These statistical fluctuations have nothing to do with the absolute "quality" of the individual test taker and everything to do with the relative performance of any individual compared to all those taking the same test. (p. 71)

Additionally, as of Fall 2015, student quantity had also increased; the number of applications to the university reached 35,572, the second highest in the university's history according to available institutional data. Overall, it is clear the profile of the University improved academically during a time where massive shifts within the athletics landscape were very public. There is no data to provide concrete evidence that the admissions statistics have been influenced by athletics, however it does appear that the Big Ten move, Kevin Plank's investment in the university, and the athletic infrastructure and facility plans might have contributed to the increases in incoming student performance as illustrated in Table 3.3.

In addition to the conference realignment and various capital spending projects, it is also important to note—consistent with the athademic imperative—the conference shift brings with it academic access via the Big Ten's Committee on Institutional Cooperation (CIC) (formerly the Big Ten Academic Alliance), an asset that Loh has touted as influential in the conference move (Grasgreen, 2012). The CIC, established in 1958, is comprised of the member universities in the Big Ten Conference, along with the University of Chicago, and through membership, Maryland students have access to 1,700 study-abroad programs and a variety of courses, research opportunities at various campuses, online access to millions of books, faster interlibrary-loan item receipt, and more than $3 million of new content due to the sharing of resources (Baillargeon & Silverman, 2015; BIG, 2016; Scharper, 2012).

In 2013, the 15 schools comprising the CIC produced more than $10 billion in funded research—an amount that exceeds that of any other conference by $4 billion (BIG, 2016). Loh has argued that the academic part of the Big Ten move is significant for the university (Scharper, 2012), and Chancellor Brit Kirwan—also a member of the Knight Commission on Intercollegiate Athletics—has explained the CIC as "unmatched in academic collaboration anywhere else save possibly for the Ivy League, so the move will advance Maryland's academic mission" (Grasgreen, 2012, ¶15). It is worth mentioning, however, that the member schools of the ACC have highly regarded academic institutions, four of which rank in the top 30 of the *U.S. News & World Report* college rankings, compared with only two in the Big Ten (Scharper, 2012). So, although this move has the potential to facilitate important academic opportunities, to say that it is a substantial improvement from the company of Maryland's ACC peers is not a fair assessment.

## Protecting the Porch: The Athademics Paradigm

July 1, 2016, marked the two-year anniversary of Maryland's Big Ten tenure. The revenue-generating marquee teams, men's basketball and football, "had better-than-expected inaugural seasons in the league" (Markus, 2015, ¶6), but in the second year, football game attendance dropped by 13%—one of the five largest dips in the 65 "Power Five" programs (Stubbs, 2015). Further, Sinha (2015, ¶4) reports "the game-day atmosphere is almost nonexistent. Students barely make it through the first half of a game, and football is still losing money. We're reliving 2011." Nonetheless, the University of Maryland administration has indicated they are on track and "very optimistic" about their ability to generate a budget surplus by 2018 (Baillargeon & Silverman, 2015, ¶36). However, Sinha (2015) raises some insightful and important points:

> After years of budget cuts, hiring freezes and employee furloughs, the athletic department is still dumping money into a program that isn't going anywhere. Not to mention that there has been little to no effort to bring back the seven varsity sports programs that were eliminated to make budget room for football in 2011. . . . Head coach firings, program spending and team cuts might not seem to directly impact the general student population, but when there's an evident lack of financial or academic benefits resulting from million-dollar investments, that becomes everyone's problem. (¶5 and 8)

To take this argument even further, we contend that with Plank's massive cash infusion and general university-related involvement, the ability to (rather easily) generate a total of $155 million for facility upgrades and capital improvements, and the increased Big Ten revenue following the realignment, that perhaps fulfilling the mission of both the university and intercollegiate athletics should involve the reinstatement of the seven intercollegiate sports that were cut in 2011. But that has yet to happen.

In fact, if the University of Maryland continues down the road it is currently on, one might wonder at what point Maryland Stadium—facing peer pressure from its 100,000+ capacity Big Ten rivals, Beaver Stadium, The Horse Shoe, and The Big House—will find a new home amid an even bigger, shinier, and more-costly Kevin Plank and Under Armour venture. Perhaps we will find the Terps sitting on the front porch alongside the Washington Redskins at the Under Armour Sports Complex in a renovated Robert F. Kennedy Memorial Stadium, a la Heinz field that serves the University of Pittsburgh and its professional football franchise, the Pittsburgh Steelers.

Speculation aside, the current context at Maryland is fantastical enough, reinforcing the "fiction of college football as education" (Gaul, 2015, p. 230), masquerading as a cooperative athademic venture. In fact, Loh has argued Maryland's competitive advantage rests squarely within this athademic mindset, explaining, "What makes us special—unique in the nation—is that we're combining this facility [The Cole Field House] together with the academic mission of the university" (Barker, 2014, ¶31). This ideology is pervasive, at least throughout the state of Maryland, with Towson University Director of Athletics, Tim Leonard, recently explaining that "so much hinges on football," and thus working to augment athletics programs will bolster everything at the university, including academics (Ordine, 2016, ¶34). Although institutional decisions would indicate otherwise, Loh has stated that Maryland's two main goals are a commitment to "No. 1, academic excellence, and No. 2, athletic excellence" (Barker, 2010, ¶8).

Interestingly, however, Maryland's most recent mission and goals statement, approved on December 16, 2015, following all of these athademic developments, states nothing about the blending of athletics and academics:

> The mission of the University of Maryland, College Park is to provide excellent teaching, research, and service. The University educates students and advances knowledge in areas of importance to the State, the nation, and the world. The University is committed to being a preeminent national center for research and for graduate education, and the institution of choice for Maryland's undergraduates of exceptional ability and promise. (Mission and Goals Statement, 2015, ¶1)

In fact, the mission of the university clearly states a distinct focus on the academic arm of its operations. Despite these public declarations and responsibilities, however, Maryland's priorities appear to promote an exploitative commitment to athletics first, to attract financing, corporate partnerships, and positive branding.

## Conclusion

This chapter argues that Maryland's national exposure via the Big Ten Conference has steadily increased the profile of new students since the realignment was announced, thus indirectly increasing the admission standards of the university and improving the national academic ranking of the school, a la the "Flutie Factor"[2] (*see* Peterson-Horner & Eckstein, 2015). But what does this really have to do with the goal of the educational enterprise that is the premiere institution in the State of Maryland? Likely it facilitates the need for increased student fees and increased class sizes, thus yielding a more costly and devalued education for these students with "exceptional ability and promise." Moreover, this contributes to the development of a campus and institutional athletic culture that Giroux and Giroux (2012) depict as:

> favor[ing] entertainment over education the more physical and destructive, the better; competition over collaboration; a worshipful stance toward iconic sports heroes over thoughtful engagement with academic leaders, who should inspire by virtue of their intellectual prowess and moral courage; and herdlike adhesion to coach and team over and against one's own capacity for informed judgment and critical analysis. (¶11)

Extending this argument, we assert that the blending of athletics and academics—our concept of athademics—a certain ramification of this neoliberal context described by Giroux and Giroux (2012), has done little to effectively support intellectual rigor and exploration at the University of Maryland. Instead, the bulk of a $155-million facility is devoted to athletics, and Under

Armour continues to use Maryland's student-athletes as a testing subjects for product development and marketing. This makes sense, however, in a corporatized university environment where "campuses have come to look like shopping malls, treat students as customers, confuse education with training and hawk entertainment and commodification rather than higher learning as the organizing principles of student life" (Giroux & Giroux, 2012, ¶14).

Ultimately, the University of Maryland's move to the Big Ten was anchored in a desire to augment the brand image—the "front porch"—of the university across the nation. There is no data, however, to support the fact that the university is a better academic institution today than it was in 2011, nor is there any concrete evidence that the Big Ten move has made the Terps any better athletically. This leads us to assert that it does not actually matter if the "front porch" argument holds true, it just matters that (1) private citizens and future students believe it; and (2) that administrators, athletics directors, and academic officers alike, work not only to carry it out but also to perpetuate it. Further, for the University of Maryland, it matters that Kevin Plank and Under Armour continue to believe it. The company's financial and leadership investment in the university relies on the metaphor of the "front porch," as the links between Under Armour's corporate sponsorship, Plank's personal involvement, and the growth of the university hinge on the successful image of the school's athletics. Although Loh attempted to "fix the front porch" by eliminating the seven varsity teams and instigating the move to the Big Ten, perhaps now the concern is to "protect the porch." Under Armour's advertising tagline has long been "Protect this House," yet its clear financial interest in the University of Maryland athletics speaks more to merely the porch rather than the rest of the (academic) house. In embracing the athademics imperative, Maryland appears to be operating with the motto of "Protect this Porch," increasingly dismissing the importance of the academic house, while bolstering the athletics infrastructure to make the porch as exclusive and successful as possible.

## Discussion

Even if research shows that athletics are not the "front porch" of an institution it remains a public truth. As an (athletic) administrator what good does it do to admit that athletics might not be as beneficial to a university as it has been suggested?

### NOTES

1. Byrd Stadium, built in 1950, was named after Harry C. "Curley" Byrd. Harry Byrd was a former Maryland football player, English and history teacher, athletic director, and university president. Despite his strong legacy at the university, he opposed racial integration. Ultimately his name was removed due to his segregationist views and

the University of Maryland's desire to demonstrate the institution's modern values (Wenger, 2015).

2. It is important to note here that, although the "Flutie Factor" is oft-used by (athletic department) administrators, there is no peer-reviewed academic study demonstrating the direct causal link between athletic success and academic improvement. It is truly a myth that has been made into reality to serve administrative ideals.

## REFERENCES

Baillargeon, R. & Silverman, E. (2015, July 2). Sweet escape, sweeter embrace. The Diamondback. Retrieved July 12, 2016, from http://features.dbknews.com/2015/07/02/maryland -terrapins-move-big-ten-analysis-anniversary/

Barker, J. (2010, August 18). New Maryland president says he'll play role in AD search. The Baltimore Sun Retrieved July 12, 2016, from http://articles.baltimoresun.com/2010–08– 18/sports/bs-sp-terps-president-athletics-0819–20100818_1_loh-search-committee- new-maryland

Barker, J. (2014, November 21). Plank's relationship with UMD is multilayered. The Baltimore Sun. Retrieved July 3, 2016, from http://www.baltimoresun.com/business/under -armour-blog/bs-bz-plank-terps-20141121-story.html

BIG. (2016). Big Ten History. Retrieved July 11, 2016, from http://www.bigten.org/school-bio /big10-school-bio.html

Bishop, G. (2013, August 3). We are the University of Nike. New York Times, p. D1.

Buzuvis, E. (2011). The feminist case for the NCAA's recognition of competitive cheer as an emerging sport for women. Boston College Law Review 52, 439–464.

Clarke, L. (2012, April 13). Title IX anniversary: Maryland cuts cheerleading, but was it ever a sport? The Washington Post. Retrieved July 19, 2016, from https://www.washingtonpost .com/sports/colleges/title-ix-anniversary-maryland-cuts-cheerleading-but-was-it -ever-a-sport/2012/04/13/gIQA5EkRFT_story.html

Clarke, L. (2012, June 28). Maryland athletics' financial woes reveal a broken college sports revenue model. The Washington Post. Retrieved July 2, 2016, from https://www .washingtonpost.com/sports/colleges/maryland-athletics-financial-woes-reveal-a -broken-college-sports-revenue-model/2012/06/28/gJQAmEvx9V_story.html

Duggan, D. (2014, November 26). Boomer Esiason on Ralph Friedgen's firing at Maryland: "He got caught in the perfect storm." NJ Advance Media. Retrieved July 12, 2016, from http://www.nj.com/rutgersfootball/index.ssf/2014/11/boomer_esiason_on_ralph _friedgens_firing_at_maryland_he_got_caught_in_the_perfect_storm.html

Eppley Recreation Center. (2008). UM Terps. Retrieved July 11, 2016, from http://www .umterps.com/fls/29700/old_site/pdf/m-swim/0708swimmgintro.pdf?DB_OEM_ID =29700

Gaul, G.M. (2015). Billion-dollar ball: A journey through the big-money culture of college football. New York: Viking.

Gerstner, J. (2012, July 3). Seven sports are eliminated at Maryland. The New York Times. Retrieved July 2, 2016, from http://thequad.blogs.nytimes.com/2012/07/03/seven -sports-are-eliminated-at-maryland/?_r=0

Giannotto, M. (2012, July 2). Maryland cuts seven sports on "sad day" in College Park. The Washington Post. Retrieved July 11, 2016, from https://www.washingtonpost.com/sports /maryland-cuts-seven-sports-on-sad-day-in-college-park/2012/07/02/gJQAqJFBJW _story.html

Giroux, H. & Giroux, S. S. (2012). Universities gone wild: Big money, big sports and scandalous abuse at Penn State. Truthout.org. January 5.

Grasgreen, A. (2012, November 20). Big terrapins. *Inside Higher Ed.* Retrieved July 2, 2016, from https://www.insidehighered.com/news/2012/11/20/maryland-departs-acc-big -ten-conference

Kirshner, A. (2015, January 26). After state pledges $25 million for Cole Field House, University of Maryland finds itself in budget crisis. *Testudo Times.* Retrieved July 3, 2016. http://www.testudotimes.com/2015/1/26/7560711/maryland-state-budget-cole-field -house-project

Listen to Ohio State's Gordon Gee's controversial remarks in their entirety. (2013, May 31). *Sports Illustrated.* Retrieved July 7, 2016, from http://www.si.com/college-football /campus-union/2013/05/31/ohio-state-gordon-gee-controversial-comments

Loh announces Maryland will join Big Ten. (2012, November 19). *The Diamondback.* Retrieved July 2, 2016, from http://www.diamondbackonline.com/news/national /article_32918b36–31fb-11e2-b0d9–001a4bcf6878.html

Mandel, S. (2014, June 23). The long play. *Sports Illustrated,* 120 (25), 53–56.

Maryland Athletics. (2014, November 21). Maryland unveils new vision for Cole Field House. *UM Terps.* Retrieved July 2, 2016, from http://www.umterps.com/ViewArticle .dbml?ATCLID=209770880

Maryland—One year later. (2012, November 8). College swimming. Retrieved July 11, 2016, from https://www.collegeswimming.com/news/2012/nov/08/maryland-one-year-later/

Markus, D. (2015, June 27). One year after joining Big Ten, Maryland on the road to solvency and success. *The Baltimore Sun.* Retrieved July 2, 2016, from http://www.baltimoresun .com/sports/bs-sp-terps-big-ten-anniversary-0628–20150627-story.html

McClure, K. R. (2015, January 12). How one building reveals what's wrong with higher education. *The Chronical of Higher Education.* Retrieved July 2, 2016, from http://chronicle .com/blogs/conversation/2015/01/12/how-one-building-reveals-whats-wrong-with -higher-education/

Mihoces, G. (2012, November 20). Maryland leaves ACC for more money. *USA Today.* Retrieved July 23, 2015, from http://www.usatoday.com/story/sports/college/2012/11/19 /maryland-leaves-acc-for-big-ten/1715635/

Mission and Goals Statement: University of Maryland, College Park. (2015, December 16). University of Maryland Office of the Provost. Retrieved July 12, 2016, from http://www .provost.umd.edu/mission_statement.cfm

Mixon, F. G., Trevino, L. J., & Minto, T. C. (2004). Touchdowns and test scores: Exploring the relationship between athletics and academics. *Applied Economics Letters* 11, 421–424.

Natatorium. (2016). University Recreation & Wellness. Retrieved July 11, 2016, from http:// recwell.umd.edu/Facilities/Aquatic-Facilities

NCAA Sport Sponsorship. (2016). NCAA. Retrieved July 11, 2016, from http://web1.ncaa.org /onlineDir/exec2/sponsorship

Olson, S. (2008). *From sidelines to center stage: The development of collegiate competitive cheer* (Unpublished master's thesis). The University of Maryland, College Park, Maryland.

Ordine, B. (2016, June 15). Tim Leonard's vision for Towson athletics. *Pressbox Online.* Retrieved September 14, 2016, from https://www.pressboxonline.com/2016/06/15/tim -leonards-vision-for-towson-athletics

Peterson-Horner, E., & Eckstein, R. (2015). Challenging the "Flutie Factor": Intercollegiate sports, undergraduate enrollments, and the neoliberal university. *Humanity & Society,* 39(1), 64–85.

Prisbell, E. (2011, November 21). Maryland accepts recommendation, will cut eight varsity sports programs. *The Washington Post.* Retrieved July 7, 2016, from https://www .washingtonpost.com/sports/maryland-accepts-recommendation-will-cut-eight -varsity-sports-programs/2011/11/21/gIQAyn1NjN_story.html

Sargeant, K. (2016, September 13). Rutgers, Maryland to play football-wrestling double-header at Yankee Stadium. *NJ.com*. Retrieved September 14, 2016, from http://www .nj.com/rutgersfootball/index.ssf/2016/09/rutgers_and_maryland_to_stage_football -wrestling_d.html

Scharper, J. (2012, November 22). Big Ten brings Maryland new chances for study, research. *The Baltimore Sun*. Retrieved July 2, 2016. http://articles.baltimoresun.com/2012–11–22/ news/bs-md-umd-academics-20121122_1_university-system-acciac-big-ten

Silverman, E. (2014, November 20). Finance committee pushes Cole Field House proposal forward, Maryland leaders react. *The Diamondback*. Retrieved July 8, 2016, from http:// www.dbknews.com/archives/article_c64c2e66–709d-11e4–9e4e-53959a4937df.html

Sinha, S. (2015, October 15). University of Maryland Athletic Department makes poor decisions. *The Diamondback*. Retrieved July 11, 2016, from http://www.dbknews.com /archives/article_58ce6bc6–7397–11e5-ae60–23cb18fe3467.html

Stubbs, R. (2015, October 11). Maryland fires football coach Randy Edsall. *The Washington Post*. Retrieved July 12, 2016, from https://www.washingtonpost.com/news/terrapins -insider/wp/2015/10/11/randy-edsall-is-fired-as-maryland-football-coach/

Tracy, M. (2015, August 26). Nike Got Ducks. Under Armour Gets Terrapins. *New York Times*, p. A1.

University of Maryland Aquatic Club. (2016). About UMAC. Retrieved July 11, 2016, from https://www.teamunify.com/SubTabGeneric.jsp?team=mdumdcp&_stabid_=90814.

University of Maryland Undergraduate Application Summary. (2012). Office of Institutional Research, Planning, & Assessment. College Park, MD: University of Maryland.

University of Maryland Undergraduate Application Summary. (2013). Office of Institutional Research, Planning, & Assessment. College Park, MD: University of Maryland.

University of Maryland Undergraduate Application Summary. (2014). Office of Institutional Research, Planning, & Assessment. College Park, MD: University of Maryland.

University of Maryland Undergraduate Application Summary. (2015). Office of Institutional Research, Planning, & Assessment. College Park, MD: University of Maryland.

Walker, C. (2012, November 20). Move to Big Ten a defining one for University of Maryland President Wallace Loh. *The Baltimore Sun*. Retrieved July 2, 2016. http://www .baltimoresun.com/sports/terps/bs-sp-big-ten-maryland-loh-1121-20121120-story .html

Weaver, T. (2014). The Privatization of Public Space: The New Enclosures. APSA 2014 Annual Meeting Paper. Retrieved July 2, 2016 http://htttps://ssrn.com/abstract=2454138

Wells, C. (2014, May 6). At College Park, an all-encompassing focus on entrepreneurship. *The Baltimore Sun*. Retrieved July 9, 2016, from http://articles.baltimoresun.com/2014-05-06 /news/bs-md-umd-loh-innovation-20140505_1_entrepreneurship-loh-honors-college

Wenger, Y. (2015, December 11). Byrd Stadium to become Maryland Stadium after regents vote. *The Baltimore Sun*. Retrieved September 12, 2016, from http://www.baltimoresun .com/news/maryland/bs-md-byrd-stadium-vote-20151211-story.html

Wolverton, B., Hallman, B., Shifflett, S., & Kambhampati, S. (2015, November 15). The $10-billion sports tab: How college students are funding the athletics arms race. *The Chronicle of Higher Education*. Retrieved May 7, 2016, from http://chronicle.com /interactives/ncaa-subsidies-main?cid=at&utm_source=at&utm_medium=en&elq =178fbfd27fd94a3dac36a8a4c8cc3c8a&elqCampaignId=1841&elqaid=6894&elqat=1& elqTrackId=37ea3dec289e45aaa8f12757d89e52c2#id=table_2014

# 4

# Football, Rape Culture, and the Neoliberal University (as) Brand

## Reflections on Institutional Governance in the Jameis Winston Rape Investigation

MATTHEW G. HAWZEN, LAUREN C. ANDERSON,
AND JOSHUA I. NEWMAN

On January 25, 2015, The Florida State University Board of Trustees—a public body corporate of the State of Florida acting for and on behalf of Florida State University (FSU)—settled a federal Title IX lawsuit with a former female student, called "Jane Doe" to protect her identity (Jane Doe vs. The Florida State University Board of Trustees, 2015). The student claimed that the university acted "deliberately indifferent" toward her allegations that she was sexually assaulted by former Florida State University quarterback Jameis Winston on the night of December 7, 2012, and that the university concealed and obstructed the investigation to allow Winston to play football (Axon, 2015; Tracy 2016).

As soon as the FSU Athletic Department was informed that Winston was being investigated for sexual assault, federal law mandates that it immediately inform university administrators. Title IX states, "[O]nce a college or university knows or reasonably should know of possible sexual harassment of students, it must take 'immediate and appropriate steps to investigate or otherwise determine what occurred' " (Hogan, 2005, pp. 319–320).[1]

According to the plaintiff,

> On January 22, 2013, the FSU Athletics Department was in contact with the Tallahassee Police and learned that Winston had been identified as the suspect in a violent sexual assault. The FSU Athletics Department called meetings involving high-ranking FSU Athletics Department and

football officials, Winston, and Winston's lawyer. On information and belief, head football coach James "Jimbo" Fisher ("Fisher") and Senior Associate Athletics Director Frances "Monk" Bonasorte ("Bonasorte") became aware of the rape accusations against Winston at that time. . . .

For the next eleven months, FSU did nothing to investigate Plaintiff's report of rape while the FSU Athletics Department continued to keep the incident a secret. Despite Plaintiff's report to the FSU Police and the FSU Athletics Department's knowledge of the suspect's identity, no one at FSU conducted any investigation into the matter. Winston, meanwhile, was named starting quarterback of the football team and, in the fall of 2013, led FSU in the pursuit of a national championship. (*Jane Doe vs. The Florida State University Board of Trustee*, 2015, pp. 3–4)

In the settlement, FSU admitted to no liability for mishandling the investigation, agreed to pay Jane Doe $950,000 in damages, and made a five-year commitment to campus-wide sexual assault awareness, prevention, and training programs. Winston was not charged by the State of Florida for sexual assault—for reasons not altogether clear, even to legal experts around the nation (*see* Luther, 2015). Nor was Winston, who came under the university's internal Title IX investigation, found in to be violation of FSU's Student Code of Conduct (Spousta, 2014).

Examining the behind-the-scenes (mis)dealings and juridical two-steps of FSU decision makers and the Tallahassee Police, journalists and critics were quick to lay bare the actions of those in power who ultimately defined the legal, moral, cultural understandings, and outcomes of the event (Axon, 2015; Bogdanich, 2014; Luther, 2015). A *New York Times* article not convinced of Winston's moral *innocence*—which is to be read differently from his legal not-guilty status—suggested, "Winston was never criminally charged in the case, in part . . . because a number of shortcomings in the police investigation left him [local prosecutor William Meggs] without the evidence needed to sustain a charge of rape" (Tracy, 2016, ¶2). Another *New York Times* report declared, "Records show that Florida State's athletic department knew about the rape accusation . . . in January 2013. . . . Even so, the university did nothing about it, allowing Mr. Winston to play the full season without having to answer any questions" (Bogdanich, 2014, ¶10).

These journalistic accounts, which call into question the integrity of the university and police investigations, provide a critical starting point from which to extend a social and cultural analysis of the interconnections between sexual violence and institutional (sport) governance in the age of big-time athletics and corporatized higher education. Extending this critical examination of the "Jameis Winston rape investigation" (as it became commonly referred to in the media, see Petchesky, 2014), this chapter argues that the various (mis)handlings of the rape investigation(s)—as depicted in publicly available testimonies, documents, and other accounts—reveal the operations of wider neoliberal governance strategies and corporate logics by which athletic departments and university officials negotiating scandals involving economically valuable student-athletes are compelled to support the smooth continuation of revenue-generating projects (Giroux, 2007) such as "big-time" college football (Andrews & Silk, 2012; King, 2012). In so doing, the authors suggest that this event—the violence described by Jane Doe, the police (and university) investigation, and the exoneration of both Winston and FSU—exemplifies particular institutional strategies, logics, and practices that prioritize the protection of the school's (brand) image, cultural legacy, and Seminole's football-consuming community over the care and support for victims and sufferers of sexual violence.[2] Our point in doing so is not to reveal new "evidence" which would prove Winston's guilt or innocence (as we do not have access to such evidence), but rather to explore the *institutional violence* perpetrated upon the female student by the Tallahassee police, Florida State University, and its various athletics constituencies.

To develop a critical understanding of institutional sexual violence, we draw upon insights developed by cultural theorist Michel Foucault (1980; 1991; 2000) and second-wave feminists, namely Susan Brownmiller (1975) and Joyce Williams (1979). Foucault developed critical perspectives on operations of power, the production of subjects and subjectivity, and governmental reasoning, or governmentality. Foucault would have us begin our analysis with the event—the violence against the female student as constituted in various physical, discursive, and political acts—because the event represents a "problematization" of institutional governance and interests, or, more precisely, a threat to the FSU college football enterprise. When the value of the college football commodity comes under threat, the operations of power and governmental (read: corporate-capitalistic) logics of the neoliberal university are put into motion in such a way that power can be ascertained. Thus, rather than moralize the investigatory practices of local authorities and FSU, we use the violent event "as a chemical catalyst so as to bring to light power relations, locate their position, find out their point of application and the methods used" (Foucault, 2000, p. 329).

We are concerned here with what Foucault might call a neoliberal university *dispositif*—a reactionary apparatus—to the production and governance of subjects, and in particular where governmental actions, rhetoric, and decisions made by athletic departments seem to privilege the interests and primacy of intercollegiate athletics over the well-being of the general student population, and in this case the well-being of women on the FSU campus. The chapter traces how, under these institutional strategies, the *dispositif* is mobilized: (1) to obscure (and thereby reconstitute) what Brownmiller, Williams, and other feminist scholars have termed "rape culture" on college campuses; (2) to initiate discursive and administrative action whereunto concern for physical violence gives way to abjection of the victim and her allies in the public sphere; and

(3) to displace both action and actors who might threaten institutional order into what Foucault might refer to as "crisis heterotopias."[3]

Our analytic strategy suggests that these moments and spaces of "crisis"— when decision makers forced to negotiate personal, ethical, scholastic, athletic, legal, and economic standards take concrete action—tell us something about the goals, objectives, and values shaping contemporary academic institutions. This, in turn, reveals the ways in which certain (student) bodies come to matter over and against others. As illustrated with the details of the Winston rape investigation (as made available through the media and court documents), it becomes abundantly clear that university and local officials were compelled to protect the valuable Seminole football commodity in lieu of an adequate search for truth about what happened to the female student that night. Although these strategies employed by FSU and local authorities paid dividends for FSU, Winston, and the wider Seminole football community, they failed to adequately address the issue of sexual violence and care for the victim.

## Managing Sexual Violence

During his brief college football career, Jameis Winston became a marquee college football icon. Winston excelled on the field, and sport media enjoyed his public persona, his "Magic Johnson-caliber smile" (Ziering & Dick, 2015). He became part of FSU's illustrious gridiron prestige and college football's preeminence in the U.S. South's popular imaginary. In the 2013–2014 season, Winston led the Florida State Seminoles football team to the school's third undefeated season and a Bowl Championship Series (BCS) National Championship victory, and became the youngest player to ever win the Heisman Trophy (awarded to college football's most outstanding player). Winston, the heralded redshirt freshman, exploded onto the national scene when he completed 25 of 27 passes for 356 yards and 4 touchdowns in the season opener against the University of Pittsburgh. His stardom culminated later that season when he brought the 'Noles back from a 20–10 halftime deficit, scoring 21 points in the fourth quarter, to lead the team to a last-minute national championship victory over Auburn University, with a score of 34 to 31.

About one year prior to that national championship winning night—on December 7, 2012, to be exact—Tallahassee police responded to Jane Doe's sexual battery complaint—and Jameis Winston later became the primary suspect. Late that night, FSU police transported the female student to the hospital for treatment, interviewing, and evidence collection. According to Jane Doe's account to police and in a later interview:

> I was at Potbelly's with [friends] Monique and Marcus. We all shared about 5 or 6 drinks. We were hanging out mostly with Marcus' friends.

One of them gave me a shot. *I was fairly certain there was something in that drink. I did not drink nearly enough to be drunk and incompetent that night.* Monique left. I texted her to see if she had my ID and my room key. She said that she left all the stuff with me. Next thing I know I was in the back of a taxi with a random guy that I have never met. There was another person in the taxi. We went to an apartment, I don't know where it was. I kept telling him to stop but he took all my clothes off. *He was on top of me. He was sexually assaulting me. He was raping me. I couldn't really breath that much. I kept saying stop, stop.* And then his roommate came in and told him *dude stop what are you doing? He picked me up and carried me to the bathroom* "because the [bathroom] door locked." *He put me on the tile bathroom floor. I was trying to push him off and kick him off but he was just too big. I said please stop multiple times and I said no. He put his hand over my face and pushed my face into the floor and he just continued to rape me. He finished and he* put my clothes on and we went outside and got on his scooter. . . . He dropped me off at Call and Stadium and then left. (Tallahassee Police Department, 2012d, p. 1; Ziering & Dick, 2015)[4]

While hospitalized, she received a rape kit from investigators to gather evidence about the assault and her assailant (Tallahassee Police Department, 2012a). Foreign blood and semen—later determined to be Winston's—were found on her underwear (Bogdanich, 2014). As Jane lay in the hospital bed, investigators and nurses watched as "several bruises began to appear on the victim," indicating recent trauma (Tallahassee Police Department, 2012a; Ziering & Dick, 2015).

What is striking is that investigators were unable to identify a suspect that night or in the weeks that followed—even though Jane Doe provided enough information for Tallahassee Police Department to locate and identify the suspect within 24 hours of the incident (Axon, 2015; Bogdanich, 2014; Ziering & Dick, 2015). About a month later, she was in class at the start of the Spring 2013 semester when she recognized her assailant—who was then identified by the instructor during the taking of attendance as Jameis Winston (Ziering & Dick, 2015). Later that day, the female student called lead investigator Scott Angulo of the Tallahassee Police Department and gave him her assailant's name—Jameis Winston.

A *New York Times* investigation noted that Angulo waited two weeks to interview Winston—*opting to call Winston on the phone*—and did not obtain Winston's DNA (Bogdanich, 2014). When Winston learned of the ongoing investigation via telephone, he informed FSU's Athletic Department. Members of the Athletic Department then referred Winston to an attorney, and they called Angulo's assistant to inquire about the case. The defense was able to prepare for the case for almost a year before the case was handed to the State—at which point, due to public records requests, the case became publicly known (Vaughan, 2014).

After Jane identified her assailant to Angulo, Jane's attorney, Patricia Carroll, requested that police obtain Winston's DNA. Angulo warned, it "might generate publicity" (Bogdanich, 2014; Portman & Burlew, 2013). According to multiple media sources, Angulo reinforced to the female student's family that "Tallahassee was a "big football town and the victim needs to think long and hard before proceeding against him [Winston] because she will be raked over the coals and her life will be made miserable" (Associated Press, 2013; Portman & Burlew, 2013, ¶21; Ziering & Dick, 2015). Obtaining DNA evidence had nothing to do with how she would be treated in the public per se, but it was when the investigation became publicly known that the accuser would be "made miserable."

On February 11, 2013, investigator Angulo suspended the rape investigation without informing Jane of the decision. Angulo's reasoning for suspending the investigation was due to "a lack of cooperation from the *victim*"—a claim later refuted by Jane's attorney (Bogdanich, 2014). From the time of the suspension of the investigation, there was an 11-month delay before the case was taken up by the state level, to prosecutor William "Willie" Meggs, on November 12, 2013. The time lost between February and November would prove pivotal in the outcomes of FSU's and the Tallahassee Police's investigations.

The clearest explanation for the 11-month delay is that Tallahassee Police had taken various missteps in the construction of a flimsy case against Winston and continued down this path—which actually met institutional protocol. According to Assistant State Attorney Georgia Cappleman, "normal procedure for criminal cases in Leon County calls for police to give information to prosecutors if there is evidence for an arrest, or if it is a 'close call.' " Cappleman explains, "police do not tell prosecutors when they have decided against pursuing an arrest" (Fineout & Copel, 2013, ¶4). Angulo's decisions technically complied, which raises some moral questions that (critical sport) scholars should be asking about the power and culture of college football surrounding incidents of sexual violence.

By the time the case reached the state level, the now-popular Winston had the 'Noles humming to a 9–0 record to the delight of FSU and the Tallahassee football community. It was also at this time that the incident and the "flawed" (as it was commonly referred to in popular media and admitted to by state officials and the Tallahassee Police) investigatory practices of local police and FSU's Athletic Department were revealed to the football-consuming public. The sexual encounter that happened almost one year earlier would become a significant storyline during the championship season. Winston's eligibility to participate in the season's critical late-season games became increasingly unlikely as the once-buried details of the night of December 7, 2012, began to emerge in the public sphere throughout the fall of 2013.

The state's reactionary investigation found "insignificant evidence" to charge Winston with sexual assault. Although DNA evidence determined that

Winston had sexual intercourse with the female student, witness accounts of the sexual encounter suggested that it was "consensual." The defense attorney working with the athletic department had the only witnesses—two FSU football players—each submit an affidavit recollecting what occurred that night (Tallahassee Police Department, 2012a; 2012b). Countering Jane Doe's word, the witness accounts—represented in composite form here—characterized the female student as a "willing participant."

> That blonde female, she was not intoxicated. She followed us out of the club and virtually invited herself into the cab with us . . . / She was able to walk, have a conversation. She was not slurring or stumbling. When we arrived at Legacy Suites, she followed Jameis into his apartment and into his bedroom. The door was broken and was partially open. I could hear them having sex. I looked through the opening and I see her giving Jameis oral sex, his hand on his hips while she was in front of him on her knees. They had only been in the room a few minutes. I witnessed them both take each other's clothes off and lay on the bed. They began having intercourse. As a joke, I busted into the room to embarrass Jameis. The girl yelled at me, "get out!" She wanted more privacy. She got up off the bed and turned off the light and tried to close the door. From what we saw, she never indicated that she was not a willing participant. From what we saw, she was a more than willing participant. After approximately 20 minutes, I could hear them leaving. They were talking to each other in a friendly manner.[5] (Tallahassee Police Department, 2012a; 2012b)

The premature suspension of the investigation and 11-month delay before Meggs was informed of the case were but two of the investigative "missteps" executed by the Tallahassee Police Department to the benefit of the Seminoles' football team (see Axon, 2015; *Jane Doe vs. The Florida State University Board of Trustees* for complete overview of the "flawed" investigation). Prosecutor Meggs publicly admonished investigators for how the investigation unfolded. He suggested that, had the investigation been done properly, the cab driver could have been identified that night; surveillance video from Potbelly's could have been obtained; an interview with Winston could have been conducted in January 2013[6]; and that if it had been conducted properly, although "we might not have a different answer or result," Meggs was confident that "we'd certainly have more clarity" about what occurred that night (Bogdanich, 2014).

## The Backlash

As is often the sentiment in highly publicized cases of alleged sexual assault by high-profile student-athletes—and particularly by football players at elite programs such as Florida State—the public condemnation of the accuser was pronounced and far reaching. Sport proponents and university advocates were quick to orchestrate what feminist scholars and critics often refer to as "slut-shaming" and "victim blaming" (*see* Rentschler, 2014). Winston's teammates and witnesses of the sexual encounter, for instance, described the accuser as a "willing participant." In his deposition on the events of that night, then–FSU cornerback Ronald Darby stated plainly and in juridically impenetrable parlance that "at no time did the girl ever indicate that she was not a willing participant. In fact, she wanted more privacy by closing the door and turning off the lights" (Darby Aff. 6, Tallahassee Police Department, 2012a). His testimony was corroborated in similar language by former FSU defensive end Christopher Casher (2013), who stated "they had only been in the room a few minutes before I witnessed her giving him oral sex" (Casher Aff. 6, Tallahassee Police Department, 2012b).

FSU football fans and classmates were public (on message boards, in newspaper and blog posts, etc.) in demonizing the accuser as a "liar," a "slut," and a "whore" (Ziering & Dick, 2015; Kruse, 2013). Many in the tomahawk-chopping football community also were supportive of Winston. A *Tampa Bay Times* headline read, "FSU fans devout in support of accused quarterback" (Kruse, 2013). "Support" for the accused was vitriol against the victim, however, as the most die-hard FSU fans and Winston-lovers claimed the accuser was "wanton" and "money-hungry"; "that they [Winston supporters] would make her life hell. They hope she pays. Gets in a car accident. Gets AIDS" (Kruse, 2013, ¶4). These epithets of the victim, as well as the hyper-aggressive and vile wishes against her well-being, reflect conservative gender ideologies and *rape myths*. She was characterized along with women more generally as prone or vulnerable to sexual on-comings of men due to the natural subordination of women's sexuality to (heterosexual) male desire (*see* Hall, 2004).

The victim-blaming, woman-bashing narratives surrounding the sexual violence at FSU do not simply reify heterosexist, patriarchal gender hierarchies by suggesting that the sexual encounter might have been rape or assault. Rather, these discourses only are made possible under certain social and cultural circumstances. For FSU, these discourses "make sense" in a football culture that Adam Weinstein (2013)—a doctoral student at FSU—described in a *Deadspin* article as "malignant." Weinstein suggested this malignant football power/culture developed alongside players' aggressive "gay-bashing," an intimidating (for faculty and students) hyper-masculinity made legitimate by administrative "handlers" whose priorities were mainly to keep "team superstars" eligible to play even if it meant "begging, browbeating, suborning intimidation, and, we all have suspected, writing assignments for the athletes" (Weinstein, 2013, ¶19).

Elsewhere, at other "big-time" college football universities, similar masculinist cultures rendering rape and female subordination as "normal" persist. In 2016, for instance, two Texas A&M football coaches were suspended for showing an offensive slideshow to an audience of hundreds of women during a fundraiser event (Khan, 2016). The slideshow included degrading remarks towards women in a parodied version of the Aggie War Hymn that stated, "We are Aggie women, we are filled with estrogen," and "Maroon and white are the colors we love, we are putting down our dish towels and taking off our gloves" (¶5–6). The slideshow also incorporated coaching tips that were coded in sexually suggestive ways, such as the "do's" of run blocking: "spread your legs," "enter-front/not-behind," "push hard," and "finish on top"; and the "don'ts" of pass blocking: "don't let him inside," "keep your hips down," and "don't go down" (Hutchins, 2016).

Backlash and heterosexist discourses against Jane Doe illustrate the victim-blaming masculinist attitudes that give rise to "rape culture." Rape culture refers to the social and cultural normalcy—*nay, spectacle*—of hyper-masculinity, misogyny, sexism, women's fear and suffering, and the legitimacy of subtle and explicit forms of physical and sexual violence against women (Rentschler, 2014; Ringrose & Renold, 2012; Ringrose & Renold, 2014). It furthermore refers to the discourses and practices that make rape thinkable and doable by some men—through justification of the ideology that the victim "deserved what she got" or was complicit in the production of the violence perpetrated upon her (Hall, 2004).[7] Relatedly, victim-blaming is a strategy for social individuals to *make sense of* rape and to sterilize its ugly insides (e.g., "when women wear short skirts, they are 'asking for it' "). As Meyers (1997) explains, "when women are on the receiving end of male violence, it is often *they*, not the perpetrator, who appear to be deviants worthy of condemnation" (p. 4). Assailants of violence and adherents of patriarchy can thus draw upon available victim-blaming discourses and logic to justify violent acts against women.

We suggest that the institutional, legal, economic, social, and cultural linkages between dominant sensibilities around gender, sexuality, sexual violence as well as the organization of commercialized "big time" college football at least in part perpetuate rape cultures on university campuses. That is to say, male student-athletes' repeated involvement in sexual violence against women, the social and cultural significance of college football in the United States, and the unique yet patterned ways in which local authorities, athletic departments, and academic institutions handle these cases create *conditions of possibility* for victim-blaming rape cultures to be sustained. In 2004, for instance, four Brigham Young University football players were indicted on gang-rape charges. The players were acquitted because jurors suggested the football players had "suffered enough" when they lost their scholarships and were no longer able to play for the team (Hyde & Walch, 2004).

In 2005, six University of Tennessee at Chattanooga football players were charged with raping a drunken student after a college party (Associated Press, 2005). Despite knowing of the rapes, Head Coach Rodney Allison "allowed the players to take the field against West Carolina University before informing chancellor Roger Brown" (Murphy, 2013, ¶22).

In 2010, the University of Montana came under investigation for violating Title IX for doing "too little" in response to sexual-assault allegations. The football coach and the athletic director were fired and one player was arrested (Robbins, 2012). That same year, at Notre Dame University, Lizzy Seeberg claimed she was sexually assaulted by a Notre Dame "Fighting Irish" football player. Whence contemplating her actions, Seeberg received a text from a friend of the accused: "Don't do anything you would regret. . . . Messing with Notre Dame football is a bad idea" (Henneberger, 2012, ¶3). Seeberg, however, did "everything that could have possibly been asked of her," including telling her friends what she alleged happened that night, going to campus police the following day, enduring an invasive physical examination, and attending counseling (Carmon, 2011, ¶6).

Despite Seeberg's efforts, Notre Dame did not adequately acknowledge her complaints. According to one report, when Seeberg initially reported the incident, Notre Dame police appeared disinterested in following up because "they were pretty busy" (Henneberger, 2012, ¶37). Once word leaked of Seeberg's allegations, her reputation was smeared across the press. A top university official reportedly called her "the aggressor in the situation," stating that "she was all over the boy" (Henneberger, 2012, ¶15). Others called her a "liar" and a "troubled girl" who had "done this before." Ten days after the sexual encounter, Seeberg committed suicide.

In August 2015, Baylor defensive end Sam Ukwuachu was found guilty on sexual assault charges and sentenced to 180 days in county jail (Ellis, 2016). During the trial, reports alleged that Ukwuachu "had transferred to Baylor from Boise State in 2013 after being kicked off the Broncos team for a previous incident of violence against a female student" (Ellis, 2016, ¶3). After Ukwuachu's conviction, the Big 12 announced plans for a new policy which would require more universities to investigate athletes' past disciplinary issues. Aside from influencing policy, the trial also drew attention to other instances in which Baylor University officials failed to respond to reports of rape and sexual assault—including the 2014 case against former defensive end Tevin Elliot, who was convicted on two counts of sexual assault and sentenced to 20 years in prison (Peterson, 2016). That same month, *ESPN*'s "Outside the Lines" alleged that Baylor University officials and coaches were aware of multiple sexual-assault allegations against players, but did not pursue disciplinary action (Sports Illustrated, 2016).

In response to public backlash against the university, in September 2015 Baylor hired Philadelphia law firm Pepper Hamilton to "conduct a thorough and independent external investigation into the university's handling of cases of alleged sexual violence" (Ellis, 2016, ¶5). The investigation revealed that university administrators failed to support victims of sexual assault, that the football program "hindered enforcement of rules and policies, and created a cultural perception that football was above the rules," and that "the University and Athletics

Department failed to take effective action in response to allegations involving misconduct by football staff" ("Baylor University Board of Regents," 2015, p. 10). Baylor fired head football coach Art Briles, demoted President Ken Starr, and placed on probation Athletic Director Ian McCaw (Ellis, 2016). Each of these cases—Brigham Young University, University of Tennessee at Chattanooga, Texas A&M, University of Montana, Notre Dame University, and Baylor University— highlight not only the prevalence of rape culture in college football, but also the differentiated yet patterned institutional (mis)handlings of sexual assault.

All this brings us back to FSU. Florida State University's management of the sexual violence and investigation was a success from a public-relations perspective, effectively insulating the incident from the public until November 2013, about nine weeks into the regular season. Once made public, however, strategies at FSU changed from suppression to opportunism; support for the accused and unwavering support for FSU football. Head Coach Jimbo Fisher reoriented the narrative of accusation and scrutiny into a type of adversity for his football team to overcome, "[i]t hasn't altered (preparation) in any way. . . . Our team is not insulated from it. We deal with it. We address those issues. We control what we can control—how we prepare and how we play. That's how we go about it" (Auerbach, 2013, ¶2).

The FSU Athletic Department showed solidarity with Winston and assured that the (potential) national championship season would not be in jeopardy: "[W]e are aware of a matter that was investigated by the Tallahassee Police Department almost a year ago. . . . We look forward to a speedy resolution of the issue. There is no change to Jameis Winston's [eligibility] status" (Rubin, 2013, ¶10). And Seminole fans were "devout" in support of Winston (see Kruse, 2014). On December 7, 2013, mere days after it was determined that Winston would not be charged with sexual assault, FSU took a different course of action than that of Baylor and rewarded their head coach with a five-year contract extension for more than $4 million per year (Schoffel, 2013). In short, the Seminole football constituency said, "play ball."

In November 2015, nearly three years after the initial report and three months prior to FSU's settlement with Jane Doe, CNN aired *The Hunting Ground*. The documentary film revealed how institutional power and indifference perpetuates sexual violence on university campuses. The FSU female student's story was central to the film's message. It highlighted her physical and emotional pain from that night, how the "system" worked her over in the three years following, and it highlighted the victim-blaming, Seminole football-loving culture at FSU. In anticipation of the national broadcast of the film, FSU President John Thrasher sent a memo to FSU students, faculty, and constituents warning that *The Hunting Ground* should not be taken seriously because it does not reflect "the truth" (Thrasher, 2015). In public-relations terms, the letter was intended to preempt and repress a critical dialogue that might emerge from the documentary's illumination of the otherwise unrevealed workings of institutional and embodied sexual violence on college campuses.

In the letter, Thrasher makes two key arguments. The first argument contends that the university's conduct throughout the Tallahassee Police's Winston rape investigation was in compliance with standards and that its own investigations also complied with institutional standards. He goes as far to argue (without substantiation), "[f]or many years, FSU's policies in this area have been a model for other universities" (Thrasher, 2015, ¶5). "Nevertheless," he continues, "we recently reviewed and improved them [the sexual assault policies], made them easier to access on the Web, bolstered bystander training, increased sexual responsibility training for incoming freshmen and hired a full-time Title IX officer to handle the investigation and adjudication of sexual assault complaints (¶5)." This, of course, leads to the question that if FSU was a model for other universities and conducted itself adequately throughout the investigation then why make such significant changes to their sexual-assault policies and procedures? In examining FSU campus safety and security history, it appears that sexual assault actually was at an all-time high around the time of the Winston rape investigation: 18 reported cases in 2013; 32 in 2014; and a total of 215 reported cases from 2001 to 2014 (U.S. Department of Education, 2015).[8]

In the second argument, Thrasher engages in what Foucault (1980) might call a "game of truth," revealing how U.S. academic institutions immersed in scandal can negotiate the politics of truth to maintain their image, profits, and power over informed citizens. This particular game of truth elicits the double standard by which the Winston rape investigation and the documentary's messages are measured. The letter specifically—and ironically—calls into question the film's investigative techniques. Thrasher suggests that the documentary cannot be trusted because, rather than telling "both sides of the story," "those making negative assertions had an agenda not supported by the evidence" (¶7). The letter further warns that the film cannot be considered a "real" documentary because it is an advocacy piece, discussing it as if documentary films were homogenous in interpretative techniques—a claim that would be wholly rejected in FSU's own communications and film departments. Thrasher goes on to criticize the film. He claims that it possesses "major distortions"; is an "inaccurate" and "incomplete picture"; and is about "blame," "advocacy," and "emotion" rather than being about an investigation to find out the truth about what occurred.

Thrasher draws upon the findings of the university's own investigations into Winston, Darby, and Casher for potential violations of student codes of conduct—which would not contradict the state's finding of Winston as being not guilty—as evidence to support his dismissal of the documentary's message. The three players were investigated for possible violations of (1) "conduct of a sexual nature that creates an intimidating, hostile, or offensive environment for another person," and (2) "acts that invade privacy of another person" (Axon,

2014, ¶5). Only Casher was found in violation of the latter and for "recording images without consent," as he recorded the sexual encounter between Winston and Jane Doe (and soon thereafter deleted it). Winston and Darby were not found in violation on any counts. The letter states, "viewers will hear an incomplete and misleading description of the University's thorough Title IX investigation, handed to an independent judge . . . who concluded there was not enough evidence to support the complainant's allegations of sexual assault." In this narrative, on the one hand, Thrasher's argument about how and why the university conducted itself adequately is supported by a 'lack of evidence'—born of flawed investigation(s)—exonerating Winston. On the other hand, Thrasher's argument about how and why *The Hunting Ground* is "mere advocacy"—which is to say that advocating for a political cause is immoral and undemocratic—is supported by the fact that the documentary did not draw upon the exact (lack of) juridical evidence and truth used to exonerate Winston in the first place.

Glossing over the organizational impetus to protect the institutional brand (and the politics thereof), Thrasher points directly to the politics of victim advocacy as a threat to the well-being of the university and its stakeholders. Within this framing, it is the university that is coming under assault from an activist media seeking to illustrate (or, in Thrasher's view, overstate) the institutionalization of cultures of rape and violence. Indeed, from this view the violence perpetrated in the Winston incident comes not from the person accused of sexual assault, but from those who look to turn the klieg light onto how this incident, the investigation, and the institutional response and incongruous support provided for the accused over the accuser reveals broader pathologies of institutional violence toward woman at FSU and beyond.

Thrasher's play to repress a critical counter-narrative around the event ought to be thought of as an instance of the institutionalization of violence. By failing to look in the proverbial mirror, the letter—preemptively re-stabilizing the status quo around sexual violence on college campuses—is concerned with how the public, faculty, and students—past, current, and future—will perceive the university's image in light of the documentary's messages. This reaction is important for the present analysis simply because this was not an inevitable or natural position to take but a particular calculated strategy in which alternatives certainly were possible. To take alternative (in)action, however, to allow the broadcast to unfold without the commentary would have been to risk the value of the hegemonic (brand) image of the university. Yet, we do not place blame on President Thrasher the individual. Instead, we understand Thrasher as operating in the role of university president and this type of strategic management is expected for the sustenance of the contemporary university that relies on college football to "keep the lights on." Though not guaranteed, people occupying Thrasher's position as president within the nexus of Florida State football, rape culture, and the neoliberal university would be pressured to react similarly.

## Football, Rape Culture, and the Neoliberal University

What does the Winston rape investigation and the institutional responses thereabout say about the contemporary university, rape culture and football, and the brand logics that define governance structures and actions in higher education? Let us first look at the links between rape culture and the neoliberal university. Kristin Bumiller, in her instructive and well-considered book, *In an Abusive State* (Bumiller, 2009), explores the effects neoliberal *doxa* in local and state governance have had on how communities and institutions deal with sexual violence. Bumiller makes the case that within the neoliberal state, feminist politics and standpoint ontologies have been rearticulated along the lines of individualization and responsibilization—meaning that sexual violence as social problem comes to be expressed as something to be managed by the individual. This dislocation of the violent act from the systems and structures (e.g., misogyny, patriarchy, sexual aggressiveness) that encumber such action thus give rise and authorization to corresponding governance machinations (institutional displacement of blame, dealing with the problem as an "individual's issue").

As a number of scholars make clear, these neoliberal logics have come to dominate institutions of higher education in the United States and elsewhere. Often, educational institutions develop policies or protocols for dealing with sexual violence on maintaining a primacy of the marketability of a safe campus to an external audience. Drawing their analysis from Susanne Gannon's (2007) study of a school excursion rape case, Davies and Bansel (2007) argue, "a school that has a market advantage is able to negate the claims of individuals who do not manage to maintain and serve their market image" (p. 258). In her chapter on sexual assault law in Canada, Gotell (2010) similarly illustrates how public institutions have come to define their policies and guidelines for investigation, treatment, and support for rape and sexual violence in ways that make the organization least culpable or liable for violence perpetrated under their guise (*see also* Meyers, 2013).

Perhaps most relevant to the present case, Cannella and Perez (2012) provide a poignant examination of the commercial imperatives and assumptions of the neoliberal university to on-campus sexual violence at Penn State University. In their analysis, they draw upon multiple stories of "capitalist violence" within and outside of higher education as facilitated by patriarchy and evidenced by the recent stories of abuse and power embedded within college football at Pennsylvania State University. They weave together the perspectives of multiple stakeholders to illustrate how sexual violence is often viewed within the university as something (1) to be managed for the purposes of promoting the image of a safe campus community, and (2) to be kept out of the public sphere for the benefit of maintaining the status quo—a culture of patriarchal violence and institutional deference and displacement. This line of critique is taken up by Gill (2008) who clearly illustrates how reporting rates and academy-based punishment rates for on-campus sexual violence acts are purposefully kept low by college administrators to maximize the perceived value of the university (as safe environment).

This brings us to the link between sport—the supposed "front porch of the university"—and the neoliberal logics which give sport such primacy within the higher-educational setting. Critical sport scholars (King, 2012; Silk & Andrews, 2012) have demonstrated the ways in which contemporary intercollegiate sport is constituted by, and constitutive of, the neoliberal university (Giroux, 2007, 2009). The neoliberal university is characterized by the transformation of academic institutions from public, democratic spaces into sites where pedagogy and research are wed to capitalist valorization and the management of academies informed by market rationality and corporate structure (Giroux, 2007, 2009); Division I college football has become a prominent enterprise and commodity within this context.

The generation of surplus value through college football increases the rates of exploitation of student-athletes, expands the power of athletic departments, and serves marketing ends for the university. Lynchpins for the valorization of college football include the NCAA's "amateur" status of student-athlete labor, cultural prestige, and on-field success (e.g., victories, championships, individual awards); conference television contracts; sponsorship deals; ticket and merchandise sales; multimillion-dollar "arms-race" investments in training facilities, stadia, and coaching staffs; as well as the careful construction and management of brand images and customer-based brand equities (see Keller, 1993, 2003, for overviews on building and managing customer-based brand equity). Sport marketers and university administrators utilize dominant symbolic meanings tied to college football brands to attract students to the university and to compel students to consume college football.

College football brand images—such as the image of Chief Osceola for FSU—become linked to patterns of spectacularized (via social media, print media, television broadcasts, and other mediums) bodily practices of beer-swilling, tailgate-partying, chanting football communities who don the colors and logos of their team. Scandals, discourses, and embodied practices that undermine these dominant cultural practices and brand images—such as a star quarterback becoming the prime suspect of a sexual-assault investigation or the need to care for and support a victim of sexual assault—represent a legitimate threat to the economic, cultural, and social value of the college football commodity. Scandals therefore must be governed and managed by the neoliberal university in a way that does not allow the situation to negatively alter perceptions about the program and school, and which might inhibit economic flows. As Welch (1997) explains, "Given the stigma and negative publicity related to violence against women, college athletics departments . . . are reluctant to acknowledge and share information about abusive athletes," and athletic departments might "go to great lengths to protect violent athletes from adverse publicity, even engaging in obstruction of justice" (pp. 395–396).

## Conclusion

Rather than interrogating the hyper-masculine, patriarchal, (hetero)sexist, victim-blaming sensibilities, or the rape culture on campus, or attending to the victim as a sufferer, FSU's reactionary apparatus to the allegations were strategies that affirmed its position as an institution concerned with profits. As illuminated in President Thrasher's letter, university representatives sought to avoid negative publicity at all costs. Administrators provided institutional and legal support for the accused, acted opportunistically about the juridical-backed not guilty legal status of the assailant, and deflected cultural and moral indictments from critical citizenry. They referred to the findings of state and university investigations as gospel, no matter how much the investigations were criticized by concerned citizenry; and, in so doing, administrators denied the existence of the victim-subject—because to admit there is a victim in need of support (e.g., emotional, physical, legal, institutional) is to admit that unwanted penetration, embodied struggle, and trauma occurred that night. Jimbo Fisher defending Winston during a press conference put it best, "There was no victim because there was no crime" (Hine, 2014, ¶1).

Jimbo's claim that there was no victim is correct in legal terms. His claim, however, does not negate the existence of suffering and pain on behalf of the accuser. We should think deeply and critically about institutional usages of juridical concepts of "evidence," "truth," "guilty," and "not guilty," and the power relations within which those concepts are employed. Because to move out from underneath the refuge of legal parlance would have allowed a critical public to penetrate FSU's brand image and open it up to question—FSU officials and profiteers certainly would not consent to such a proposition. These potentialities might have given voice to the "victim," offering the female student's police report and vivid, lachrymose testimony about what happened that night social, cultural, and perhaps legal legitimacy in college-football America. At the end of the day, according to juridical, institutional, and Fisher's logic, we are left with a paradox: How do we consider the production of a sufferer of sexual violence absent an agent of force? If we continue to manage the sport-sexual assault nexus at FSU and elsewhere within the confines of legal concepts in the context of "big-time" college football, we risk allowing popular discourses to continually characterize victims as "money-hungry liars and sluts" because, within neoliberal college football rape cultures, this *makes sense.*

## Discussion

The rape allegation that Jameis Winston eluded while at Florida State University exposed a grim reality—administration continues to place the best interests of the institution over the best interests of individuals in the student body. Should they? Meaning that if an institution admits that sexual assaults happen on its campus, and deeply investigates accusations by alleged victims of assault, when—quite literally—many other institutions continue denying that it is happening on *their* campuses, then what should administrative leadership do?

NOTES

1. "Sexual harassment is 'unwelcome conduct of a sexual nature. [It] can include unwelcome sexual advances, requests for sexual favors, and other verbal, nonverbal, or physical conduct of a sexual nature" (Hogan, 2005, p. 319).

2. The authors acknowledge the difficulties of language construction in accounts of violence against women. Feminist scholars (*see* Meyers, 1997) warn against the use of passive voice structure when describing accounts of sexual violence, because doing so reduces the agency of abusers. Although referring to rape as an "incident," "event," or "alleged rape" is problematic—mainly because these terms reinforce notions of victim blaming—given the legal outcomes of the Winston rape investigation, the authors cannot refer to the incident as "rape."

3. Foucault (1984) refers to crisis heterotopias as

    privileged or sacred or forbidden places, reserved for individuals who are, in relation to society and to the human environment in which they live, in a state of crisis: adolescents, menstruating women, pregnant women, the elderly. . . . For example, the boarding school, in its nineteenth-century form, or military service for young men, have certainly played such a role, as the first manifestations of sexual virility were in fact supposed to take place "elsewhere" than at home. For girls, there was, until the middle of the twentieth century, a tradition called the "honeymoon trip" which was an ancestral theme. The young woman's deflowering could take place "nowhere" and, at the moment of its occurrence the train or honeymoon hotel was indeed the place of this nowhere, this heterotopia without geographical marker. (p. 4)

4. The authors recreated this composite testimony of two separate testimonies the female student gave of the incident, one from the publicly accessible Offense Reporting Form and the second from her interview in *The Hunting Ground* (Ziering & Dick, 2015). Italicized text represents her account from the documentary film. All other text is from the Offense Reporting Form.

5. The authors recreated a composite account of the two separate yet incredibly similar accounts from the two key witnesses, Christopher Casher and Ronald Darby, for the purposes of conciseness and to emphasize how the seemingly professionally prepared statements provided investigators with symmetrical and impenetrable witness accounts. For instance, the accounts follow a similar logical order where paragraph six of both accounts is where claims of Jane Doe as a willing participant are made. The full (yet edited) interview accounts read:

    the female was pursuing Jameis . . . she did not want him to leave. . . . She was able to walk out of the club, have a conversation . . . [and] got in the cab with us. . . .

When we returned to our apartment building, she followed Jameis into his . . . bedroom . . . the door was partially open . . . the girl told Chris to get out. . . . Chris and I could hear her and Jameis having sex. At no time did the girl ever indicate that she was not a willing participant. In fact, she wanted more privacy by closing the door and turning off the lights. (Tallahassee Police Department, 2013a)

That blonde female . . . [f]ollowed us out of the club. . . . And virtually invited herself in [to the cab with us]. She was not intoxicated. She was able to have a conversation with us. She was not slurring or stumbling. . . . When we arrived at Legacy Suites, she . . . [f]ollowed Jameis into his . . . bedroom. Since the door was partially open, I looked through the opening and we could see her giving Jameis oral sex. They had only been in the room a few minutes before I witnessed her giving him oral sex. . . . I witnessed them both take each other's clothes off and lay on the bed. . . . [They] began having intercourse. As a joke, I busted into the room to embarrass Jameis. The girl yelled at me, "get out." She got up off the bed and turned off the light and tried to close the door. . . . From what I saw, she was a more than willing participant. After approximately 20 minutes . . . I could hear [them] leaving. They were talking to each other in a friendly manner" (Tallahassee Police Department, 2013b).

6. Meggs called Angulo's decision to call Winston on the phone "insane." He continued, "you don't call someone on the phone and have any level of control" (Bogdanich, 2014).

7. Although rape culture is a problem at U.S. universities, recently, widespread protests of rape culture have made their way to many campuses. In June 2016, for example, Stanford University students protested the minimal six-month sentence that Brock Turner—the university's star swimmer—received for brutally raping an unconscious woman (Brennan, 2016). During the university's graduation ceremony, students held signs that read, "Stanford protects rapists" and "rape culture has deep roots." Another example of protests occurred in September 2016 at the University of Pennsylvania, when students covered the campus with flyers that read, "THIS IS WHAT RAPE CULTURE LOOKS LIKE" and "WE ARE WATCHING" (Amatulli, 2016, ¶1). These statements were typed over a sexually suggestive e-mail that was sent to several female freshman students by an off-campus fraternity.

8. Prior to 2015, statistics for sex offenses were combined into two categories: "Rape" and "Fondling" were combined under "Sex offenses—Forcible," and "Incest" and "Statutory Rape" were combined under "Sex Offenses—Nonforcible." As of the 2015 data collection, these statistics were no longer combined. Four separate categories of data were recorded, including "Rape," "Fondling," "Incest," and "Statutory Rape." All 32 reported cases of sexual assault in 2014 fell under the category of rape (U.S. Department of Education, 2015).

## REFERENCES

Andrews, D. L., & Silk, M. L. (2012). *Sport and neoliberalism*. Philadelphia, PA: Temple University Press.

Amatulli, J. (2016, September 8). UPenn is covered with "This Is What Rape Culture Looks Like" flyers. *The Huffington Post*. Retrieved May 13, 2017, from http://www.huffingtonpost .com/entry/upenns-campus-is-covered-with-this-is-what-rape-culture-looks-like -flyers_us_57d1a480e4b03d2d459926b5?section=&

Associated Press. (2005, November 9). Six Tenn. football players charged with gang rape [Text Article]. Retrieved August 31, 2016, from http://www.foxnews.com/story/2005/11 /09/six-tenn-football-players-charged-with-gang-rape.html

Associated Press. (2013, November 21). Victim's lawyer critical of cops in Winston case. Retrieved August 19, 2016, from http://www.nydailynews.com/sports/college/victim -lawyer-critical-cops-winston-case-article-1.1523939

Auerbach, N. (2013, December 1). Jimbo Fisher: Winston investigation not affecting preparation. Retrieved September 21, 2016, from http://www.usatoday.com/story/sports /ncaaf/2013/12/01/jimbo-fisher-florida-state-jameis-winston-sexual-battery -investigation/3797361/

Axon, R. (2014, June 5). FSU finds one Jameis Winston teammate responsible. Retrieved September 21, 2016, from http://www.usatoday.com/story/sports/ncaaf/2014/06/04 /florida-state-jameis-winston-ronald-darby-chris-casher-code-of-conduct/9972737

Axon, R. (2015, January 25). Florida State agrees to pay Winston accuser $950,000 to settle suit. Retrieved February 1, 2016, from http://www.usatoday.com/story/sports/ncaaf /2016/01/25/florida-state-settles-title-ix-lawsuit-erica-kinsman-jameis-winston /79299304/

Baylor University Board of Regents: Findings of fact. (2016). Retrieved from http://www .baylor.edu/rtsv/doc.php/266596.pdf

Bogdanich, W. (2014, April 16). A star player accused, and a flawed rape investigation. *The New York Times*. Retrieved May 13, 2017, from http://www.nytimes.com/interactive /2014/04/16/sports/errors-in-inquiry-on-rape-allegations-against-fsu-jameis-winston .html

Brennan, C. (2016, June 13). Stanford students protest Brock Turner sentence, sexual assault on campus during graduation ceremonies. *NY Daily News*. Retrieved May 13, 2017, from    http://www.nydailynews.com/news/national/stanford-students-protest-rapist -brock-turner-graduation-article-1.2671260

Brownmiller, S. (1975). *Against our will*. New York: Simon and Schuster.

Bumiller, K. (2009). *In an abusive state: How neoliberalism appropriated the feminist movement against sexual violence*. Durham, NC: Duke University Press.

Cannella, G. S., & Perez, M. S. (2012). Emboldened patriarchy in higher education feminist readings of capitalism, violence, and power. *Cultural Studies ↔ Critical Methodologies*, 12(4), 279–286.

Carmon, I. (2011). "Life, sweetness, hope" lost in Notre Dame sex assault case. Retrieved September 18, 2016, from http://jezebel.com/5748113/life-sweetness-hope-lost-in -notre-dame-sex-assault-case

Davies, B., & Bansel, P. (2007). Neoliberalism and education. *International journal of qualitative studies in education*, 20(3), 247–259.

Ellis, Z. (2016, May 26). A timeline of the Baylor sexual assault scandal. Sports Illustrated. Retrieved May 14, 2017, from http://www.si.com/college-football/2016/05/26/baylor -art-briles-sexual-assault-ken-starr

Fineout, G., & Copel, K. (2013, November 14). Prosecutors received Jameis Winston case on Tuesday. Retrieved September 12, 2016, from http://www.nbcmiami.com/news/local /Prosecutors-Received-Jameis-Winston-Case-on-Tuesday-231999151.html

Foucault, M. (1980). Truth and power. In *Power/knowledge: Selected interviews and other writings*, 1972–1977. New York, NY: Vintage.

Foucault, M. (1991). Governmentality. In *The Foucault Effect: Studies in governmentality*. Chicago, IL: University of Chicago Press.

Foucault, M. (2000). The subject and power. In J. D. Faubion (ed.), *Michel Foucault: Power* (pp. 326–348). New York, NY: The New Press.

Gannon, S. (2007). The market, the media and the family in a school excursion rape case. *International Journal of Qualitative Studies in Education*, 20(3), 355–369.

Gill, R. (2008). Culture and subjectivity in neoliberal and postfeminist times. *Subjectivity*, 25(1), 432–445.

Giroux, H. A. (2007). *University in chains: Confronting the military-industrial-academic complex*. New York, NY: Routledge.

Giroux, H. A. (2009). Democracy's nemesis: The rise of the corporate university. *Cultural Studies ↔ Critical Methodologies*. Retrieved June 19, 2017, from http://doi.org/10.1177/1532708609341169

Gotell, L. (2010). Canadian sexual assault law: Neoliberalism and the erosion of feminist-inspired law reform. *Rethinking rape law: International and comparative perspectives*, 209–223.

Hall, R. (2004). "It can happen to you": Rape prevention in the age of risk management. *Hypatia*, 19(3), 1–18. Retrieved June 19, 2017, from http://doi.org/10.1111/j.1527-2001.2004.tb01299.x

Henneberger, M. (2012). Reported sexual assault at Notre Dame campus leaves more questions than answers (News). *National Catholic Reporter*. Retrieved September 17, 2016, from https://lockerdome.com/8730587087387969/

Hine, C. (2014, October 13). Emotional Jimbo Fisher defends FSU QB Jameis Winston. Retrieved September 21, 2016, from http://www.chicagotribune.com/sports/college/chi-jimbo-fisher-jameis-winston-20141013-story.html

Hogan, H. (2005). What athletic departments must know about Title IX and sexual harassment. *Marquette Sports Law Review*, 16(2), 317–351.

Hutchins, A. (2016, July 29). Texas A&M suspends 2 football coaches after "failed attempt at humor" during women's clinic. *SB Nation*. Retrieved May 13, 2017, from http://www.sbnation.com/2016/7/29/12329726/texas-aggies-suspension-coaches-chalk-talk-women-clinic

Hyde, J., & Walch, T. (2004, December 4). 4 former Y. players indicted in scandal. Retrieved August 31, 2016, from http://www.deseretnews.com/article/595110063/4-former-Y-players-indicted-in-scandal.html?pg=all

Jane Doe v. The Florida State University Board of Trustees, No. 4:15-cv-00235-MW-CAS (United Sates District Court Northern District of Florida October 22, 2015).

Keller, K. L. (1993). Conceptualizing, measuring, and managing customer-based brand equity. *The Journal of Marketing*, 1–22.

Keller, K. L. (2003). Understanding brands, branding and brand equity. *Interactive Marketing*, 5(1), 7–20.

Khan, S. (2016, August 1). Texas A&M suspends 2 assistant coaches over slideshow, apologizes. *ESPN*. Retrieved May 13, 2017, from http://www.espn.com/college-football/story/_/id/17175699/texas-aggies-suspend-assistant-coaches-degrading-slide-show

King, S. (2012). Nike U. In *Sport and neoliberalism* (pp. 75–89). Philadelphia, PA: Temple University Press.

Kruse, M. (2013). FSU fans devout in support of accused quarterback Jameis Winston. Retrieved September 17, 2016, from http://www.tampabay.com/news/fsu-fans-devout-in-support-of-accused-quaterback-jameis-winston/2154074

Luther, J. (2015, April 17). The Jameis Winston rape lawsuit has some damaging new information [Sport News Media]. Retrieved August 23, 2016, from https://sports.vice.com/en_us/article/the-jameis-winston-rape-lawsuit-has-some-damaging-new-information

Meyers, M. (1997). *News coverage of violence against women: Engendering blame*. Thousand Oaks: Sage Publications.

Meyers, M. (2013). The war on academic women: Reflections on postfeminism in the neoliberal academy. *Journal of Communication Inquiry*, 37(4), 274–283.

Murphy, T. (2013, December 5). College football's sexual assault problem is worse than you thought. Retrieved August 30, 2016, from http://www.motherjones.com/media/2013 /12/college-football-sexual-assualt-jameis-winston

Petchesky, B. (2014). Everything the cops didn't do in the Jameis Winston rape investigation. Retrieved September 17, 2016, from http://deadspin.com/everything-the-cops -didnt-do-in-the-jameis-winston-rape-1563730510

Peterson, C. (2016, May 25). Baylor sexual assault timeline story. Retrieved June 19, 2017, from    http://collegefootball.ap.org/article/correction-baylor-sexual-assault-timeline -story

Portman, J., & Burlew, J. (2013). Accuser's attorney calls for inquiry in Jameis Winston case. Retrieved September 12, 2016, from http://www.usatoday.com/story/sports/ncaaf/2013 /12/13/family-of-accuser-statement-jameis-winston-case/4008855/

Rentschler, C. A. (2014). Rape culture and the feminist politics of social media. *Girlhood Studies 7*(1), 65–82.

Ringrose, J., & Renold, E. (2012). Slut-shaming, girl power and "sexualisation": Thinking through the politics of the international SlutWalks with teen girls. *Gender and Education 24*(3), 333–343.

Ringrose, J., & Renold, E. (2014). "F** k rape!": Exploring affective intensities in a feminist research assemblage. *Qualitative Inquiry*, Online First.

Robbins, J. (2012, May 22). Handling of sexual assault claims brings new scrutiny to Montana. *The New York Times*. Retrieved May 14, 2017, from http://www.nytimes.com/2012 /05/23/sports/ncaafootball/handling-of-sexual-assault-claims-brings-new-scrutiny-to -montana.html

Rubin, R. (2013, November 13). Scrutiny intensifies on Jameis Winston allegations. Retrieved September 21, 2016, from http://www.usatoday.com/story/sports/ncaaf/acc/2013/11/21 /jameis-winston-sexual-assault-tallahassee-police-heisman-trophy/3669637/

Schoffel, I. (2013, December 7). Florida State, Jimbo Fisher agree to new deal. Retrieved September 22, 2016, from http://www.usatoday.com/story/sports/ncaaf/2013/12/07 /jimbo-fisher-florida-state-new-contract/3905847/

Sports Illustrated. (2016, May 26). Baylor fires head coach Art Briles amid rape scandal. Retrieved May 14, 2017, from http://www.si.com/college-football/2016/05/26/baylor -art-briles-coach-fired-rape-scandal

Spousta, T. (2014, December 21). Jameis Winston is cleared in hearing over student's rape accusation. *The New York Times*. Retrieved May 13, 2017, from http://www.nytimes.com /2014/12/22/sports/ncaafootball/jameis-winston-is-cleared-in-florida-state-hearing .html

Tallahassee Police Department. (2012a). *Incident Report* (Affidavit of Ronald Darby). (p. 25). Tallahassee, FL.

Tallahassee Police Department. (2012b). *Incident Report* (Affidavit of Christopher Casher). (p. 26). Tallahassee, FL.

Tallahassee Police Department. (2012d). *Offense Reporting Form* (Police Report No. 12– 032751) (p. 8). Tallahassee, FL.

Thrasher, J. (2015, November 16). FSU President John Thrasher statement on CNN and "The hunting ground." Retrieved May 13, 2017, from https://www.fsu.edu/the-hunting -ground/

Tracy, M. (2016, January 25). Florida State settles suit over Jameis Winston rape inquiry. *The New York Times*. Retrieved May 13, 2017, from http://www.nytimes.com/2016/01/26 /sports/football/florida-state-to-pay-jameis-winstons-accuser-950000-in-settlement .html

Vaughan, K. (2014, October 10). Police, Florida State hampered Jameis Winston investigation, documents show. Retrieved August 22, 2016, from http://www.foxsports.com
/college-football/story/jameis-winston-florida-state-tallahassee-police-hindered
-investigation-documents-101014

Weinstein, A. (2013). Jameis Winston isn't the only problem here: An FSU teacher's lament.
Retrieved September 17, 2016, from http://deadspin.com/jameis-winston-isnt-the
-only-problem-here-an-fsu-teac-1467707410

Welch, M. (1997). Violence against women by professional football players: A gender analysis of hypermasculinity, positional status, narcissism, and entitlement. *Journal of Sport
& Social Issues 21*(4), 392–411.

Williams, J. (1979). Sex role stereotypes, women's liberation and rape: A cross-cultural analysis of attitudes. *Sociological Symposium 25*, 61–97.

Ziering, A., & Dick, K. (2015). *The hunting ground*. Los Angeles, CA: Chain Camera Pictures.

# 5

# College Athletes as Employees and the Politics of Title IX

ELLEN J. STAUROWSKY

Mention the prospect of acknowledging "big-time" college football players as employees who have a right to collectively bargain for purposes of shaping the rules that govern their lives or basketball players as deserving of having their value recognized for the contributions they make to the multi-billion-dollar industry of college sport and somewhere in the conversation Title IX[1] comes up. In an interview with *espnW* in April of 2016, consultant and lobbyist Donna Lopiano commented that litigation filed by college athletes seeking fair recognition of their market value and employment rights—most particularly *Northwestern University and College Athletes Players Association* (Petitioner) (Pearce, Miscimarra, Hirozawa, Johnson, & McFerran, 2015); *In re: NCAA Athletic Grant-in-Aid Cap Anti-Trust Litigation* (2015); *Jenkins et al. v. National Collegiate Athletic Association et al.* (2014); and *O'Bannon v. NCAA* (2015)—"is the biggest potential game-changer" the college sport industry confronts (McManus, 2016, ¶15).

Depicting those lawsuits as simple attempts on the part of players to "get paid" rather than efforts to gain control and influence over an exploitative system, Lopiano presented a foreboding consequence (McManus, 2016). She claimed that the revenue needed to respond to athletes challenging the NCAA structure that unilaterally imposes rules that limit player value in the most lucrative sports and serve as mechanisms to redirect revenue to other areas of the enterprise could "hurt men's and women's sports," with that effect being more pronounced because Title IX compliance would require that female athletes receive compensation as well (McManus, 2016).

Other college sport officials have offered similar warnings. As a case in point, former Baylor University President Kenneth Starr testified in May 2014 before the U.S. House Education and Workforce Committee discussing the potential consequences of college athletes unionizing that, "it really is raising a host of serious questions. I think it could, in fact, at a minimum cause programmatic curtailments" and disrupt an important "gender balance in athletic programs that threatened public policy and perhaps violated the law" (Kline, 2014). Law professor Ron Katz (2016) reached the same conclusion, arguing that it would be impossible to reconcile compensating college football and men's basketball players beyond the limits imposed by the NCAA with the mandate of Title IX barring sex discrimination. He went further in writing, "Title IX will prevent such salaries from being paid to football and men's basketball players" (Katz, 2016) because women's college sports do not have the capacity to generate as much revenue.

Confronted with football players signing union cards at Northwestern and seeking the right to organize and collectively bargain in January 2014 (Staurowsky, 2014a), the NCAA developed a media campaign characterizing college football player unionization efforts as a money grab that had the potential to undermine other college sports (NCAA, 2014). Issuing a set of talking points to athletics administrators around the United States under the headline "Pay for Play/Unionization" (NCAA Staff, 2014), the NCAA urged them to write op-eds and to convey the message to media outlets that athletic scholarships would be reduced, championship opportunities would be cut back, "smaller sports" would lose funding, and athletic support services (academic support, counseling, tutoring) would be eliminated or severely cut. By way of countering the threat of college football players attempting to affect the balance of power in the decision-making structure of the industry, the NCAA and its thousands of spokespeople were urged to send a message that college football player empowerment would "signal to society and high school students that making money is the reason to come play a sport in college, as opposed to getting an education . . ." (NCAA Staff, 2014, ¶4).

But are the interests of college athletes in the sports of football and men's basketball really on a collision course with female college athletes and sports that have come to be referred to as the "smaller sports" by the NCAA? Is advocacy for the employment rights of a labor force in the sports that have been selected by NCAA member institutions to generate revenue that forms the basis for the business model of college sport a zero-sum game? Is it really the case that employment status represents an automatic forfeiture of educational opportunities for college football and basketball players in the sports that serve as the financial anchors for the college sport industry? On what basis did college sport officials determine that recognizing the employment status of certain college athletes would bankrupt the system for others?

In this chapter, several underlying myths that play out in discussions regarding the rights of college athletes as employees are explored.

- The first myth is that all college sports are the same.
- The second myth is that all college sport programs operate under the same model.

- The third myth is that the sports of big-time college football and men's basketball are extracurricular activities.
- The fourth myth is that lack of perceived profitability means that the economic model in college sport is unsustainable.
- The fifth myth is that recognizing college athletes as employees jeopardizes the educational interests of the athlete labor force.

The purpose of examining these myths is to understand their influence on efforts to achieve meaningful and impactful change within the college sport industry. In the conclusion, an argument is made that the acceptance of a default Title IX position on the issue of college athletes and employment rights covers over a more nuanced conversation about whether the law applies to certain potential scenarios (Staurowsky, 2012). Flowing from that, a final thought to consider is whether Title IX has been used as a tool in blocking rather than facilitating change that would allow for the creation of twenty-first-century models of college sport.

## Myth #1: All College Sports Are the Same

The prevailing narrative about college sport is one put forward by the National Collegiate Athletic Association (NCAA). As an entity that symbolically bears responsibility for shaping understandings of college sport, the NCAA assumes the position of a governance structure that has the authority to impose a regulatory system that controls college athletes. NCAA officials questioned about the business practices of college sport are quick to cite that their work is reflective of the wishes of the Association's membership which includes 1,121 colleges and universities, 99 voting athletics conferences, and 39 affiliated organizations (NCAA Staff, "What is the NCAA?" 2016a). According to the NCAA, "More than 460,000 college athletes make up the 19,000 teams that send more than 54,000 participants to compete each year in the NCAA's 90 championships in 24 sports across all 3 divisions" (NCAA Staff, "What is the NCAA?" 2016a). In fact, however, data reported for the 2015–2016 academic year reveals that 486,859 athletes compete on teams sponsored by NCAA member institutions (Irick, 2016).

Emblematic of the public representation of how the NCAA does business, the Association's president, Dr. Mark Emmert, testified before the U.S. Senate Commerce, Science, and Transportation Committee in July 2014 that discussions focusing on improving college sport required an understanding "that the NCAA is a democratically governed membership led association" where college presidents serve as the "ultimate decision makers" and NCAA staff fulfill their wishes (Rockefeller, 2014).[2] Dr. Emmert depicted the NCAA's deliberations on issues as being a one-way channel, with membership initiating and proposing legislation and the NCAA staffers passively responding to those as they arise, as reflected in his assurance to the U.S. Senate Commerce Committee that neither he nor his staffers vote.[3] There is far more agenda-setting done by NCAA staffers, however, than Dr. Emmert's streamlined depiction suggests.

NCAA staffers prepare briefing documents, interpret legislation, provide oversight for compliance efforts, conduct investigations of schools and individuals accused of wrongdoing, and offer legal advice regarding policy development and strategy. In effect, the NCAA is not a neutral party. For NCAA staffers, college sport is a full-time job. For college presidents, it is a part of a much larger portfolio of concerns. Conservatively estimated, 34% of college presidents have little to no expertise in college sport (Woodhouse, 2015).[4] Thus, the NCAA itself has a significant stake in the overall financial health of the industry, employing more than 500 people in the home office in Indianapolis, Indiana, and a staff of lobbyists handling government relations in Washington D.C. (Berkowitz, 2015; Trahan, 2014).[5]

Underneath the overarching NCAA narrative of college sport as a monolithic entity that services more than a thousand institutions and nearly a half a million athletes, there is the narrow assignment of responsibility for the financial welfare of the entity. That task is codified in the NCAA's Division I philosophy statement, which distinguishes institutions in that division as those that:

> Sponsor(s) at the highest feasible level of intercollegiate competition one or both of the traditional spectator-oriented, income-producing sports of football and basketball. In doing so, members of Division I recognize the differences in institutional objectives in support of football; therefore, the division provides competition in that sport in the Bowl Subdivision and the Championship Subdivision (NCAA Academic and Membership Affairs Staff, 2016, p. 339).

Thus, the sports of football and basketball (at an economic level, men's basketball, in particular[6]) are distinguished and strategically designed to perform a function that other sports are not assigned, namely to serve as what college officials refer to as the "front porch" of their institutions. In effect, the principle way that colleges and universities create a public media and marketing presence national in scale is through these sports (Bass, Schaeperkoetter, & Bunds, 2015; DeLuca & Maddox, [this volume]; Moody's Investment Services, 2013).[7] Men's college basketball, the property that is the source of the NCAA's 22-year $19.6 billion broadcast deal with CBS and Turner that extends through 2032, is not like all other sports because it serves as the funding source for the NCAA to exist, furnishing revenue to the tune of a $1 billion a year (Sherman, 2016).

The labor of only 1% of the athletes (5,472 Division I men's basketball players) effectively supports the NCAA's industry brand itself, the 89 other championships sponsored by the NCAA for the remaining 99% of the athletes under its umbrella, and other services.[8] That money also pays for the salaries of those working in the NCAA home office as well as the legal and lobbying services that work to undermine college athletes who seek greater representation of their interests, fair compensation, safer work conditions, accountability regarding education, and health/medical coverage.

The philosophy statement alludes to a further distinction between the most powerful football programs in the country, Division I Football Bowl Subdivision (FBS), and those that seek to play among the most powerful but fall into a tier below that (FCS). That complication speaks to the relationship between the football power conferences, known as the Power Five (Atlantic Coast Conference, Big Ten, Big 12, PAC-12, and Southeastern Conference), and the Group of Five (American Athletic Conference, Conference USA, Mid-America Conference, Mountain West Conference, Sunbelt Conference) and the NCAA. Notably, the NCAA has never awarded a national championship to top teams in the most elite football-playing institutions. Of the 90 championships offered by the NCAA (45 women's, 42 men's, and 3 co-ed) (Johnson, 2015), none are for the 15,320 players who compete in the 127 most elite college-football programs (as reported by Irick, 2016), those players who compete on teams designated as Football Bowl Subdivision teams.

A separate governance structure embodied in the College Football Playoff organization, an organization outside of the NCAA, is comprised of presidents and chancellors from 10 FBS conferences and the University of Notre Dame ("Overview," 2016). Known as the CFP Board of Managers, that group oversees a championship format that "increases revenue for all conferences and independents" ("Overview," 2016, ¶5). A network of other post-season bowls provides further competition for top programs that are not selected as one of the four teams to compete for a national title. Revenue from the College Football Playoff (CFP) and other bowls is not shared with the NCAA.

Consequently, the governance structure of college sport actually is a set of self-reinforcing decision-making bodies with interlocking power bases. The NCAA accommodates the football powers with an autonomy structure that provides for those institutions that run top-tier football programs the latitude to pass rules that will allow that business to thrive (Hosick, 2014), their autonomy is further preserved by ensuring that revenues generated from the College Football Playoff and other bowl appearances are retained solely for those within those conferences (and the scant few schools that remain independent and have been able to compete at that level). College football is not like all other sports because its governance structure is entangled within the NCAA but also outside of it, anchored in the conferences.

Recognizing these sports as being different from other college sports provides a window to explore the veracity of the notion that the interests of college athletes in what Southall and Weiler (2014) refer to as the profit sports of football and men's basketball are the same as other athletes and oppositional to the interests of female athletes. Such an assertion might be less about gender than about different models of college sport.

## Myth #2: Men's and Women's College Sport Are the Same

Since its earliest origins in the 1850s, men's college sport has been the production of the entrepreneurial spirit of its caretakers (Crowley, 2006; Sack & Staurowsky, 1998; Smith, 1990). In the beginning, male college students attending all-male institutions devised sporting activities to provide entertainment for themselves, to balance out long and tedious hours of studying subjects that they viewed as boring or of questionable relevance in their lives, and to experiment with new and innovative social and cultural forms (Sack & Staurowsky, 1998; Smith, 1990). Over time, as students graduated, they relied increasingly on networks of alumni to help fund their athletic ventures and to assist in locating athletic talent. Most specifically, the sport of football came under increasing scrutiny in the early 1900s because of the brutality associated with the game. Although student football captains and coaches balked at giving up control of the sport, a push by U.S. president Theodore Roosevelt lent momentum to calls for reform from college authorities (Sack & Staurowsky, 1998; Smith, 1990). Factions supporting a campus ban on football were opposed almost in equal measure by those invested in the game.

According to Palmer J. Pierce (1907), president of the NCAA's predecessor organization, the Intercollegiate Athletic Association of the United States (IAAUS), the first meeting resulted in the creation of a football committee whose charge was to assure the public that the violence in the sport would be addressed. Reluctant college football leaders like Yale's Walter Camp, conceded ground by going along with the creation of the NCAA and its football committee but worked to resist efforts to undermine their power in controlling the future of the game.[9] Pierce (1907) also reported that one of the primary goals of the Association was to shift responsibility for "student athletic sports" away from students into the hands of college authorities.

In the years ahead, through every era, college football reflected the sensibilities of military strategy and American business acumen (Kish, 2000; Oriard, 1998; 2002; 2009; Montez, 2013; Smith, 2008; Staurowsky, 2004; Watterson, 2002). Publicity in the press was sought after, and was used to market all-male colleges and universities as they sought to stabilize and increase enrollment (Smith, 2011; Thelin, 1996; Sperber, 2002). Land-grant colleges formed in the aftermath of the Morrill Act of 1862 emerged as state universities that used the marketing potential of college football to establish brand identity and to serve as an anchor for regional rivalries that solidified state identity (Thelin, 1996; Sack & Staurowsky, 1998). Thus emerged "classic" games between inter-region teams that have lasted for more than 100 years, such as the Red River Showdown, featuring the Longhorns of Texas and the Oklahoma Sooners—a rivalry that dates back to the 1900s (AT&T Red River Showdown, 2016). Large sporting spectacles sponsored by colleges and universities became sites for the convergence of high-powered political and economic interests with loyalties growing with each passing generation (Loftin, 2014; Williams, 1969). Men's college sport grew in parallel to the evolution of media technologies throughout the latter part of the 1800s through the twentieth century, providing content for newspapers, radio, and television, eventually forming the basis for digital television networks across multiple platforms and 24–7 media coverage in the twenty-first century (Glier, 2012; Huma & Staurowsky, 2013; Oriard, 1998; Oriard, 2002: Oriard, 2008; Smith, 2003; Smith, 2003; Sperber, 2002; Yost, 2009).

Those spectacles were built as commercial enterprises. Ticket sales, media coverage, competitive advantage, and player performance fueled the need to present athletic programs that paid lip-service to amateur ideals discouraging player subsidization, recruitment, and professional coaching but embraced all three behind the scenes as a matter of survival. "The first decades of the twentieth century witnessed a relentless professionalization of collegiate sport" in response to membership's open defiance of "amateur principles" (Sack & Staurowsky, 1998, p. 32). Further, "many of the organization's [NCAA's] actions, especially after 1948, can best be understood as rearguard accommodations to professionalism rather than efforts to preserve amateur ideals" (Sack & Staurowsky, p. 32).

After years of failed attempts to discourage compensation for athletes, with the result being a fracturing of the NCAA membership with schools across the spectrum offering "subsidies" in various forms, a political détente on the question was achieved with the formalization of a compensation scheme within the NCAA manual in 1956 regarding the terms and conditions for the awarding of athletically-related aid, understood by its architects to constitute "pay for play" (Byers, 1995).[10] Walter Byers (1995), the first full-time executive director of the NCAA, wrote in his memoir that by creating the grant-in-aid, "We were forswearing old amateur principles without admitting it" (p. 74). He credited then University of Michigan athletic director Fritz Crisler with the understanding that "We're saying that these youngsters are amateurs and nobody should be permitted to professionalize them except the colleges. The *colleges* can pay them to play" (Byers, 1995, p. 74).

The story of the evolution of women's college sport is a very different one. In contrast to college men's sports, women's college sport emerged out of physical education and health movements of the late 1900s. Crafting rationales to allow women to pursue education, women's physical education offered assurances to a concerned public that women would not jeopardize their femininity by attending school. Whatever serious "brainwork" women might take on would be put to good social use in support of their roles as wives and mothers. Fear that too warm an embrace of sporting activities would threaten female dispositions and attractiveness and might interfere with reproduction tempered approaches to physical activity for women. Attention to posture and decorum were thought important qualities to cultivate in young women and were reflected in the activities, such as hygiene and posture testing, thought suitable for them (Sack & Staurowsky, 1998).

The careful regulation of sport for women was considered the domain of women physical educators. Through their professional associations, they carved out a space for women's college sport that eschewed the practices of the men's college sport model, opting instead for a model of sport that was not commercial, focused on the health of participants, was not spectator-oriented, moderate, sponsored for the enjoyment of the participant, and was run by women. Although not all women agreed with the notion that women collegians should participate in "restrained' forms of competition, the prevailing belief was one of "a girl in every sport, and a sport for every girl" (Sack & Staurowsky, 1998). In 1974, three years after the passage of Title IX, sport historian Ellen Gerber wrote,

> To date there has never been an NCAA sponsoring women's sport in the colleges. Nor has there been any other authority totally divorced from physical education specifically seeking to control college women's sport. Thus far, the physical educators have had carte blanche to control the national development and organization of collegiate sport programs (p. 8).

Although women's sport did not have an NCAA at that time (the NCAA was still an all-male organization), it did have the Association for Intercollegiate Athletics for Women (AIAW). As per Gerber's (1974) report, in 1971 the AIAW had been proposed by the Division of Girls and Women in Sport, a section of the Alliance for Health, Physical Education, and Recreation, otherwise known as AAPHERD which was a part of the National Education Association (NEA).

This grounding of women's college sport in educational associations influenced the model under which women's college sport developed. "Proceeding from the premise that whatever model they adopted had to place the interests of female students at the core, AIWA leaders embarked on a journey to forge a new model of college sport distinct from that in place for men" (Staurowsky, 2012, p. 586).

> This perspective resulted in a set of policies that ran counter to those espoused by the NCAA. . . . The ideological centerpiece of the AIAW's educational model of college sport was its original prohibition on athletic scholarships. Drawn from the 1969 DGWS position paper on the topic, the ban on athletic scholarships was designed to avoid the perceived problems associated with men's college sport, including "pressure recruiting, the possibility of exploiting athletes, and the increased

financial costs associated with buying athletic talent." In the estimation of AIAW leadership, offering athletic scholarships was antithetical to a model of amateur, educational athletics. Within months of Title IX's passage, the AIAW's model of college sport for women would be challenged on several fronts, starting with the rule barring athletic scholarships. (Staurowsky, 2012, p. 286)

Within 10 years of its founding, the AIAW was taken over by the NCAA, but the differing models of college sport continue to have resonance as reflected in the NCAA's philosophy statement that carves out a role for the business as embodied in the sports of "big-time" football and men's basketball (Sack & Staurowsky, 1998; Wushanley, 2004). These two models both operate within college sport, but in different ways and for different reasons. The "educational" model gives cover to the commercial "business" model, insulating it both from being viewed as the profit-seeking entity that it is, and from considering the athletes who work in it to be employees. Although those working within the business model often are depicted as privileged, competing interests buffet their existence. The profit-seekers need them to be as productive as possible in service to a media-entertainment industry that competes favorably with other professional sport entities for market share and audience. At the same time, the "educational" side of the university program pulls at the revenue-generators to siphon off a portion of their earnings. College sport officials justify this practice by claiming that the revenue generated through the labor of athletes in the two income-producing sports is used for "educational purposes," but the practice itself is akin to non-professional teams in local areas expecting the pro franchise in town to pay for its championships by taking money away from the players.

### Myth #3: "Big-Time" College Football and Basketball Are Extracurricular Activities

According to the NCAA's principle of amateurism, "Student participation in intercollegiate athletics is an avocation and student-athletes should be protected from exploitation by professional and commercial enterprises" (NCAA Academic and Membership and Affairs Staff, 2016, p. 4). The term "avocation"— meaning that athletic participation is not a vocation or job but a hobby or pastime—forms a bridge to the related assertion that all college sport programs fall into the category of being "extra-curricular activities." This link is a recurring theme in responses filed by parties supporting Northwestern University in its opposition to a favorable ruling by the National Labor Relations Board (NLRB) regional director on behalf of football players there who had signed union cards and sought to collectively bargain as employees (Sung Ohr, 2014).

Among the parties assisting Northwestern in its opposition to the notion that its football players are employees were the Big Ten Conference (Rosenman, Netter, & Wolf, 2014), the Higher Education Council (Jones, Reid, Mathison, & Salsburey, 2014), the National Association of Collegiate Directors of Athletics and Division I-A Athletics Directors Association (DiPalma, Cohen, & Maxfield, 2014), a group of eight private institutions (including Baylor, Rice, Southern Methodist, Stanford, Tulane, the University of Southern California, Vanderbilt, and Wake Forest) (Durham, 2014), and six Republican members of the U.S. Congress (Livingston, Klimesh, Kramer, & Harris, 2014).

Arguing that the volitional nature of athlete participation disqualifies it from being viewed as employment, the amicus brief on behalf of Republican congressional members stated:

> Colleges and universities offer and students participate ('perform services') in these extracurricular programs because they are "valuable" to both the student and the institution. Students participate in intercollegiate athletics because they want to, not because it is a "job" (Livingston, Klimesh, Kramer, & Harris, 2014, p. 5).

In an amicus brief filed by the National Association of Collegiate Director of Athletics and the Division I Athletic Directors Association (2014), the NLRB regional director's determination that the university exerted "strict and exacting" control of scholarship football players was countered with the argument that such control "however it is described, is no different than the control exercised over other students who also participate in extracurricular activities at the university" (DiPalma, Cohen, & Maxfield, 2014, p. 10).

> The Higher Education Council of the Employment Law Alliance argued in turn, "But even assuming the common law test can provide some illumination on this issue, applying it correctly in light of all of the incidents of the relationship similarly reveals that the student-athletes here are students and not statutory employees with collective bargaining rights over the terms and conditions of their extracurricular education" (Jones, Reid, Mathison, & Salsburey, 2014, p. 13–14).

Connecting the logic to Title IX, the brief further notes that activities that are not academic are still regarded as educational not just as a matter of common usage and common sense, but as a principle embodied in federal law. In mandating equal access and non-discrimination in educational programs receiving federal funding, Title IX, for example, defines "education" to include not only academic and research activities, but also extracurricular programs such as intercollegiate athletics. 34 C.F.R. §§ 106.31(a); 106.41(a) (Jones, Reid, Mathison, & Salsburey, 2014, p. 9).

Across the briefs supporting Northwestern, college football players were compared to members of the debate team and to students working on college newspapers, as well as to artists and musicians (Staurowsky, 2015). Although some argued for "common sense" understandings to prevail, an easy acceptance that college football players performing in a multibillion-dollar industry are just like every other student on campus pursuing recreational interests strains under the weight of several realities.

First, although campuses have their share of debaters, musicians, artists, poets, activists, movie buffs, knitters, tobacco enthusiasts, and politicians,[11] those interests do not brand students in any way that could be construed as equal to college sport celebrities. There is, however, a special effort to brand college athletes as "student-athletes" (*see* Southall, Southall, & Dwyer, 2009). That effort is not without intention or meaning. Following a spate of legal challenges from college football players and their families in the 1950s and 1960s seeking relief for injuries suffered while playing or participating in the sport, NCAA officials worked with a legal team to devise the term "student-athlete" and avert what Byers referred to as "the dreaded notion" that athletes might gain workers' compensation coverage (Byers, 1995; Staurowsky & Sack, 2005). In his memoir, Walter Byers (1995) elaborated, saying

> We crafted the term student-athlete, and soon it was embedded in all NCAA rules and interpretations as a mandated substitute for such words as players and athletes. We told college publicists to speak of "college teams," not football or basketball "clubs," a word common to the pros (p. 69).

Drawing an analogy between debaters and football players working in the industry of "big-time" college sport as being the "same" obscures the very real differences between a corporate business entity that commodifies players and student activities that can be pursued at leisure.

According to NCAA data for the 2015–2016 season, FBS football drew paying crowds of more than 38,000,000 attendees. Six FBS teams (University of Michigan, Ohio State, Texas A&M, LSU, Alabama, and Tennessee) averaged more than 100,000 fans per home game. In contrast, no professional football franchise in the National Football League (NFL) drew more than 91,000 fans in a single game in 2015 (ESPN Staff, 2015).[12] In the fall of 2016, college football experienced its most successful kickoff weekend, which extended from Thursday, September 1, through Monday, September 5, and featured key matchups around the country. In total, 81.2 million viewers watched college football on ESPN's networks (combined television and streaming) (Volner, 2016). Both college football and NCAA men's basketball compete favorably with the most lucrative sports properties in the United States for audience share and advertising revenue.

In an ongoing Harris Poll of American's favorite sports, the NFL has held steady in the number one position for many years, with college football in the third position and college basketball in the seventh position (ESPN Staff, 2015; Staff, 2015). As sports properties, college football and men's basketball are among the 10 most lucrative in the United States. Although some argue that they do not wish to see college sport become "minor league" entities, there is nothing about the economic and corporate interest in those sports that is *minor league*. Their economic peers are major-league professional entities. Navigating an environment where millions of people, countless companies, and media conglomerates have a stake in the outcomes of the games played by college athlete employees establishes a different set of expectations and vulnerabilities. Betting lines are not published on a weekly basis for debate competitions, but professional oddsmakers monitor "big-time" college sport for the purposes of facilitating and harvesting billions of dollars. Estimates indicate that $60 to $70 billion is wagered each year on college football (Spear, 2013), and the American Gaming Association (2016) projected that the 2016 NCAA Division I Men's Basketball Tournament (colloquially known as March Madness) drew $9.6 billion.

Limits are placed on the movement of players; little opportunity exists outside of the sports themselves for players to pursue other interests; public opinion regarding players can shift rapidly, depending on the outcomes of games; and the scrutiny that comes from being in such a highly publicized activity dictates a professional level of expectations. This is evidenced in the recruitment process that leads to the signing of "big-time" college football and basketball talent. Top high school recruits in these sports are publicly rated and throughout their careers are followed on websites such as *247 Sports, Rivals.com, and Scouts.com,* in which news of high school player prospects is covered just like the stock market; offers extended to athletes are catalogued; there is ongoing monitoring of the caliber of team recruiting classes; and player commitments are updated on a daily—sometimes hourly—basis (Staurowsky, 2015).

Selected college football recruits that have high ratings from *247 Composite* are featured every July in ESPN's *The Opening* and the *Elite 11*. The events are designed to introduce the next wave of potential college and NFL stars, are followed closely by college-football recruiting staffs, and are hosted on the Nike campus in Beaverton, Oregon (Kirshner & Berkes, 2016). In the sport of basketball, Nike sponsors the Elite Youth Basketball League composed of 40 clubs that play throughout the spring, leading into the Peach Jam tournament held each summer in North Carolina. Both Adidas and Under Armour sponsor similar circuits. Nowhere on these websites are statistics kept about the academic prowess or intentions of the players. The attention is on the business of player development and personnel. Such programming also aids in extending the coverage of college football and basketball over a 12-month period, maintaining audience interest and corporate investment in those sports on a year-round basis.[13]

Second, leveling the experience of athletes working in the "big-time" college sport industry to students who participate in an array of elective activities renders invisible the forces of commodification that are the hallmarks of college athlete employees. The NLRB regional director found that football players at Northwestern were employees under common law because the institution exerted substantial control over their lives, expected performance for compensation, and in accordance with a contractual agreement (all characteristics of employee status under common law) (Sung Ohr, 2014). Documentation of work weeks at or exceeding 40 hours; regimented time commitments and schedules post-season, in-season, and out-of-season; and a handbook delineating rules and regulations for conduct with penalties for misconduct reinforced the finding. As noted in Staurowsky (2014a):

> Great effort is made to ensure that college football players appear to be working 20 hours when they are actually engaged in team-related activities 40 to 60 hours per week during pre-season, over 40 hours per week during regular season, and far more than the eight hours per week legislated by NCAA rules in the "off-season." Through creative accounting, a job that requires college football players to work more than the average American work week is presented as a tidy 20 hour package with one day off per week in season. . . . On game days, regardless of the number of hours expected, only three are calculated in the weekly total as per the NCAA definition of time.

The regional director further determined that a "grant-in-aid" (the regulatory term used by the NCAA to describe an athletic scholarship) was not financial aid but compensation for athletic performance. In the decision, he wrote:

> the facts here show that the Employer never offers a scholarship to a prospective student unless they intend to provide an athletic service to the Employer. In fact, the players can have their scholarships immediately canceled if they voluntarily withdraw from the football team (Sung Ohr, 2014, p. 20).

Chilling stuff indeed.

Third, in the sports of football and basketball, college athlete–employee relationships with institutions are markedly different as a result of the economic and corporate investment in the designated revenue-producing sports. There is a reason that college and university websites list athletic departments as separate entities in their search menus, separate from other "student activities." College athletes are enveloped in a growing bureaucracy unlike any in existence for extracurricular activities.[14] That bureaucracy is designed to surveil athlete behavior in ways more intrusive than any found for the general student body. Athletes are required to report to athletic officials what type of cars they drive, and the details of their living situations (2016–2017 Compliance Forms, 2016). They are encouraged to provide access to their bank accounts to athletic department personnel who investigate and monitor their financial activity (Bishop, 2012).[15] Coaching staffs monitor players on social media, and some programs institute social media bans for portions of the year (Clapp, 2016; Keepfer, 2015).[16] Athletes in some "big-time" programs are required to wear GPS tracking devises to monitor their class attendance (Wolverton, 2015). National Labor Relations Board Associate General Counsel Barry Kearney (2016) found that sections of the *Northwestern University Football Handbook* violated section 8(a)(1) of the National Labor Relations Act.

Students participating in extracurricular activities are not subjected to that level of behavioral regulation and monitoring nor are they subjected to the complexities of a regulatory system contained within the more than 450-page NCAA Manual (NCAA Academic and Membership Affairs Staff, 2016; Staurowsky, 2014c). No other student sector anywhere within U.S. higher education has been commodified in this manner, sold for profit by Fortune 500 companies, and subjected to such regulation. "Big-time" football and basketball players participate in a workplace, not an extracurricular activity. "In the final analysis, the distinction between college football players and college debaters is the fact that the industry would like college football players to remain silent. Denying them their rightful status as employees accomplishes just that" (Staurowsky, 2014b, p. 140).

## Myth #4: College Athletic Department Economic Models: Profitability versus Sustainability

The Big Ten's amicus brief argued that affording Northwestern football players employee status "could endanger institutions' athletic budgets and discourage continued support for robust, highly competitive athletics programs" (Rosenman, Netter, & Wolf, 2014). Onerous in tone, this is a standard response that college sport authorities give whenever change is proposed. In the 1970s, when Title IX was passed, there were predictions that the sport of football would be destroyed or diminished. Senator Roman Hruska is famously to have queried during a congressional hearing in 1975, "are we going to let Title IX kill the goose that lays the golden eggs in those colleges and universities with a major revenue-producing sport?" (Ware, 2014, p. 5). Since then, college football has become a multibillion-dollar industry, and opportunities for female athletes have grown to record numbers.

And yet, fears about excessive spending and an industry perched on the brink of financial collapse persist. In the assessment by economist Andrew Zimbalist, litigation against the NCAA on matters pertaining to concussions, athlete compensation, and unionization represent significant threats that could lead to a bursting of the college sports financial bubble. Alternatively, Jeff Orleans, former executive director of the Ivy Group and consultant (who cowrote the federal regulations for Title IX) has said, "there's so much out there, it is hard to feel comfortable. On the other hand, it could be like the Cold War. For 50 years we had all kinds of ways the world could have blown to hell, and somehow we survived it" (Brady, Berkowitz, & Upton, 2016, ¶7).

Since 1989, the Knight Commission on Intercollegiate Athletics has called for greater financial transparency in the college sport industry. One of the commission's long-standing conclusions has been that athletic department expenditures are unsustainable and that efforts need to be made to control costs and to bring expenses more in line with the rest of the university (Knight Commission on Intercollegiate Athletics, 2016).

This is manifest in aggregate reporting on the broad relationship between operating expenses and revenues for NCAA Division I athletic departments. In an analysis of 228 public schools in NCAA Division I, both revenues and expenses were reported to have increased for most schools in 2015 (Brady, Berkowitz, & Upton, 2016). Among 50 public schools located in the Power Five conferences, expenses were reported to have exceeded revenue by $28 million ($332 million in expenses and $304 million in revenues). For 128 public schools outside of the Power Five, the gap between revenues and expenses was $19 million ($218 million in expenses and $199 million in revenue). According to the NCAA, "fewer than two dozen public schools can cover their annual operating expenses without money from university coffers, government sources or student fees" (Brady, Berkowitz, & Upton, 2016, ¶3).

Unpacking what this all means, however, is a complicated matter (see King-White, this volume). More to the point, the veracity of the accounting methods used to produce the results cited above has been questioned by several economists. Schwartz (2013) wrote that the decisions made regarding the definitions used to guide accounting in athletic departments are "likely designed for the purposes of hiding the profits, as schools face the tradeoff between justifying their programs (so a bean counter doesn't cancel sports) vs. justifying why they cannot share the profits (for obvious reasons)." Schwartz (2014) further explains:

> Athletic departments are trying to walk a rhetorical tightrope. They want to hide their profits to make it easier to keep them away from other would-be claimants. They also want to avoid looking so poor that other stakeholders within academia use sports' apparent poverty to strip them of power. Rhetoric that turns a price into a cost, and a transfer of profit into a loss of money, helps play a role in confusing things enough that the moment in the magic trick where the profit is moved from one pocket to the other gets obscured.

Thus, the long-held belief that college athletic departments "lose money" is not as straightforward as it seems.

Offering a deeper understanding of what the term "deficit" means, Goff and Wilson (2013) instructively explain that:

> athletic "deficits" reflect the accounting practices of universities or the flow of revenues back into expenses rather than the inability of revenues to meet costs. . . . Within athletic departments it can flow into salaries for athletic staff (coaches, athletic directors, support personnel) or into facilities. Beyond the athletic department, it can appear in the general revenue fund as a transfer for grants-in-aid or be embedded in any number of intra-university transactions between athletic accounts and other accounts (p. 17).[17]

For non-profit entities, what would the alternatives be? If they report that programs are profitable, they jeopardize their tax status. They no longer can be said to be operating as a non-profit, thus there is little to no incentive, unlike in other business contexts, to "show a profit."

Moody (2013) adds further nuance noting that the commercial value of programs also determines when they are operating in the negative, operating in the positive, or are flat. In keeping with that idea, Duke University economist Charles Clotfelter (2015) cautions that it is important to understand that college athletics has not one, but two definitions. He argues that one definition refers to activities that are provided principally for the players where "the ratio of spectators to players in most of our [college] sports is very low." The second definition refers to those sports, primarily "big-time" football and basketball (men's and women's), which have "become a core function of universities like Nebraska, like North Carolina, and like Duke" (Clotfelter, 2015). Thus, although the "vast majority of athletic departments operate at a loss, requiring university subsidies," it is also the case that "revenue from high-profile sports has grown significantly" and "expenses from less commercially prominent sports are still large enough such that most athletic departments generate negative net income each year" (Moody's, 2013, p. 3).[18]

Just as there are two different definitions of college sport, so too are there two different economic models operating within college sport. This is important in determining where the threats to sustainability are within each of those models. As Schwartz (2014) and Maxcy (forthcoming) point out, although some predict that an employment model for "big-time" college sports would threaten financial viability, this is an industry that has evidenced considerable resilience and continued expansion for decades. Between 2003 and 2014, FBS football realized a 72% increase in profit (Maxcy, forthcoming). In the sport of NCAA Division I men's basketball, growth in profits fluctuated year to year but remained largely stable in growth (Maxcy, forthcoming). According to an analysis in *Forbes* (Alsher, 2016), the Power Five conferences brought in more than $250 million during 2015 and 2016, representing a 33% increase in revenue in one year

TABLE 5.1

**Power Five Conference Revenue Streams and Payouts**
**to Individual Member Schools**

| Conference | TV Deals | NCAA Tournament | Bowl Game | Total | Payouts |
|---|---|---|---|---|---|
| Atlantic Coast Conference (ACC) | $212M | $21M | $98M | $331M | $22.1M |
| Big 12 | $162M | $19M | $72M | $253M | $25.3M |
| Big Ten | $279M | $21M | $86M | $386M | $27.6M |
| PAC-12 | $215M | $11M | $81M | $307M | $25.5M |
| Southeastern Conference (SEC) | $347M | $17M | $112M | $476M | $34M |

(Data drawn from Alsher, 2016)

(Solomon, 2016). Broken down by conference, major revenue streams for those conferences include revenue from bowl games, the NCAA tournament, and television rights deals (see Table 5.1 for details on each conference).

According to ESPN (Lavigne, 2016, ¶1), "The nation's richest athletic departments—those in the Power Five conferences—pulled in a record $6 billion last year, nearly $4 billion more than all other schools combined." The financial largesse of programs in that tier of schools has opened the door for the lucrative salaries for head coaches, lavish facilities, and layers of specialized personnel. Over a decade, between 2004 and 2014, average salaries for the commissioners of the Power Five Conferences increased by more than $2 million, with percentages of increases for individual commissioners going from 258% for John Swofford (ACC commissioner) to 542% for Larry Scott (PAC-12 commissioner) (Hobson & Rich, 2016).

It is not unusual that head coaches of "big-time" football and basketball programs are the most highly paid public employees within their states. In a state-by-state analysis conducted by *24/7 Wall Street* (Comen, Frohlich, & Sauter, 2016), 60% of the highest paid state employees (30 out of 5) were college coaches. The average salary for head football coaches in 2015 was $1.8 million, an increase of more than 90% since 2006 (Comen, Frohlich, & Sauter, 2016). Coaches' salaries provide only one measure of compensation. With generous bonus structures, coaches stand to earn significantly more if they win a certain number of games, are named coach of the year, place well within their conference, and compete for conference titles and national titles. As a comparison, when Penn State football became eligible to play for the Big Ten Conference

Championship in the fall of 2016, Head Coach James Franklin received a $250,000 bonus with the opportunity to increase the bonus amount depending on how far the team went in the post-season (Pickel, 2016).

Within this system, the notion that just compensation for college athletes who fulfill the definition of an employee would be denied that status because of affordability ring hollow when considered in light of accepted industry practice relative to increasing compensation for others who work alongside of the athlete labor force. The denial of such affirms what Crisler understood about the system, that it works to increase profit for itself while reserving the right to exploit athletes, as it does (Byers, 1995). Maxcy (2016) argues that:

> The concern that universities cannot afford reasonable and competitive wages for its football and basketball athletes is specious. Equally illogical is that should these athletes be reasonably paid, resources would be diverted from non-revenue sports, or the university's academic mission. Universities investing in big time sports are classified as non-profit organizations, but like some other enterprises within a university, e.g. hotels, bookstores and hospitals, football and basketball programs reflect commercial activity, generate substantial revenue *and* often a profit (p. 1).

In other words, there is more than enough money to compensate college athletes; it would simply need to be redirected.

## Myth #5: Recognition of College Athlete Employees Precludes Earning College Degrees

College sport industry officials opposed to the employment status of football and basketball players have put forward a position that there is an imperative that intercollegiate athletics be about, in the words of a Big Ten campaign, "education first, athletics second" (Delany, 2015). Among the talking points issued by the NCAA in making its case to the public about the threat of college football players being recognized as employees was a caution that high school students would get the impression that they could make money playing in college and that would undermine their intention of getting an education (NCAA Staff, 2014).

Division I athletic directors asserted in their opposition to the Northwestern football players' bid to collectively bargain that the educational process would be undermined because players would be in position, for example, to negotiate the terms and conditions of their academic engagement. According to Division I athletic directors, such a scenario would put players in control of contesting conflicts between practices and classes. Such a possibility would result in the "educational process" suffering and the "student-athlete model of education" (DiPalma, D., Cohan, M. C., Maxfield, H. O., 2014, p. 20) being undermined. In a panel on college sport at the Marquette Law School, the associate director at the Office of the Committees on Infractions for the NCAA, Dino Pollock, stated that as a former football player at the University of Illinois he was offended by the idea that college football players were exploited and that conferring employment status would result in athletes not being able to get an education (author's notes, October 21, 2016).

These arguments reflect a classic management response when labor seeks to exert influence over what is happening in the lives of workers. There was nothing in the Northwestern football players' attempt to unionize that even hinted at a desire on the part of the players to relinquish the opportunity to get an education. Positioning employment status as antithetical to education is a false narrative, as damaging as fake news, one that is particularly troubling within higher education where many employees are also students. The college and university workplace expressly provides for employees to be enriched and invested in the educational system within which they work. Those working in higher education routinely receive tuition benefits as part of their compensation package. Employment status for football and basketball players would not foreclose educational opportunities unless colleges and universities departed from their own well-established employment practices. Further, among undergraduate students, 60% to 80% work at a paying job (Staurowsky, 2014b).

If deconstructed further, how would the ability of athletes to receive academic degrees be diminished if they were employees? It is well known that college football and basketball players, as an entire group, have not received the full benefit of the educational promises made in the current bargain that was struck for them. Historically, these groups of athletes, many of whom are racial minorities, have lower graduation rates than nearly any other NCAA athlete cohort and, depending on the metric used, substantially so (Harper, 2016; Southall, Eckard, Nagel, Keith, & Blake, 2014; Southall & Southall, this volume; Staurowsky & Southall, 2015).

At a logical level, in a scenario where athletes are compensated more fairly and negotiate more favorable work conditions that ensure their health, safety, and well-being, it would seem there would be a greater likelihood that athletes would graduate with meaningful degrees. As it stands, athletes in these sports work more than 40 hours per week in physically demanding jobs, in high-stress situations, and under intense scrutiny. Additional hours might be spent recovering from injury and the physical toll of playing in high-contact sports. Why insist under those circumstances that those athletes give the appearance that the circumstances are optimal for them to reap the benefits of the educational opportunities available?

## Conclusion

In 1972, at the time of Title IX's passage, U.S. congressional leadership and the shapers of Title IX's athletic regulatory system could not anticipate what the college sport industry of the twenty-first century would be. At the time, the NCAA had just adopted a federated system that established Divisions I, II, and III. The intention was to accommodate differing philosophical views regarding the ways business would be conducted as well as the relationship that athletes had with their institutions. It was a time when the NCAA controlled the television rights to college football. Disputes over the value of football properties led to a confrontation between the NCAA and the football powers in 1984 in the Board of Regents case, wherein the University of Oklahoma and the University of Georgia challenged the NCAA's restrictive practice of limiting the number of football games that could be televised and limiting the capacity of conferences and member schools from negotiating contracts on their own behalf (*NCAA v. Board of Regents*, 1984).

With a U.S. Supreme Court ruling that such restrictions violated antitrust law, the era of expansive coverage of college football led to a break of the football powers from the NCAA, and with that exit went football money. To follow would be media conglomerates, such as CBS, ESPN, FOX, and Turner, that would build part of their sport media empires on lucrative college sport football and basketball properties. In the digital age, college conferences with ever-expanding power bases of their own then mirrored their professional counterparts in the NFL and NBA with the creation of niche television networks that fed growing fan bases and corporate profits.

Those who harken back to the failed attempts on the part of the revenue producers to receive an exemption from the reach of Title IX point out that the question has been asked and answered definitively over the years, that Title IX does not assess the capacity of a sport to generate revenue but merely requires that the benefits accrued to athletes through revenue are distilled into equitable experiences (Carpenter & Acosta, 2005). That assumes, however, that all athletes are participating in the same type of activities, that all college sports operate within the same model and are extracurricular activities, and that all athletes are the same—assumptions that are fundamentally and fatally flawed. The issue that not all sports are the same has been addressed under Title IX in the sport of cheerleading (*Beidiger v. Quinnipiac*, 2013). There the determination has been that although there are various forms of physical activity, not all sports are acknowledged under Title IX.

An area that has gone unexamined in the analysis is what happens if the relationship between athlete and institution does not fall under existing definitions. What happens if the sports of football and basketball are not extracurricular activities and the relationship between player and university is that of employee to employer? Would Title IX apply to a professional team? Until asked, the answer remains uncertain but it likely would be "no."

In NLRB Regional Director Sung Ohr's (2014) finding in the Northwestern case, he noted that "Employer never offers a scholarship to a prospective student unless they intend to provide an athletic service to the Employer" (p. 20). In effect, this means college football players are paid to play football. In support of his determination, he also noted that NCAA rules specifically provide that if an athlete voluntarily chooses not to play, the athlete no longer retains the right to the scholarship. Title IX analyses hinge on an understanding of the athletic scholarship as access to education. Orh's finding reveals that the scholarship is payment for service. The connection to education is mandated not by the earning of compensation but by the requirement imposed by NCAA rules that workers must spend that compensation in restricted ways that the NCAA exclusively determines.

Such a unilaterally imposed financial arrangement is not volitional and it ought not obscure the labor who earn it. This is not "access to education," but is denial of employee status under the guise of education with the express purpose of controlling a labor force and suppressing player value. It is a direct manifestation of what Fritz Crisler observed at the time athletic scholarships were adopted by the NCAA in the 1950s (Byers, 1995), that it was a tool of player control that assigned the right of exploitation to the colleges themselves to the exclusion of others.

Reverting automatically to a position that Title IX simply will not allow college athletes to be deemed employees or that the requirements of Title IX requires that female athletes be compensated the same presents a two-edged problem.[19] First, it blocks opportunities to recognize the different models that operate in college sport, one commercial and the other educational. Depending on the model in which athletes participate in, that should drive recognition of their status as employees. That status then might or might not implicate Title IX. Regardless of the dictates of Title IX, female athletes have a stake in the clarity that could come from being clearer about how this industry works. If some college athletes are employees, and some female athletes are included in that group, then they stand to benefit. Second, the use of Title IX as a political weapon in defending the economic exploitation of college athlete employees suggests a commitment to fairness and equity that the college sport industry has been hard put to convincingly demonstrate.

When former Baylor University chancellor and president, Kenneth Starr, testified in the congressional hearing on the implications of college athletes unionizing, his cautionary tale that there could be very serious implications for Title IX was met with questioning from U. S. Representative John Tierney (D-MA). Regarding Baylor's public record of compliance with Title IX as reflected in the federally required Equity in Athletics Disclosure Report, Tierney asked Mr. Starr to address the issue of disproportionately high allocations of athletically-related financial aid favoring male athletes. In his response, Mr. Starr indicated that such allocations were fluid and changed from year to year prompting Tierney query "So you're saying this is a temporary issue . . . ?" with Starr suggesting as much. The significance of this exchange is that "Title IX regulations require an allocation within 1% of what the representation for males and females are within the athlete population (in theory, if there are 50% female athletes, the allocation of existing athletically related financial aid should be within one percentage point of 50%—either 49% or 51%)" (Staurowsky, 2015). In an analysis of Baylor's allocation of athletically related financial aid between 2004 and 2014, I (Staurowsky, 2015, p. X) reported, "these were not small discrepancies that might be accounted for with modest fluctuations in athlete movement within the program. These were double digit discrepancies that ordinarily suggest that there is a Title IX violation."

The distillation of the litigation efforts of college football and basketball players into a bumper sticker slogan of "pay for play" which pits male athletes against female athletes obscures the real issue. Although it should hardly be objectionable in the United States that workers seek to reap the fruits of their labor, and this can result in college athlete employees receiving paychecks, the issue is not about "pay" but power. What college football and basketball players seek is the opportunity to bargain for better labor conditions that is in their interests. As it stands now, this is a system that has the financial wherewithal to use money generated from the labor of players seeking their value to hire lobbyists to protect the decision makers in the centers of power in Washington D.C. and state legislatures and to actively suppress the value of those who work for them, employing the full scale of their relationships with media conglomerates to monopolize the national discussion. Title IX should be used for a much more just purpose than to deny college athlete workers their fundamental rights.

## Discussion

What real changes would occur if student-athletes were considered employees and earned compensation? Would the cost come at the expense of the coaching staff? Students via athletics fees? Would more "non-revenue" teams be cut?

### NOTES

1. Title IX of the Education Amendments of 1972 is a federal law that prohibits sex discrimination in schools that receive federal financial assistance.
2. In response to Dr. Emmert's comments, U.S. Senator Claire McCaskill observed, "I can't tell whether you are in charge or whether you are a minion" (Kerkhoff, 2014).
3. Dr. Emmert's depiction of the NCAA president's role in voting within the Association is not wholly accurate. According to Article 4.1.1 of the 2016–2017 NCAA Division I Manual, Article 4.1.1. The NCAA president and the chairs of the Division I Council and the Division II and Division III Management Councils shall be ex officio nonvoting members, except that the NCAA president is permitted to vote in the case of a tie among the voting members of the Board of Governors present and voting.

4. According to Woodhouse (2015), the presidential search firm Witt/Keifer estimated that 66% of presidents working in universities with powerhouse Division I football programs have experience working at similar universities. That said, not all of those individuals would have been working as university presidents at the time they were hired. Thus, although 66% of those university presidents might have worked at institutions with a football culture, that should not be interpreted to mean that those individuals had dealt with athletics and the complexities of athletic conferences and the NCAA.

5. According to the NCAA's self-report (NCAA Staff, 2016b), of the more than $1 billion in revenues that funded its budget in 2015–2016, $776.6 million came from the Division I men's basketball championship television and marketing rights, with an additional $119.8 million coming from a total of $119.8 million from championship ticket sales. Of the total revenue, $44.8 million is dedicated to general and administrative expenses for the NCAA itself and $43.9 is allocated to Association-wide legal services, communications, and business services. Of the 90 championships, only 5 either meet or exceed expenses: men's basketball, men's ice hockey, men's lacrosse, wrestling, and the College World Series.

6. During a visit to Utah State University in April of 2016, NCAA president Mark Emmert stated that women's basketball loses $14 million per year (McIntyre, 2016). Dosh (2013) reported that one of the distinctions between "big-time" women's college basketball as compared to football and men's basketball is program donations. She wrote, "even the most successful [women's] teams on the court struggle with donor support" (Dosh, 2013, second paragraph, third line). In men's basketball, attendance for the 2016 tournament was 703,854 with the Final Four total of 149,845 (2016 NCAA Men's Basketball Attendance). Attendance for the 2016 NCAA women's basketball tournament, in comparison, was 224,189 (2016 NCAA Women's Basketball Attendance).

7. In an interview with *espnW*, Eastern Michigan University Athletic Director Heather Lyke stated, "Whether we want to believe it or not, football drives the attention, viewership, enrollment, fundraising" (Kahn, 2016, ¶7).

8. In 2014–2015, of the 90 championships, only 5 either meet or exceed expenses: men's basketball, men's ice hockey, men's lacrosse, wrestling, and the College World Series (NCAA Staff, 2016a).

9. There appears to be no dispute in the historical literature regarding the violence in college football in the 1900s. There is, however, dispute over the reporting done regarding deaths of college football caused by participation in the game (Gordon, 2014; Watterson, 2002).

10. In a November 2016 article written by Brad Wolverton and published in the *Chronicle of Higher Education*, more than seven decades after the passage of the NCAA's athletic scholarship legislation, coaches still understand that the athletic scholarship is payment for work. Coaches indicated that they favored less than full scholarships so that they were not "overpaying" athletes, expressing concerns that athletes on full scholarship "just quit and sat on their money," that scholarships provided incentives for athletes to "work their way up the ladder" forcing athletes to "earn their money."

11. The references to poets, activists, movie buffs, knitters, and tobacco enthusiasts reflect student clubs at various colleges and universities. At Ithaca College, students organized the John Cusack Club, devoted to the work of that actor. Another group organized the Cigar Club, where students shared their interest in cigars. At James Madison, a club included individuals who were interested in the art and craft of knitting.

12. Stadium seating capacity for top college teams is more than 100,000 people. NFL stadiums typically have seating capacities that hold less than 100,000 people. Cowboys Stadium—which serves the NFL's Dallas franchise—has a seating capacity of 80,000 with ability to expanded capacity to 111,000 people. The stadium designers took into account not only the seating capacity for games of the professional football team but also included capacity for college bowl games (Staff, 2009).

13. In contrast, the Harvard College Debating Union (HDU) states on its website that "HDU holds tryouts at the beginning of each academic year. No prior experience necessary, just commitment to the team and intellectual promise" (retrieved from http://www.hcdu.org/get_involved). The Stanford Debate Society notes that "[p]eople start debate in college all the time, and we accept people with no experience every year" (retrieved from https://debate.stanford.edu/join). At the University of Michigan, students wondering whether they must be a high school debate star to participate on the team are assured that "[n]othing could be further from the truth. A good deal of our most successful debaters have been little known in high school" (retrieved from http://www.michigandebate.com/prospectivestudents.php).

14. It was once the case that administrators in athletic departments were in the minority. That is no longer the case. As a measure of the growth of the bureaucracy within college sport, consider the expansion of the National Association for Athletics Compliance (NAAC). In 2006, it had a membership of less than 100. By 2016, its membership had grown to more than 1,200 (Bradenburg, 2016). This type of similar trajectory has occurred in every area of administration and management.

15. In 2012, Ohio State "strongly advised" athletes in the sports of football and basketball (men's and women's) to make their financial records available (Kahn, 2012).

16. Texas Tech head football coach Kliff Kingsbury stated in an interview that his staff creates fake social media accounts using "cute girls" to infiltrate players account so that they can be monitored (Clapp, 2016).

17. Michigan State President Lou Anna Simon said, "Admittedly it's a little bit easier dealing with academic units because the criteria for judging success and the business model of each college are much more similar than those for intercollegiate athletics" (Belzer, 2015). Presidents simply can't treat the athletics department as just another university unit, because the consequences of a misstep are far greater where all eyes congregate.

18. In Moody's (2013) report, size comparisons of athletic department budgets to total university operations excluded two areas of operations—research and patient-care expenses.

19. Katz, Vaughn, and Gilleran (2013) seem to acknowledge the different business models that exist in college sport, but revert to the position that Title IX requires that male and female athletes be compensated equally. Once the business model of college sport as recognized as such, distinguished from an educational model, I argue that Title IX in fact might not apply.

## REFERENCES

2016 NCAA Men's Basketball Attendance. Indianapolis, IN: National Collegiate Athletic Association. Retrieved May 27, 2017, from http://fs.ncaa.org/Docs/stats/m_basketball _RB/Reports/attend/2016.pdf

2016 NCAA Women's Basketball Attendance. Indianapolis, IN: National Collegiate Athletic Association. Retrieved May 27, 2017, from http://fs.ncaa.org/Docs/stats/w_basketball _RB/reports/Attend/2016.pdf

2016–2017 Compliance Forms. (2016). Boulder, CO: University of Colorado Department of Athletics. Retrieved May 27, 2017, from http://www.cubuffs.com/sb_output.aspx ?form=25

"AT&T Red River Showdown." (2016). Press Release. Retrieved May 27, 2017, from http://www.texassports.com/news/2016/6/14/tickets-available-for-at-t-red-river-showdown -against-oklahoma.aspx

Alsher, J. (2016, October 21). 5 college conferences that bring in over $250 million. *Cheatsheet.com*. Retrieved May 27, 2017, from http://www.cheatsheet.com/sports/the-5-most -valuable-conferences-in-college-sports.html/?a=viewall

American Gaming Association (2016, March 14). March Madness betting to total $9.2 billion this year. Press release. Retrieved May 27, 2017, from https://www.americangaming .org/newsroom/press-releasess/march-madness-betting-total-92-billion-year

Bass, J., Schaeperkoetter, C., & Bunds, K. (2015). *The "front porch": Examining the increasing interconnectedness of university and athletic department funding*. Monograph. Hoboken, NJ: John Wiley & Sons.

Belzer, J. (2015, November 3). The priorities of university presidents: Where do college athletics fit? *Forbes.com*. Retrieved May 27, 2017, from http://www.forbes.com/sites /jasonbelzer/2015/11/23/the-priorities-of-university-presidents-where-do-college -athletics-fit-in/#1b839b8131b9

*Beidiger v. Quinnipiac University*. (2013). Case no. 3:09cv21 (SRU). United States District Court District of Connecticut. Retrieved May 27, 2017, from http://courtweb.pamd.uscourts .gov/courtwebsearch/ctxc/KX330R32.pdf

Berkowitz, S. (2015, January 20). NCAA drastically increases its spending on lobbying. *USA Today*. Retrieved May 27, 2017, from http://www.usatoday.com/story/sports/college /2015/01/20/ncaa-lobbying-expenditures-congress-capitol-hill-washington/22078773/

Bishop, G. (2012, December 17). Ohio State's monitoring of athletes' spending raises concerns. *New York Times*. Retrieved May 27, 2017, from http://www.nytimes.com/2012/12 /18/sports/ncaafootball/ohio-states-monitoring-of-athletes-spending-raises-privacy -concerns.html

Bradenburg, N. (2016, November 9). Notice of annual meeting of members of National Association for Athletics Compliance. Email (on file with author).

Brady, E., Berkowitz, S. & Upton, J. (2016, April 17). Can college athletics continue to spend like this? *USA Today*. Retrieved May 27, 2017, from https://www.usatoday.com/story /sports/college/2016/04/17/ncaa-football-basketball-power-five-revenue-expenses /83035862/

Byers, W. (1995). *Unsportsmanlike conduct: Exploiting college athletes*. Ann Arbor, MI: University of Michigan.

Carpenter, L., & Acosta, V. (2005). *Title IX*. Champaign, IL: Human Kinetics.

Clapp, M. (2016, August 26). Texas Tech uses fake accounts with "cute girls" to monitor players on social media. *Thecomback.com*. Retrieved May 27, 2017, from http://thecomeback.com/ncaa/texas-tech-uses-fake-accounts-with-cute-girls-to-monitor -players-on-social-media.html

Clotfelter, C. (2015). Law symposium: What the future may hold: College athletics in the ESPN era [starts at 33.54 minutes into the program]. Durham, NC: Duke University. Retrieved May 27, 2017, from https://law.duke.edu/video/what-future-may-hold -college-athletics-espn-era

Comen, E., Frohlich, T. C., & Sauter, M. C. (2016, September 20). The highest paid public employee in every state. *24wallstreet.com*. Retrieved May 27, 2017, from http://247wallst .com/special-report/2016/09/20/the-highest-paid-public-employee-in-every-state/

Crowley, J. (2006). *In the arena: The NCAA's first century.* Indianapolis, IN: National Collegiate Athletic Association. Retrieved May 27, 2017, from https://www.ncaapublications.com /p-4039-in-the-arena-the-ncaas-first-century.aspx

Delany, J. (2015). Education first, athletics second: The time for a national discussion is upon us. Chicago, IL: The Big Ten Conference. Retrieved May 27, 2017, from http:// i.usatoday.net/sports/college/2015-4-17-Education%20First%20Athletics%20Second .pdf

DiPalma, D., Cohan, M. C., Maxfield, H. O. (2014). *Amicus brief by National Association of Collegiate Directors of Athletics and DIA Athletic Directors' Association.* Retrieved May 27, 2017, from https://www.nlrb.gov/case/13-RC-121359

Dosh, K. (2013, October 15). Why women's college basketball operates at a deficit. *The Business of College Sports.* Retrieved May 27, 2017, from http://businessofcollegesports.com /2013/10/15/why-womens-college-basketball-operates-at-a-deficit/

Durham, D. (2014). *Brief of amicus curiae: Baylor University et al.* Retrieved May 27, 2017, from https://www.nlrb.gov/case/13-RC-121359

ESPN Staff. (2015). NFL attendance. *ESPN.com.* Retrieved from http://www.espn.com/nfl /attendance/_/year/2015

Gerber, E. (1974). The controlled development of collegiate sport for women: 1923–1936. *LA 84 Sports Library.* Retrieved May 27, 2017, from http://library.la84.org/SportsLibrary /JSH/JSH1975/JSH0201/jsh0201b.pdf

Glier, R. (2012). *How the SEC became goliath: The making of college football's most dominant conference.* New York: Howard Books.

Goff, B., & Wilson, D. (2013, March). Estimating the MRP of college athletes from professional factor shares. Presentation at the Southern Economists Association Conference.

Gordon, A. (2014, January 22). Did football cause 20 deaths in 1905? Re-investigating a serial killer. *Deadspin.* Retrieved May 27, 2017, from http://deadspin.com/did-football-cause -20-deaths-in-1905-re-investigating-1506758181

Harper, S. (2016). *Black male student-athletes and racial inequities in NCAA Division I college sports.* Philadelphia, PA: University of Pennsylvania. Retrieved May 27, 2017, from http:// www.gse.upenn.edu/equity/sites/gse.upenn.edu.equity/files/publications/Harper _Sports_2016.pdf

Hobson, W., & Rich, S. (2016, January 9). Salaries for some NCAA commissioners are skyrocketing. Here's why. *Washington Post.* Retrieved May 27, 2017, from https://www .washingtonpost.com/sports/colleges/good-to-be-commish-salaries-for-power-five -conference-bosses-soar/2016/01/08/8b5dfe1c-b569-11e5-a76a-0b5145e8679a_story .html

Hosick, M. (2014, August 7). Board adopts new Division I structure. *NCAA.org.* Retrieved May 27, 2017, from http://www.ncaa.org/about/resources/media-center/news/board -adopts-new-division-i-structure

Huma, R., & Staurowsky, E. J. (2013). *The $6 billion heist: Robbing college athletes under the guise of amateurism.* Riverside, CA: National College Players Association.

*in re: NCAA Athletic Grant-in-Aid Cap Anti-Trust Litigation* (2015). Case number 4:2014cv02758. United States District Court, Northern District of California (Oakland). Retrieved May 27, 2017, from http://www.leagle.com/decision/In%20FDCO%2020151207C18/IN %20RE%20NATIONAL%20COLLEGIATE%20ATHLETIC%20ASSOCIATION%20ATHLETIC %20GRANT-IN-AID%20CAP%20ANTITRUST%20LITIGATION

Irick, E. (2016). *2015–2016 NCAA sports sponsorship and participation rates report.* Indianapolis, IN: National Collegiate Athletic Association. Retrieved May 27, 2017, from http:// www.ncaa.org/about/resources/research/sports-sponsorship-and-participation -research

Knight Commission on Intercollegiate Athletics. (2016). About. Washington, DC: Knight Commission on Intercollegiate Athletics. Retrieved May 27, 2017, from http://www .knightcommission.org/about

Jenkins, Moore, Perry, Tyndall et al. v. National Collegiate Athletic Association, Athletic Coast Conference, Big Ten Conference, Big 12 Conference, PAC 12 Conference and Southeastern Conference (2014). Case number 4:2014cv02758. United States District Court, Northern District of California (Oakland). Retrieved May 27, 2017, from https://dockets.justia .com/docket/california/candce/4:2014cv02758/278361

Johnson, G. (2015, September 17). NCAA DII, DIII membership approves sand volleyball as 90th championship. Press release. Indianapolis, IN: National Collegiate Athletic Association. Retrieved May 27, 2017, from http://www.ncaa.com/news/beach-volleyball /article/2015–01–17/ncaa-dii-diii-membership-approves-sand-volleyball-90th

Jones, P. A., Reid, F., Mathison, M., & Salsburey, J. (2014). Brief of amicus curiae: The Higher Education Council of the Employment Law Alliance. Filed in support of Northwestern University in College Athletes Players Association v. Northwestern University, Case No. 13-RC-121359. Retrieved May 27, 2017, from https://www.nlrb.gov/case/13-RC-121359

Kahn, A. (2016, November 22). Rebuilding a football program—with a wrench and a hammer. espnW.com. Retrieved May 27, 2017, from http://www.espn.com/espnw/culture /feature/article/18111706/rebuilding-football-program-wrench-hammer

Katz, R. (2016, October 7). O'Bannon, Title IX, and student-athlete compensation. Retrieved May 27, 2017, from Collegeathleticsclips.com.

Katz, R., Vaughn, I., & Gilleran, M. (2013). Nine points to consider regarding the payment of athletes. Santa Clara Law Blog. Retrieved May 27, 2017, from http://law.scu.edu/sports -law/should-college-athletes-be-paid/

Kearney, B. (2016, September 16). Memorandum: Northwestern University. Case no.: 13-CA-157467. Washington, DC: National Labor Relations Board. Retrieved May 27, 2017, from http://blog.cupahr.org/2016/10/nlrb-general-counsel-advises-northwestern -unlawful-rules/

Keepfer, S. (2015, August 14). Shutting it down: Clemson players ready for the season without social media. USA Today. Retrieved May 27, 2017, from http://www.usatoday.com /story/sports/college/clemson/2015/08/14/shutting-clemson-players-ready-season -without-social-media/31729463/?hootPostID=9512a542a00e81ee6fc15aef3f193fb1

Kerkhoff, B. (2014, July 9). NCAA president Mark Emmert gets an earful from Claire McCaskill in Senate hearing. Kansas City Star. Retrieved May 27, 2017, from http://www .kansascity.com/sports/college/article700050.html

Kirshner, A., & Berkes, P. (2016, July 6). Here are the 2017 QB recruits considered the country's best by Elite 11. SBnation.com. Retrieved May 27, 2017, from http://www.sbnation .com/college-football-recruiting/2016/7/6/12104828/elite-11-roster-time-format -competition-2016

Kish, B. (2000). Knute Rockne: The coach-maker. UND.com. Retrieved May 27, 2017, from http://www.und.com/sports/m-footbl/spec-rel/111200aad.html

Kline, J. (2014, May 8). Hearing on unionizing student athletes. Washington, DC: U.S. House Committee on Education and the Workforce. Retrieved May 27, 2017, from https:// www.c-span.org/video/?319264–1/unionizing-student-athletes

Lavigne, P. (2016, September 6). Rich get richer in college sports as poorer schools struggle to keep up. ESPN.com. Retrieved May 27, 2017, from http://www.espn.com/espn/otl /story/_/id/17447429/power-5-conference-schools-made-6-billion-last-year-gap -haves-nots-grows

Livingston, B. L., Klimesh, M. K., Kramer, R. J., & Harris, A. D. (2014). Brief for amici curiae: Members of the United States Committee Health Education Labor and Pensions and the

*United States House of Representatives Committee on Education in the Workplace.* Retrieved May 27, 2017, from https://www.nlrb.gov/case/13-RC-121359

Loftin, R. B. (2014). *The 100-year decision: Texas A & M and the SEC.* Indianapolis, IN: Dog Ear Publishing.

Maxcy, J. (forthcoming). College sport workplace economics: Suppressing player compensation to increase profits. In Staurowsky, E. J., Karcher, R., Maxcy, J., Nagle, M., & Southall, R. (forthcoming). *Big time college athletes, labor, and the academy.* Columbia, SC: University of South Carolina Press.

McIntyre, J. (2016, April 20). Women's college basketball loses $14 million a year, says Mark Emmert. *The Big Lead.* Retrieved May 27, 2017, from http://thebiglead.com/2016/04/20/womens-college-basketball-loses-14-million-a-year-says-mark-emmert/

McManus, J. (2016, April 19). Pressure to pay student-athletes carries question of Title IX. *Espnw.com.* Retrieved May 27, 2017, from http://www.espn.com/espnw/culture/feature/article/15201865/pressure-pay-student-athletes-carries-question-title-ix

Montez, J. (2013). *Discipline and indulgence: College football, media, and the American way of life during the Cold War.* New Brunswick, NJ: Rutgers University Press.

Moody's Investment Services. (2013). Eye on the ball: Big-time sports pose growing risks for universities. Retrieved May 27, 2017, from https://www.insidehighered.com/sites/default/server_files/files/Sports%20Pose%20Growing%20Risk%20for%20Universities.pdf

*NCAA v. Board of Regents,* 468 U.S. 85 (1984). U.S. Supreme Court. Retrieved May 27, 2017, from https://supreme.justia.com/cases/federal/us/468/85/case.html

NCAA Academic and Membership Affairs Staff. (2016). *2016–2017 NCAA Division I manual.* Indianapolis, IN: National Collegiate Athletic Association. Retrieved May 27, 2017, from https://www.ncaapublications.com/p-4435-2016–2017-ncaa-division-i-manual-august-version-available-august-2016.aspx

NCAA Staff. (2014, April 10). Pay-for-play/unionization background. Indianapolis, IN: National Collegiate Athletic Association. Retrieved May 27, 2017, from http://www.al.com/sports/index.ssf/2014/04/what_do_ncaa_talking_points_ab.html

NCAA Staff. (2016a). What is the NCAA? *NCAA.org.* Retrieved May 27, 2017, from http://www.ncaa.org/about/resources/media-center/ncaa-101/what-ncaa

NCAA Staff. (2016b). Where does the money go? *NCAA.org.* Retrieved May 27, 2017, from http://www.ncaa.org/sites/default/files/97910_NCAA101_MoneyGo_v8.pdf

*O'Bannon v. National Collegiate Athletic Association and Electronic Arts* (2015). Nos. 14–16601; 14–17068. D.C. 4:09–03329-CW. Appeal from the United States District Court for the Northern District of California, Claudia Wilken, Senior District Judge, Presiding. Opinion. Retrieved May 27, 2017, from http://www.scotusblog.com/wp-content/uploads/2016/04/ncaa-op-below.pdf

Oriard, M. (1998). *Reading football: How the popular press created an American spectacle.* Chapel Hill, NC: University of North Carolina Press.

Oriard, M. (2002). *King football: Sport and spectacle in the golden age of radio and newsreels, movies and magazine, the weekly and daily press.* Chapel Hill, North Carolina: University of North Carolina Press.

Oriard, M. (2009). *Bowled over: Big time college football from the Sixties to the BCS era.* Chapel Hill, NC: University of North Carolina Press.

"Overview." (2016). Irving, TX: College Football Playoff. Retrieved May 27, 2017, from http://www.collegefootballplayoff.com/overview

Pearce, M., Miscimarra, P., Hirozawa, K., Johnson, H., & McFarran, L. (2015). *Northwestern University and College Athletes Players Association* (Petitioner). Decision on review and order. Washington, DC: National Labor Relations Board. Retrieved May 27, 2017, from https://www.aaup.org/sites/default/files/files/NLRB-Board-Decision-8-15.pdf

Pickel, G. (2016, November 26). The bonus James Franklin earned on Saturday night, and how it can grow for the Penn State coach. *Pennlive.com.* Retrieved May 27, 2017, from http://www.pennlive.com/pennstatefootball/index.ssf/2016/11/whats_james_franklins_big_ten.html

Pierce, P. J. (1907). The International Athletic Association of the United States: Its origin, growth and function. A paper read before the Second Annual Convention, New York City, December 28, 1907. Reprinted in *Procedures of the Annual Convention of the National Collegiate Athletic Association.* Ann Arbor, MI: University of Michigan Library.

Rockefeller, J. (2014, July). *Hearing on college athletes and academics.* Washington, DC: U.S. Committee on Commerce, Science & Transportation. Retrieved May 27, 2017, from https://www.c-span.org/video/?320346-1/hearing-college-athletes-academics

Rosenman, A., Netter, B., & Wolf, T. (2014). *Brief of amicus curiae: The Big Ten Conference.* Retrieved May 27, 2017, from https://www.nlrb.gov/case/13-RC-121359

Sack, A. L., & Staurowsky, E. J. (1998). *College athletes for hire: The evolution and legacy of the NCAA amateur myth.* Westport, CT: Praeger Press.

Schwartz, A. (2013). Illuminating the obscure: Accounting change looming at NCAA? *Sportgeekonomics.com.* Retrieved May 27, 2017, from http://sportsgeekonomics.tumblr.com/post/53439422488/illuminating-the-obscure-accounting-change

Schwartz, A. (2014, May 2). How athletic departments (and the media) fudge the costs of scholarships. *Deadspin.com.* Retrieved May 27, 2017, from http://deadspin.com/how-athletic-departments-and-the-media-fudge-the-cost-1570827027

Sherman, R. (2016, April 26). The NCAA's new March Madness TV deal will make them a billion dollars a year. *SBnation.com.* Retrieved May 27, 2017, http://www.sbnation.com/college-basketball/2016/4/12/11415764/ncaa-tournament-tv-broadcast-rights-money-payout-cbs-turner

Smith, R. (2003). *Play by play: Radio, television and big-time college sport.* Baltimore, MD: The Johns Hopkins University Press.

Smith, R. (2008). *Sports and freedom: The rise of big-time college athletics.* Oxford, England: Oxford University Press.

Smith, R. (2011). *Pay for play: A history for big-time college athletic reform.* Champaign, IL: University of Illinois Press.

Solomon, J. (2016, May 27). Power Five conferences see revenue grow by 33 percent in one year. *CBSSports.com.* Retrieved May 27, 2017, from http://www.cbssports.com/college-football/news/power-five-conferences-see-revenue-grow-by-33-percent-in-one-year/

Southall, R., & Weiler, J. (2014). NCAA Division-I Athletic departments: 21st century company towns. *Journal of Issues in Intercollegiate Athletics 7,* 161–186. Retrieved May 27, 2017, from http://csri-jiia.org/documents/publications/ research_articles/2014/JIIA_2014_7_08_161_186_21st%20Century.pdf

Southall, R., Eckard, W., Nagel, M., Keith, E., & Blake, C. (2014, March 12). 2013–2014 Adjusted Graduation Gap Report: NCAA Division I basketball. Columbia, SC: University of South Carolina. Retrieved May 27, 2017, from http://csri-sc.org/wp-content/uploads/2014/03/2013–14_MBB-WBB_AGG-Report_3–12–14.pdf

Southall, R. M., Southall, C., and Dwyer, B. (2009). 2009 Bowl Championship Series telecasts: Expressions of big-time college-sport's commercial institutional logic. *Journal of Issues in Intercollegiate Athletics, 2,* 150–176. Retrieved May 27, 2017, from http://csri-jiia.org/old/documents/publications/research_articles/2009/JIIA_2009_9_BCS_Institutional_Logics.pdf

Spear, G. (2013, July 15). Think sports gambling isn't big money? Wanna bet? *NBCnews.com*. Retrieved May 27, 2017, from http://www.nbcnews.com/news/other/think-sports -gambling-isnt-big-money-wanna-bet-f6C10634316

Sperber, M. (2002). *Shake down the thunder: The creation of Notre Dame football*. Bloomington, IN: University of Indiana Press.

Staff. (2009, September 22). What costs $1.3 billion, holds 111,000 people and has the world's biggest TV? *Twisted Sifter*. Retrieved May 27, 2017, from http://twistedsifter.com/2009 /09/new-dallas-cowboys-stadium/

Staff. (2015, January 28). Harris poll: NFL remains king among U.S. adults, a gap with baseball closer. *Street & Smith's Sports Business Daily*. Retrieved from http://www .sportsbusinessdaily.com/Daily/Issues/2015/01/28/Research-and-Ratings/Harris-Poll .aspx

Staurowsky, E. J. (2004). Piercing the veil of amateurism: Commercialisation, corruption, and US college sports. In Slack, T. (ed.), The commercialization of sport, pp. 143–169. NY, NY: Routledge.

Staurowsky, E. J. (2012). "A radical proposal:" Title IX has no place in college sport pay-for-play discussions. *Marquette Sports Law Review*, 575–595. Retrieved from http:// scholarship.law.marquette.edu/cgi/viewcontent.cgi?article=1560&context= sportslaw

Staurowsky, E. J. (2014a). The significance of college athletes signing union cards. *Huffington Post*. Retrieved from http://www.huffingtonpost.com/ellen-j-staurowsky/the -significance-of-college-athletes_b_4701486.html

Staurowsky, E. J. (2014b). An analysis of Northwestern University's denial of rights to and recognition of college football labor. *Journal of Intercollegiate Sport 7*, 134–142.

Staurowsky, E. J. (2014c). College athletes in the age of the super conference: The case of the All Players United campaign. *Journal of Intercollegiate Sport 7*, 11–34.

Staurowsky, E. J. (2015, January 20). College football players as employees: About this there should be no debate. *Huffington Post*. Retrieved June 19, 2017, from http://www .huffingtonpost.com/ellen-j-staurowsky/college-football-players-_1_b_6506392.html

Staurowsky, E. J., & Sack. A. L. (2005). Reconsidering the use of the term student-athlete in academic research. *Journal of Sport Management* 19 (2), 205–214.

Staurowsky, E. J. & Southall, R. (2015). *College Athletes Rights and Empowerment Faculty Coalition Statement*. Retrieved June 19, 2017, from http://care-fc.org/care-fc-statement/

Sung Ohr, P. (2014). *Decision and direction of election: College Athletes Players Association v. Northwestern University*. Chicago, IL: National Labor Relations Board Regional Office.

Thelin, J. (1996). *Games colleges play: Scandal and reform in intercollegiate athletics*. Baltimore, MD: The Johns Hopkins Press.

Trahan, K. (2014, June 13). Report: NCAA hires D.C. lobbying firm to try to save amateurism. *SBnation.com*. Retrieved June 19, 2017, from http://www.sbnation.com/college-football /2014/6/13/5807700/ncaa-lobbyists-congress-washington-dc

Volner, D. (2016, September 8). More than 81 million viewers reached throughout ESPN/ ABC's best college football kickoff weekend. *ESPN.com*. Retrieved June 19, 2017, from http://espnmediazone.com/us/press-releases/2016/09/81-million-viewers-reached -throughout-espnabcs-best-college-football-kickoff-weekend/

Ware, S. (2014). *Title IX: A brief history with documents*. NY: Waveland Press.

Watterson, J. S. (2002). *College football: History, spectacle, controversy*. Baltimore, MD: The John's Hopkins University Press.

Williams, T. H. (1969). *Huey Long*. New York: Alfred Knopf.

Wolverton, B. (2015, June 17). Electronic checking on athletes in class sparks debate about privacy. *The Sport Digest*. Retrieved June 19, 2017, from http://thesportdigest.com/2015/06/electronic-checking-on-athletes-in-class-sparks-debate-about-their-privacy/

Woodhouse, K. (2015, April 16). NCAA novices: When universities that are sports powerhouses appoint presidents with little experience in intercollegiate athletics, new leaders face a steep learning curve. *Inside Higher Education*. Retrieved June 19, 2017, from https://www.insidehighered.com/news/2015/04/16/some-presidents-face-steep-learning-curve-athletics

Wushanley, Y. (2004). *Playing fair and losing: The struggle for control of women's intercollegiate athletics 1960–2000*. Syracuse, NY: University of Syracuse Press.

Yost, M. (2009). *Varsity green: A behind the scenes look at the culture and corruption in college athletics*. Palo Alto, CA: Stanford University.

# PART TWO

## Emerging Concerns

# 6

# The National Collegiate Athletic Association's "Nothing Short of Remarkable" Rebranding of Academic Success

RICHARD M. SOUTHALL AND CRYSTAL SOUTHALL

Almost since the founding of the National Collegiate Athletic Association (NCAA), college sport leaders have noted "an inherent tension between the intellectual independence of the academy and the use of corporate dollars to support any aspect of higher education" (National Collegiate Athletic Association [NCAA], 2010b, ¶ 2). In 2012, Wally Renfro (former NCAA vice president and policy advisor) declared, "commercial activity within the context of intercollegiate athletics is as old as the games themselves and it is growing" (Renfro, 2012, p. 33). He also stated, "participation in college sports enhances the educational experience of student-athletes and that such educational value is the only rational reason for the continued support of intercollegiate athletics in higher education" (Renfro, 2012, p. 33).

Justifying commercial activity, NCAA administrators proclaim that, contrary to public perceptions, college athletes are fully integrated into universities' academic communities and enjoy greater academic success than regular students. Since the introduction of its academic reform program in 2004, the NCAA has characterized its reform efforts as "nothing short of remarkable . . . with a record percentage of student-athletes achiev[ing] graduation, the ultimate goal of entering college" (Hosick, 2014, ¶3). In sworn court testimony, the NCAA has gone further and declared that its academic reform efforts have been especially beneficial to athletes from disadvantaged backgrounds:

> Integrating student-athletes into the academic community improves their educational experience. Full participation in that experience—not just meeting academic requirements, but also studying, interacting with

faculty and diverse classmates, and receiving academic support such as tutoring and mentoring—generally leads student-athletes, especially those from disadvantaged backgrounds, to reap more from their education, including enjoying higher graduation rates and better job prospects (*O'Bannon v. NCAA*, November 14, 2014, p. 11).

In the midst of explosive commercial activities, including record media-rights deals (e.g., eight-year, $8.8 billion NCAA Men's Basketball Tournament extension with CBS/Turner [NCAA, 2016a]) and coaching compensation (e.g., Mike Krzyzewski and Nick Saban both earned more than $7 million in 2016 [Berkowitz, Upton, Schnaars, Doughtery, & Neuharth-Keusch, 2016a; 2016b]), during his 2012 State of the Association address Emmert obliquely invoked Robert Frost, declaring college sport was at a:

> curious fork in the road, and we have to decide. Are we going to take the collegiate model, maximize our values, make the changes we need to make, but bring the collegiate model up to the 21st century consistent with our values as academic enterprises. Or are we going to wave the white flag, throw in the towel and say it's too much (Emmert, 2012, p. 13).

Answering his rhetorical question, Emmert declared critics' calls for "big-time" college sport to adopt a "professional model" was admitting defeat after more than 100 years of college sport successes, including the unparalleled recent academic success of the NCAA's cherished Collegiate Model of Athletics (Southall & Staurowsky, 2013).

Throughout its history, the NCAA has continually rebranded its most visible product—"big-time" college sport—as the antithesis of an exploitative commercial enterprise; it is a pathway to opportunity, which everyone wants. According to this rebranding narrative, supported by *sepia tone* or greyscale images on the NCAA website public service announcements during NCAA events, and YouTube and Twitter video vignettes (*see* http://www.ncaa.org/opportunity/#opportunity), NCAA college sport provides athletes a *pathway to opportunity* "by prioritizing academics, well-being and fairness" (NCAA, 2016b). Further, the NCAA characterizes its academic-reform efforts as having resulted in "nothing short of remarkable" (Hosick, 2014, ¶ 3) progress.

The NCAA's academic rebranding has made use of targeted statistical methodologies and analyses, coordinated public-relations strategies, messaging discipline, and elements of institutional propaganda. Although the NCAA has sought to rebrand academic success to assuage college sport fans, the media, and public officials, this chapter critically examines this rebranding strategy and offers an alternative hypothesis to the "nothing-short-of-remarkable" narrative: The NCAA's quarter-century rebranding has significantly harmed both higher education and—most troublingly—college athletes.

## The NCAA Brand

The NCAA[1] (i.e., "the all-encompassing blue disk" [Stark, 2015, ¶1]) is a globally recognized, multifaceted institutional brand (i.e., 1,121 colleges and universities) that encompasses several sub-brands (i.e., NCAA Divisions I, II, and III), 24 sports, and 90 championship products (e.g., football, soccer, volleyball, lacrosse). As an institution, the NCAA engages in strategic brand-management decision making in conjunction with 99 athletic conferences, 39 affiliated organizations, and numerous corporate partners (NCAA, "What is the NCAA?" [n.d.]).

The NCAA's brand-management decisions include those in which institutions, organizations, and executives normally engage: (1) developing brand positioning, (2) integrating brand marketing, (3) assessing brand performance, (4) growing sub-brands, and (5) strategically managing the brand (Keller & Lehmann, 2006, p. 740). In several subtle ways, however, the NCAA brand is unique—reflecting a bifurcated college-sport experience in which some athletes are revenue-generating employees, and other athletes are primarily benefit-accruing consumers. Additionally, although for many college sport consumers the NCAA brand is synonymous with U.S. college sport, the NCAA national office does not directly administer its members' most lucrative and widely consumed college sport product: NCAA Division I Football Bowl Subdivision (FBS) football.

The NCAA national office, member institutions, conferences, and affiliated organizations, however, do engage in coordinated brand-management strategies consistent with an expressed core value: support of "[t]he collegiate model of athletics in which students participate as an avocation, balancing their academic, social and athletics experiences" (NCAA, "Core Values," n.d.). Additionally, the NCAA disseminates a primary brand attribute: "athlete success on the field, in the classroom and in life" (see ncaa.org public homepage). In support of these attributes, the NCAA's organizational website[2] provides short vignettes, graphics, social media postings (e.g., YouTube, Twitter), and navigable hyperlinks.

As Keller and Lehmann (2006) note, "brands can simplify choice, promise a particular quality level, reduce risk, and/or engender trust" (p. 740). Former NCAA executive director, Walter Byers, understood the need for an NCAA brand that reduced the legal and financial risks posed by "the dreaded notion that NCAA athletes could be identified as employees by state industrial commissions and the courts" (Byers & Hammer, 1995, p. 69). For more than 50, years the NCAA national office has provided "focused, centralized leadership" (NCAA, 2010a, ¶1) in advancing this brand strategy through the consistent use of the term "student-athlete."

Numerous researchers have contended that such consistency in messaging is part of what Qualter (1962) identified as a crucial part of rebranding via institutional propaganda, which is described as a "deliberate attempt . . . to form, control, or alter attitudes" (Qualter, 1962, p. 27). Many scholars have chronicled the NCAA's use of rebranding/propaganda tactics to support its notion of amateurism (Byers & Hammer, 1995; McCormick & McCormick, 2006; Oriard, 2009; Sack, 2008; Sack & Staurowsky, 1998; Southall & Staurowsky, 2013; Sperber, 1990, 2000; Staurowsky & Sack, 2005; Telander, 1996; Thelin, 1994; Yaeger, 1991; Yost, 2009; Zimbalist, 1999). Further, such efforts are reinforced through the creation and consistent use of institutional rhetoric, in the form of language and images to convey their message (Rein, Shields, & Grossman, 2015).

As Kuhn (1991) noted, such branding/rebranding efforts are effective because they exploit consumers' reluctance to intellectually engage with oppositional or alternative views. Additionally, consistent with Jowett and O'Donnell's (1992) analysis of propaganda techniques, the NCAA's branding and rebranding efforts utilize symbols and *mythos* to systematically shape and manipulate consumer perceptions, cognitions, and behaviors to achieve the association's desired intent—college-sport consumption. As Armstrong (2000) noted, mythos is non-rational and reflects a spiritual truth that is personal and subjective. For rabid fans—as well as for many college presidents and trustees—college sport is the world of their dreams, hopes, fears, and imaginations. College sport's mythos, encapsulated in the concept of the "student-athlete," is the unseen tie that binds fans and alumni—through their university athletic teams—to the university community.

In response to what former NCAA President Cedric Dempsey identified as a "level of cynicism over the commercialization of our most visible athletic programs [that] has reached epidemic proportions" (Carter, 2001, ¶8)—since 2003 the NCAA (both the national office and the association) has responded to this brand crises by creating, disseminating, and imbedding a redefinition of amateurism (Southall & Staurowsky, 2013), that was rebranded as its "Collegiate Model of Intercollegiate Athletics" (Southall & Staurowsky, 2013). This rebranding campaign demonstrated the NCAA's commitment to "(a) a shared understanding of how individual initiatives should both reflect and connect to the brand, and (b) the discipline to stay on message and on brand" (NCAA, 2010a, ¶1). Consequently, through example setting, persuasion, and coercion (Snidal, 1985) the NCAA has achieved "spontaneous consent" from college sport consumers and the general public to its collegiate model.

## Branding and Rebranding

Extending these two efforts, today the NCAA has formulated several branding and rebranding strategies to portray college athletes as being just like other college students—fully integrated into the academic community (Hosick, 2014). As Merrilees and Miller (2008) note, *branding* is the "initial coherent articulation of the corporate brand and can occur at any time" (p. 538). Extending this concept, *rebranding* is the dislocation and reformulation of a brand, resulting in a new or slightly altered brand articulation. A change in the vision or values associated with a brand often requires (or results from) a change in an organization's management process or leadership. Not surprisingly, developing a coherent institutional brand involves making sure a brand articulation is consistent with institutional logic(s) and ceremonial facades (Southall et al., 2008). Consequently, any rebranding necessitates "moving" an institution—and relevant stakeholders—from established dominant logic(s) to a new or hybrid logic.

Since the 1950s, the NCAA national office has conducted periodic situational analyses and initiated internal brand re-visioning discussions to identify its brand's essential elements. While continually rebranding itself, the NCAA also has sought to maintain continuity with past brand meanings, often framing NCAA college sport as the "tie that binds" generations of college athletes, students, alumni, and fans. The effectiveness of this nostalgic brand association can be seen clearly in the Knight Commission's "College Sports 101" chapter on "myths and intangibles," in which intercollegiate athletic contests are viewed as community builders and "Logos, nicknames, and television appearances brand institutions locally and nationally" (Knight Commission on Intercollegiate Athletics [KCIA], 2009, ¶1). Many college-sport reformers advocate for a return to a more "amateur" era (an interesting mythos world view), arguing that a restoration of educational values and priorities would strengthen accountability for intercollegiate athletics. They want to "make academic values a priority, and [treat] college athletes as students first and foremost—not as professionals" (KCIA, 2010, ¶5).

What is striking about such reform efforts is how they are framed or situated almost exclusively with an NCAA institutional-brand perspective. Consistently, reformers utilize the NCAA's language—most notably its created terms, such as "student-athlete" and "collegiate model." Adamson (1980) refers to an institution's use of language as its "armor of coercion." Consistent with Gramsci (1971) hegemonic analysis, the consent and homage given by reformers to the NCAA's collegiate model is a logical result of the prestige the model enjoys, not only because of its position and function, but because so many reformers are ensconced within the model's governance structure (e.g., current or former college presidents, athletic directors, administrators, coaches, and athletes). The NCAA's hegemony is so complete even U.S. district and appellate court judges consistently and repeatedly use NCAA language (i.e., student-athlete) in decisions that find the NCAA's collegiate model a criminal conspiracy in violation of the Sherman Act (*O'Bannon v. NCAA*, 2014, 2015).

According to the NCAA, its institutional brand[3] "is a collection of the Association's messages, visual presentation, decisions, actions, behaviors, relationships and experiences" (NCAA, 2010a, ¶2). Consistently, the NCAA's national office coordinates the implementation of a chosen brand strategy or series of rebranding strategies with conferences, other associated organizations, as well as individual colleges or universities. The NCAA clearly understands that by utilizing various communication platforms, it can strategically and aggressively advocate for its brand (NCAA, 2010b). Although advertising or public-service announcements are part of its issues management and branding model, it has consistently utilized public relations to brand and rebrand itself and its products.

Successfully implementing a rebranding strategy involves insuring internal brand understanding and consistently executing selected rebranding activities focused at the general public, college-sport consumers, and external and internal stakeholders. While simultaneously obtaining stakeholder buy-in and methodically implementing a rebranding campaign, the NCAA most often does not completely sever ties to past brand meanings. An example of this has been the recent subtle de-emphasis of Walter Byers' (former NCAA executive director) 1950s branding term "student-athletes," which was "created by the NCAA to convince workers' compensation boards, as well as the general public, that scholarship athletes are students like any others" (Staurowsky & Sack, 2005, p. 105).

Recognizing how deeply imbedded the term "student-athlete" is in the public lexicon, the NCAA national office no longer mandates the exclusive use of the term, now using it interchangeably with "college athlete." Although it is still the preferred NCAA moniker for both *profit* and *loss* athletes[4] (i.e., consumers of a NCAA "Olympic" college athletic experience), in a July 7, 2016, Atlantic Coast Conference (ACC) press release, entitled: *Commissioners Announce Agreement For Changes In How Much Time Students Play Sports* (Atlantic Coast Conference [ACC], 2016), the term was noticeably absent, with college athletes instead referred to as "students who play sports" (ACC, 2016, ¶1), positioning them—seemingly—alongside "students who play guitars."

To cement the new rebranding strategy, the NCAA has gained stakeholder buy-in and developed specific reputational management tactics consistent with its reimagined and rebranded "core" values, vision, mission, and goals (NCAA, 2010b; Southall & Staurowsky, 2014). In all likelihood, the NCAA understands the importance of utilizing internal and external marketing mixes (including language, symbolism, and visual and auditory imagery) to convey the rebranded NCAA, which offers "pathways to opportunity, while prioritizing academics, [athlete] well-being, and fairness" (see http://www.ncaa.org/opportunity/). The NCAA's 2016b *pathways to opportunity* public service announcement (PSA) campaign is a great example of such rebranding.

## Historic NCAA's Rebranding Responses to Reputational Triggers

Despite an obvious disconnect between the college-sport enterprise and NCAA members' educational missions, the NCAA and its members' athletic departments have attempted to position their business practices as non-exploitative and educational (Huma & Staurowsky, 2012). Historically, NCAA college sport has been criticized for low athlete-graduation rates and questionable academic standards (KCIA, 2010). However, many college sport "reformers" criticize college athletics for not adhering to the NCAA brand's stated core values:

> Despite our deep concern about this problem,[5] we believe firmly that—at their best—intercollegiate sports bring enormous benefits to their universities and communities. Indeed, we take as our starting point the mission articulated by James L. Knight, Chairman of the Knight Foundation in 1989: "We recognize that intercollegiate athletics have a legitimate and proper role to play in college and university life. Our interest is not to abolish that role but to preserve it by putting it into perspective" (KCIA, 2010, ¶4).

Although the KCIA and other college sport "reformers" longed to return to a time when college sport was at its best, by 2003, NCAA members and associated organizations increasingly struggled to reconcile "big-time" college sport's rampant and increasing commercialism with the NCAA's historic notion of amateurism: "As the scale of both revenue generation and spending has grown over the past few decades, there is a general sense that 'big-time' athletics is in conflict with the principle of amateurism" (NCAA, 2010a, ¶3).

In response to this institutional "angst," Brand and the NCAA national office developed a rebranding campaign in which they redefined amateurism: "Critical for the future of intercollegiate athletics will likely be a better understood definition of amateurism that isolates the principle to the way in which student-athletes are viewed without imposing its avocational nature on revenue-producing opportunities" (NCAA, 2010a, ¶3). Brand proudly proclaimed he "wanted to change the way people talked about intercollegiate athletics" (NCAA, 2010a, ¶1).

Throughout Brand's tenure, the national office and senior NCAA leadership rebranded college sport not as what had historically been referred to as "amateur" intercollegiate athletics, but as the NCAA's collegiate model of athletics. The NCAA's marketing mix consistently has proclaimed the collegiate model as a sacred American tradition inextricably tied to the nation's colleges and universities, who have a moral obligation to preserve this myth that protects college athletes from the corrosive influences and exploitation of commercialism. Just as the term "student-athlete," the collegiate model is an example of mythos. On a rational or *logos* level, the general public—and college-sport fans in particular—"know" the collegiate model is not a truly accurate representation of college sport. However, the collegiate model is a part of a college-sport mythology that "believers" reenact "in stylized ceremonies that worked aesthetically upon participants and, like any work of art, introduced them to a deeper dimension of existence" (Armstrong, 2009, p. xii).

To insure internal understanding and consistent execution of its mythological rebranding activities, the NCAA national office staff developed and disseminated a briefing document that succinctly summarized the collegiate model's major elements:

> As a descriptor for intercollegiate athletics, The Collegiate Model of Athletics is intended to impart two principles: (1) Those who participate in college sports are students, and (2) intercollegiate athletics is embedded in the values and mission of higher education. According to the NCAA, a comparison of the collegiate model vs. the professional model runs like this: In the professional model, the athletes are a work force, a commodity that can be traded from team to team. In the collegiate model, the athlete is a student. In the professional model, the goal is to generate revenue through entertainment. In the collegiate model, the goal is to acquire an education, including learning the value of hard work and teamwork, self-sacrifice and self-discipline, resilience and persistence, and the pursuit of excellence. In the professional model, the team is connected to a community only so long as the community supports the franchise through the building and maintenance of facilities and the purchase of tickets. In the collegiate model, the team is enduringly connected to a community through the sponsoring college or university (NCAA, 2010c, ¶2).

Since 2003, NCAA senior leadership has often referred to specific talking points from this template in public statements, as well as in depositions and court testimony.

As part of the NCAA's rebranding of amateurism, increased attention was paid to the "460,000 student-athletes going pro in something other than sports," subtly differentiating these "loss" athletes—from D-I Olympic sports, as well as D-II and D-III—from the minority of "pre-professional" athletes who generate the vast majority of the revenue for the college-sport enterprise. Whenever possible, these true "student-athletes" were described as the rationale for the NCAA's revenue generation activities. One such example of this utilitarian rebranding was NCAA president Mark Emmert's 2014 testimony before the United States Senate Committee on Commerce, Science, & Transportation, in which he called attention to a core truth of intercollegiate athletics.

> Before I address the challenges, I want to begin by highlighting a core truth of intercollegiate athletics. For the vast majority of those who participate in NCAA sports—more than 460,000 young men and women each year at 1,084 institutions across three divisions and in 23 different sports—the experience is exactly what it is intended to be: a meaningful extension of the educational process that provides the opportunity

for students to compete fairly against other students, in an educational environment (Emmert, 2014, p. 2).

Although admitting college sport has "challenges," Emmert made clear Brand's college sport amateurs were truly students; even though the enterprise might be professional, participants were students, just like all other students (Emmert, 2014).

Initially viewed as a combative and surly "loose cannon," Emmert now consistently stays on message in speeches and during media appearances. He is no longer the preeminent face of the NCAA, but the NCAA national office's Public and Media Relations team provides Emmert and all other NCAA senior national office leaders with strategic and practical talking points regarding the NCAA brand that highlight how member schools protect athletes' health and safety, create opportunities for academic success, and involve "students" in NCAA governance. Additionally, NCAA spokespersons and senior administrators consistently emphasize gains made in academic reform, increased graduation success rates, and higher academic standards for incoming athletes. Recent policy changes (i.e., cost of attendance, multi-year grants-in-aid, unlimited meals) also are touted as major improvements to athletes' lives (Schwarb, 2015).

## Rebranding Academic Success:
## The NCAA's Graduation Success Rate

Although NCAA D-I college football and men's basketball players historically have graduated at significantly lesser rates than the general student body (NCAA, 1991), it was not until the mid-1980s that this phenomenon among "big-time" college football and men's basketball players became a well-chronicled and embarrassing public issue (Byers & Hammer, 1995; *Hall v. University of Minnesota*, 1982; *Ross v Creighton University*, 1992). At the time, Nyad (1989) and other media sources reported 76% to 92% of professional football and men's basketball players lacked college degrees. In the late 1980s, former NCAA and Olympic basketball players, believing prospective college athletes and their parents had a right to information about their likelihood of graduating, began lobbying members of Congress to force U.S. colleges and universities to publish college athletes' graduation rates (Selingo, 2012).

Public scrutiny intensified when several high-profile athletes testified before Congress that they were functionally illiterate (Jacobson, 1992). Subsequently, the *1990 Student Right-to-Know and Campus Security Act* included a Department of Education (DOE) administered program, which mandated colleges and universities collect and disseminate student graduation rates (i.e., Federal Graduation Rates [FGRs]). After initially voicing concerns over the program, the NCAA acquiesced and agreed to make athlete graduation rates public (Selingo, 2012). The NCAA has engaged in similar public "hand wringing" when it has been forced to make "reforms" as the result of public pressure or court cases (e.g., Title IX, Cost of Attendance, etc.).

In response to this public-relations crisis, and prior to the passage of the Student Right-to-Know Act, the NCAA commissioned a series of research projects that examined college-athlete graduation rates (NCAA, 1991). One project was the NCAA Academic Performance Study (APS), which began in 1985 (NCAA, 1994). One of the first reports, published in 1991, highlighted the five-year

### TABLE 6.1

### Five-Year Graduation Rates for 1984–85 NCAA Athletes by Group

| Group | Total Persons N | % | Number Graduated | Overall Graduation Rate (N=3288) | Adjusted Graduation Rate (N=2198)* |
|---|---|---|---|---|---|
| Overall Racial Group | 3,288 | 100.0% | 1,504 | 45.7% | 68.4% |
| Whites | 2,453 | 74.6% | 1,282 | 52.3% | 77.0% |
| Blacks | 835 | 25.4% | 222 | 26.6% | 41.6% |
| Sex | | | | | |
| Males | 2,314 | 70.4% | 979 | 42.3% | 63.7% |
| Females | 974 | 29.6% | 525 | 53.9% | 79.4% |
| Sport | | | | | |
| Male Revenue | 1,314 | 40.0% | 553 | 42.1% | 62.5% |
| Male Nonrevenue | 1,018 | 31.0% | 436 | 42.8% | 65.3% |
| Female All | 956 | 29.1% | 515 | 53.9% | 79.5% |
| Separate Groups | | | | | |
| White Male Revenue | 751 | 22.8% | 412 | 54.9% | 78.5% |
| White Male Nonrevenue | 895 | 27.2% | 407 | 45.5% | 69.3% |
| White Female All | 807 | 24.5% | 463 | 57.4% | 83.9% |
| Black Male Revenue | 563 | 17.1% | 141 | 25.0% | 39.5% |
| Black Male Nonrevenue | 123 | 3.7% | 29 | 23.6% | 35.8% |
| Black Female All | 149 | 4.5% | 52 | 34.9% | 54.2% |

Notes: All percentages based on sample size listed.

* N for adjusted graduation rate is based on total sample minus eligible dropouts.

graduation rates of a sample of NCAA athletes ($N$ = 3,288) who "entered NCAA Division-I institutions in the fall semester of 1984 or 1985" (NCAA, 1991, p. 6). The employed methodology was similar to that eventually used in the six-year FGR: "The graduation rates for the following tables were calculated by dividing the number of graduates after five years by the number of student-athletes who had entered that institution as freshmen in the initial year of the survey" (NCAA, 1991, p. 6). However, the study also reported an "adjusted graduation rate . . . calculated by removing all student-athletes who left their institutions in good academic standing from the group of initially entered freshmen" (NCAA, 1991, p. 6).

In this initial report, athletes removed from the initial graduation-rate cohort were referred to as *eligible dropouts* (NCAA, 1991, p. 10). As shown in Table 6.1, this adjustment removed approximately 33% of athletes from the sample and resulted in an overall adjusted graduation rate of 68.4%—an improvement of 22.7%. For male revenue sport athletes, the adjustment (the precursor of the GSR) resulted in a 20.4% jump, from 42.1% to 62.5%. In subsequent peer-reviewed articles (i.e., McArdle & Hamagami, 1994) as well as NCAA reports (*see* http://www.ncaa.org/about/resources/research/academic-initial-eligibility-research) there was no mention of eligible dropouts or an adjusted graduation rate. Inextricably, the "eligible dropout" label had been forgotten, just another statistical analysis in yet another report. Or perhaps it was not consistent with the branding efforts associated with the Graduation Success Rate.

## Twenty-First Century Rebranding

When the NCAA "launched a major academic reform program in 2003" (LaForge & Hodge, 2011, p. 219) however, the eligible-dropout adjustment reappeared as the cornerstone of the NCAA's new Graduation Success Rate (GSR). The rationale for the adjustment was "the federally mandated rate is an inaccurate graduation measure" (Brand, 2004, ¶53). In virtually every NCAA document, communiqué, or press release since 2003, the GSR has been identified as an improved and more accurate metric that was developed at the request of NCAA members, particularly presidents and chancellors. This narrative initially was established in both the 2003 and 2004 NCAA state of the association addresses, when NCAA president Myles Brand highlighted the GSR as evidence of the newly instituted reform agenda's success (Brand, 2003, 2004).

Subsequent to the GSR's introduction, it has been consistently portrayed as a more accurate measure of academic success. To one degree or another, the tagline "NCAA graduation rates: A quarter-century of tracking academic success" (Brown, 2014) has been embedded in almost every graduation-rate related press release and news story on the NCAA.org website, in the mainstream media, and on university athletic-department websites. Additionally, the NCAA and its members' athletic departments consistently describe the FGR as being divorced from reality, and understating and misstating graduation results: "The NCAA also devised a new metric for measuring graduation in an effort to amend the shortcomings of the federally mandated methodology" (Brown, 2014, ¶11).

With each release of NCAA graduation "success" rates, (*see* Figure 6.1) the degree to which the NCAA's rebranding strategy has been implemented is readily apparent. Somewhere in almost every NCAA D-I athletic department's discussion of its athletes' graduation rates, the GSR will be described as a more

---

### Examples of Graduation Success Rate Accuracy Claims

#### University of Notre Dame

The GSR [Graduation Success Rate] was created to *more accurately reflect actual graduation rates* [emphasis added] by including transfer data in the calculation. College and university presidents asked the NCAA to develop a new methodology that takes into account the mobility among students in today's higher education environment. Research indicates that approximately 60 percent of all new bachelor's degree recipients are attending more than one undergraduate institution during their collegiate careers.

http://www.und.com/genrel/102914aac.html

#### Atlantic Coast Conference

The Graduation Success Rate was developed by the NCAA as part of its academic reform initiative as *a better measure of student-athlete academic success....* [emphasis added].

The *federal graduation rate, which is less accurate than GSR* [emphasis added] because it counts transfer students as academic failures, is the only rate that allows comparison between the general student body at a school and its student-athletes.

http://www.theacc.com/#!/news-detail/acc-teams-continue-to-set-high-graduation-success-rate-2014-10-28

#### University of Alabama–Tuscaloosa

The NCAA GSR and the Academic Success Rate (ASR) were developed in response to college and university presidents who wanted graduation data that *more accurately reflected* [emphasis added] the mobility among college students today. *Both rates improve on the federally mandated graduation rate* [emphasis added] by including students who were omitted from the federal calculation.

http://www.rolltide.com/genrel/102814aaa.html

accurate and better measure that *proves* athletes are achieving academic success. Doing so is integral to rebranding efforts that highlight that the collegiate model is consistent with and upholds NCAA member institutions' educational missions.

## Rebranding Academic Success

Although the NCAA has "established itself as a strong brand, with its own unique attributes" (NCAA, 2010a, ¶4), over the past 25 years the NCAA increasingly has been challenged to protect its brand in both the court of public opinion and U.S. federal court. The importance the NCAA places on its quarter-century academic success rebranding strategy is reflected in its status as the first outcome-oriented goal (i.e., "Goals are outcome-oriented statements that represent what will constitute the organization's future successes" [NCAA, 2004, p. 6]) in the NCAA's 2004 Strategic Plan: "Student-athletes will be better educated and prepared for increased life-long achievement and success" (NCAA, 2004, p. 6). Consistent with fundamental strategic-management principles the NCAA strategic plan also outlined several objectives, including: "1.2 Increase the number of student-athletes who succeed academically" (NCAA, 2004, p. 6).

Not surprisingly, NCAA national office staff members consistently adhere to this developed rebranding strategy in communicating with internal stakeholders (e.g., university presidents and faculty athletic representatives). Additionally, on July 8, 2014—amid increased congressional scrutiny and a significant legal challenge to its collegiate model (i.e., *O'Bannon v. NCAA*)—NCAA president Mark Emmert utilized this rebranded definition of academic success throughout his testimony before the U.S. Senate Committee on Commerce, Science & Transportation. Coming at a time when the NCAA faced "pressure from multiple fronts to reform how athletes are treated and compensated" (Associated Press, 2014, ¶7), the committee's goal was to gain a better understanding of "how the NCAA is integrating athletics with academics and to determine if student-athletes are being exploited in the process" (McGuire, 2014, ¶1). Leading up to the hearing, several committee members had expressed concern about the NCAA's policies, oversight of member institutions, and potential exploitation of athletes.

In this challenging environment (Herndon, 2014) Emmert focused on the association's "first and foremost [mission] . . . to promote student-athlete success in the classroom" (NCAA, 2014, ¶2). He also unilaterally proclaimed that for the vast majority of college athletes the collegiate model provides educational opportunities for students to compete fairly against other students in an educational environment (NCAA, 2014). Highlighting this success, he noted "participants in athletics are more likely to go to college, to stay and graduate from college, to secure a good job after college, and earn more money within a few years after college and for a lifetime" (NCAA, 2014, ¶6).

Although Emmert noted that most Americans view college sport in a positive light, however, he diminished concerns about issues and challenges associated with the experiences of NCAA Division-I FBS football and men's basketball players at 123 well-known institutions in the larger conferences, contending these athletes "represent only 3.5 percent of all NCAA student-athletes" (NCAA, 2014, ¶9). Subsequently, Emmert touched upon a host of issues and concerns and mentioned two key points that he felt often go unnoticed or unmentioned: (1) NCAA sports provide access to higher education for a significant number of first-generation students, including "many whose financial situation would have otherwise prevented them from attending college" (NCAA, 2014, ¶13), and (2) the NCAA has substantially increased support of college athletes' academic success (NCAA, 2014).

Contending that the NCAA had made tremendous progress in addressing historic academic concerns, he offered several success stories, including annual spending of $2.1 billion on athletic scholarships, increased initial eligibility requirements, mandatory progress toward degree requirements, as well as stringent Academic Progress Rates (APRs) and "record" GSRs. As LaForge & Hodge (2011) noted, however, "Comparing the GSR of an athletic team to the institutional FGR generally casts the athletic team in a more favorable light. This comparison is invalid, however, because the two measures use different cohort groups in the computation (p. 228). Additionally, throughout his remarks, Emmert failed to address any of the following four points that Southall (2014) outlined.

1. Neither the FGR nor the GSR is perfect or inherently a more accurate metric; they utilize different sampling and statistical analyses to examine different cohorts. In short, they are different graduation rates.

2. The GSR consistently returns a "success" rate 12% to 25% higher than the FGR. As far back as 1989 (NCAA, 1991), the NCAA knew that removing one-quarter to one-third of "eligible dropouts" from a "graduation rate" sample would result in a markedly higher "success" rate.

3. A comparison of published FGRs of NCAA athletes and the general student population includes a significant number of part-time students at many schools. This is problematic because NCAA athletes must be "full-time" students making progress toward a degree. Without adjusting for the possible downward "part-timer bias" in the student-body rate, any comparison is likely distorted—or somewhat skewed. Because part-time students take longer to graduate, general student-body FGRs might be significantly lower, making the relative rate of college athletes at many schools and conferences appear more favorable.

4. Finally, there is no comparable national-level GSR for the general student body. Consequently, GSR and FGR data should NOT be reported simultaneously in press releases or news accounts. The NCAA's consistent comingling of FGR-student and GSR-athlete in press releases or dataset tables invites inappropriate comparisons and fosters confusion (pp. 4–5).

Although the NCAA exclusively utilizes its GSR metric, other statistical analyses have been developed to address FGR and GSR limitations. One such analysis—The Adjusted Graduation Gap (AGG)—initially was developed by Dr. E. Woodrow Eckard (Eckard, 2010) and extended by Dr. Eckard and colleagues with the *College Sport Research Institute* (CSRI). The AGG addresses FGR and GSR limitations (*see* Figure 6.1a). The AGG compares an adjusted FGR for full-time students and the reported FGR for college athletes AGG Reports regarding FBS football, as well as NCAA D-I basketball (*see* Figure 6.1b), baseball (*see* Figure 6.1c) and softball, are released at various times during the year (CSRI, 2016). The AGG analysis of FBS football players, as well as NCAA D-I men's basketball and baseball players' graduation rates reveals that these athletes' graduation rates are overwhelmingly poor compared to other full-time male students at their universities (Frisella, Eckard, Woodman, Nagel, & Southall, 2015; Frisella, Eckard, Southall, Nagel & Woodman, 2015; Southall, Eckard & Nagel, 2016).

Although the 2015–16 College Football Playoff (CFP) yielded more than $500 million for participating FBS athletic departments (College Football Playoff, 2015) and the NCAA grosses nearly $800 million per year as a result of its multibillion-dollar March Madness contract (Clarke, 2013), through a purposeful statistical methodology, which excludes alternative analyses, the NCAA has successfully rebranded itself as an educational association focused on academic

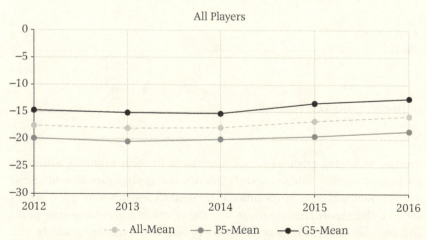

FIGURE 6.1 (a) Trend-Lines of NCAA Athletes' Adjusted Graduation Gaps—FBS Football

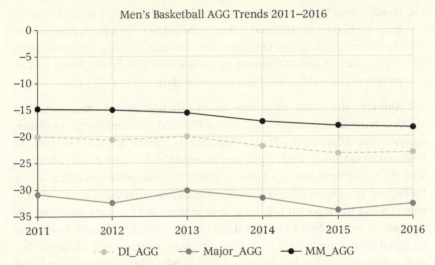

**FIGURE 6.1** (b) NCAA D-I Men's Basketball

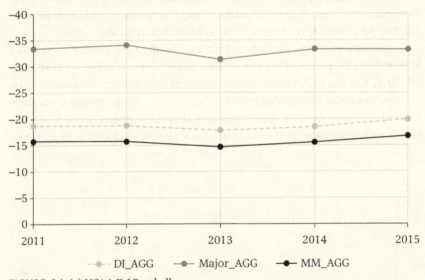

**FIGURE 6.1** (c) NCAA D-I Baseball

success, by forcing graduation rate discussions to occur primarily within its graduation "success" rate framework. This rebranding propaganda has obscured its institutional hegemony (Gramsci, 1971; Southall & Staurowsky, 2013), which allows college sport fans, sponsors, and the courts to comfortably view profit athletes who generate billions of dollars in revenue as merely "students who play sports" (ACC, 2016, ¶1).

## Conclusion

To maintain the mythology that it maintains a clear line of demarcation between its collegiate model and professional sport, the NCAA has successfully restricted our view of academic success to the prism of its Graduation "Success" Rate. This tactic transforms the GSR into what Adamson (1980) described as an "armor of coercion," designed to deliberately form, control, and alter the attitudes of those within college sport's institutional field. The NCAA national office, as well as member athletic departments, consistently position the GSR as the "best" or "most accurate" graduation rate and offer "record" GSR and APR scores as evidence that "big-time" college sport has one clear focus—education. Although GSR data is aggregated to support the collegiate model's mythos, graduation rates disparities between profit-athletes and the general student body, as well as large-scale clustering of such athletes are not part of the rebranding.

For a quarter century, the NCAA national office has sought to disseminate a rebranded definition of academic success to position the economic exploitation of NCAA profit athletes (Rascher & Schwarz, 2000; Schwarz, 2015) as simply a proper part of the overall enterprise (Brand, 2006). By continually rebranding its collegiate model of athletic as well as its definition of academic success, the NCAA and its corporate partners have successfully convinced the American public to ignore the college-sport industry's profit-seeking tendencies—as well as its exploitation of NCAA profit-athletes. Although such systematic and sustained rebranding is not inherently unethical, it has allowed the profit-seeking business of college sport to portray itself as a not-for-profit educational enterprise (Gramsci, 1971; Southall & Staurowsky, 2013).

Fundamentally, the NCAA—through its rebranding efforts—is attempting to maintain the status quo. Or at least slow any fundamental change to its collegiate financial model of athletics to a glacial pace. To accomplish this, it must maintain a veneer of educational legitimacy. Most importantly, any rebranding of academic success must offer evidence to support the claim that graduation rates for African American male athletes (who are disproportionally present in the profit sports of FBS football and NCAA D-I men's basketball). Such rebranding maintains the mythos that the NCAA is delivering on its promise of "world-class" educational opportunities for these players, whose athletic skills power the entire operation. Although not all myths are wholly false, calculated representations of college metaphors or models as literally and completely true are disingenuous at best, patently and cynically immoral at worst.

## Discussion

If using creative accounting to brand the NCAA as a conglomerate that helps facilitate student-athlete success is unacceptable then how do you propose it should promote itself? Are there ways that would be less disingenuous that would be acceptable methods of promoting the NCAA or is it too corrupt to possibly acceptably brand itself in a positive light?

## NOTES

1. In this chapter, references to the NCAA brand include the overall institution (Southall, Nagel, Amis & Southall, 2008), which is comprised of the "association" (e.g., member athletic departments, conferences, governance structure, and affiliated entities), "membership" (e.g., colleges and universities), and the "national office" (NCAA, 2004, p. 2).
2. The NCAA maintains both ".org" and ".com" websites. The ncaa.org site is the institution's association and national office website, and the .com website is a fan-friendly commerce website.
3. The focus of this chapter is the NCAA as an institutional brand, with conference brands subsumed under the overall NCAA brand. Consequently, the developed analysis utilizes branding/rebranding theories on a corporate or organizational level, as well as an institutional branding/rebranding level. Such usage is consistent with the literature, in which similar properties are applied to corporate, organizational, retail, service, and institutional brands (Berry, 2000; Birtwistle & Freathy, 1998).
4. Profit athletes are college athletes whose market value exceeds the value of their grant-in-aid (GIA). The value of a loss athlete's GIA exceeds the athlete's athletic market value. Loss athletes can appropriately be viewed as college-sport consumers.
5. This financial arms race threatens the continued viability of athletics programs and the integrity of our universities (Knight Commission on Intercollegiate Athletics, 2010, ¶3).

## REFERENCES

Adamson, W. L. (1980). *Hegemony and revolution: A study of Antonio Gramsci's political and cultural theory*. Berkeley: University of California Press.

Armstrong, K. (2000). *The battle for God: A history of fundamentalism*. New York: Random House Publishing Group.

Armstrong, K. (2009). *The case for God*. New York: Alfred A. Knopf.

Associated Press. (2014, July 9). *NCAA President Mark Emmert calls for "scholarships for life," other reforms*. Retrieved June 19, 2017, from http://www.ncaa.com/news/ncaa/article/2014–07–09/ncaa-president-mark-emmert-calls-scholarships-life-other-reforms

Atlantic Coast Conference. (2016, July 7). Commissioners announce agreement for changes in how much time students play sports. Retrieved June 19, 2017, from http://www.theacc.com/news/commissioners-announce-agreement-for-changes-in-how-much-time-students-play-sports-07–07–2016

Berkowitz, S., Upton, J., Schnaars, C., Doughtery, S., & Neuharth-Keusch, A. J. (2016a). NCAA salaries: NCAAF coaches. *usatoday.com*. Retrieved June 19, 2017, from http://sports.usatoday.com/ncaa/salaries/

Berkowitz, S., Upton, J., Schnaars, C., & Doughtery, S. (2016b). NCAA salaries: NCAAB coaches. *usatoday.com*. Retrieved June 19, 2017, from http://sports.usatoday.com/ncaa/salaries/mens-basketball/coach/

Berry, L. (2000). Cultivating service brand equity. *Journal of the Academy of Marketing Science, 28*(1), 128–137.

Birtwistle, G., & Freathy, P. (1998). More than just a name above the shop: a comparison of the branding strategies of two UK fashion retailers. *International Journal of Retail & Distribution Management (26)*8, 318–323, https://doi.org/10.1108/09590559810231788.

Brand, M. (2003, January 20). State of the association address. *NCAA News*. Retrieved from http://fs.ncaa.org/Docs/NCAANewsArchive/2003/Association-wide/state+of+the +association+address+-+1–20–03.html

Brand, M. (2004, January 19). Brand address: Fortify bond between academics, athletics. *NCAA News*. Retrieved from http://fs.ncaa.org/Docs/NCAANewsArchive /2004/Associationwide/brand%2baddress%2b%2bfortify%2bbond%2bbetween %2bacademics%2bathletics%2b-%2b1–19–04.html

Brown, G. (2014, October 28). NCAA graduation rates: A quarter-century of tracking academic success. Retrieved June 19, 2017, from http://www.ncaa.org/about/resources/research /ncaa-graduation-rates-quarter-century-tracking-academic-success?division=d3

Byers, W. & Hammer, C. (1995). *Unsportsmanlike conduct: Exploiting college athletes*. Ann Arbor: The University of Michigan Press.

Carter, D. M. (2001). Commentary: And you thought you were watching football. *Bloomberg*. Retrieved from http://www.bloomberg.com/news/articles/2001–0128/commentary -and-you-thought-you-were-watching-football

Clarke, P. (2013, March 21). NCAA tournament 2013: Breaking down the business behind March Madness. *Bleacher Report: Sport Business*. Retrieved June 19, 2017, from http:// bleacherreport.com/articles/1575128-ncaa-tournament-2013-breaking-down-the -business-behind-marchmadness

College Football Playoff. (2015). 2015–16 Revenue Distribution. Retrieved June 19, 2017, from http://www.collegefootballplayoff.com/revenue-distribution

Eckard, E. W. (2010). NCAA athlete graduation rates: Less than meets the eye. *Journal of Sport Management, 24*(1), 45–58.

Emmert, M. (2012). 2012 State of the association: President Emmert. Retrieved from http:// www.ncaa.org/wps/wcm/connect/public/ncaa/pdfs/2012/final+state+of+association +transcript

Emmert, M. A. (2014, July 9). Written testimony of Dr. Mark A. Emmert president of the National Collegiate Athletic Association before the Senate Commerce, Science, and Transportation Committee. Retrieved June 19, 2017, from http://www.ncaa.org /sites/default/files/2014_Sen_Commerce_Committee_Written_Testimony_Final %20Version.pdf

Frisella, R., Eckard, E. W., Woodman, M., Nagel, M. S., & Southall, R. M. (2015, September 28). 2015 adjusted graduation gap report: NCAA D-I softball and baseball. *College Sport Research Institute (CSRI)*. Columbia, SC.

Frisella, R., Eckard, E. W., Southall, R. M., Nagel, M. S., & Woodman, M. (2015, October 21). 2015 adjusted graduation gap report: NCAA FBS football. *College Sport Research Institute (CSRI)*. Columbia, SC.

Gramsci, A. (1971). *Selections from the prison notebooks* (Q. Hoare & G. N. Smith, eds.). New York: International Publishers.

Herndon, M. (2014, July 10). NCAA president Mark Emmert challenged by Senate committee. Retrieved June 19, 2017, from http://www.al.com/sports/index.ssf/2014/07/ncaa _president_mark_emmert_cha.html

Hosick, M. (2014, October 28). Student-athletes earn diplomas at record rate: Graduation success rate jumps two points, virtually every demographic improves. *News Articles*. Retrieved June 19, 2017, from http://www.ncaa.org/about/resources/media-center /news/student-athletes-earn-diplomas-record-rate

Huma, R., & Staurowsky, E. J. (2012). The $6 billion heist: Robbing college athletes under the guise of amateurism. A report collaboratively produced by the National College Players Association and Drexel University Sport Management. http://www.ncpanow.org

Jacobson, S. (1992, October 8). Manley finally gets a read on education he missed. *The Sun.* Retrieved June 19, 2017, from http://articles.baltimoresun.com/1992-10-08/sports /1992282145_1_dexter-reading-the-menu-ottawa-sun

Jowett, G. S. & O'Donnell, V. (1992). *Propaganda and persuasion* (2nd ed.). Newbury Park, CA: Sage.

Keller, K. L., & Lehman, D. R. (2006). Brands and branding: Research findings and future priorities. *Marketing Science, 25*(6), 740–759.

Knight Commission on Intercollegiate Athletics. (2009). Chapter 8: Myths and intangibles. *College sports 101.* Retrieved June 19, 2017, from http://www.knightcommission.org /collegesports101/chapter-8

Knight Commission on Intercollegiate Athletics (KCIA). (2010). Letter of transmittal. *Restoring the balance: Dollars, values, and the future of college sport.* Retrieved from http://www .knightcommission.org/restoringthebalance/letter-of-transmittal

Kuhn, D. (1991). *The skills of argument.* Cambridge, UK: Cambridge University Press.

LaForge, L., & Hodge, J. (2011). NCAA academic performance metrics: Implications for institutional policy and practice. *The Journal of Higher Education, 82*(2), 217–235.

McArdle, J. J., & Hamagami, F. (1994). Logit and multilevel logit modeling of college graduation for 1984–1985 freshman student-athletes. *Journal of the American Statistical Association, 89,* 1107–1123.

McCormick, R. A., & McCormick, A. C. (2006). The myth of the student-athlete: The college athlete as employee. *Washington Law Review, 81,* 71–157.

McGuire, K. (2014, July 9). NCAA president being grilled by Senate committee. *Collegefoot balltalk.nbcsport.com.* Retrieved June 19, 2017, from http://collegefootballtalk.nbcsports .com/2014/07/09/ncaa-president-being-grilled-by-senate-committee/

Merrilees, B., & Miller, D. (2008). Principles of corporate rebranding. *European Journal of Marketing, 42*(5/6), 537–552. doi.org/10.1108/03090560810862499

National Collegiate Athletic Association. (1991, June). *NCAA academic performance study: Report 91–01—A description of college graduation rates for 1984 and 1985 freshman student-athletes.* Overland Park, KS: NCAA.

National Collegiate Athletic Association. (1994, July). *NCAA research report: Report 91–07—Executive summary of reports 91–01 to 91–06.* Overland Park, KS: NCAA.

National Collegiate Athletic Association. (2004, April). *NCAA strategic plan: NCAA executive committee.* Indianapolis, IN: NCAA

National Collegiate Athletic Association (NCAA). (2010a). Branding and communications major NCAA challenges from group perspective. President's Briefing Documents. Retrieved from http://fs.ncaa.org/Docs/newmedia/2010/Emmert/Part3/BC.html

National Collegiate Athletic Association. (2010b). Branding and communications group functional description. Retrieved from http://fs.ncaa.org/Docs/newmedia/2010 /Emmert/Part3/BC/BC1.html

National Collegiate Athletic Association. (2010c). Protecting the collegiate model. Retrieved from http://fs.ncaa.org/Docs/newmedia/2010/Emmert/Part5/protecting.html

National Collegiate Athletic Association (2014, July 9). *NCAA president's testimony on value of college model: NCAA President Mark Emmert testified Wednesday about the value of college sports before the U.S. Senate Committee on Commerce, Science & Transportation.* Retrieved June 19, 2017, from http://www.ncaa.org/about/resources/media-center/news/ncaa -president%E2%80%99s-testimony-value-college-model

National Collegiate Athletic Association [NCAA]. (2016a). Turner, CBS and the NCAA reach long-term multimedia rights extension for NCAA Division I men's basketball championship: New agreement extends television, digital and marketing rights through 2032. *ncaa.com*. Retrieved June 19, 2017, from http://www.ncaa.com/news/basketball -men/article/2016–04–12/turner-cbs-and-ncaa-reach-long-term-multimedia-rights

National Collegiate Athletic Association [NCAA]. (2016b). Pathway to Opportunity. Retrieved June 19, 2017, from http://www.ncaa.org/opportunity/#opportunity

National Collegiate Athletic Association. [n. d.]. NCAA core values. Retrieved June 19, 2017, from http://www.ncaa.org/about/ncaa-core-values

National Collegiate Athletic Association [n. d.]. What is the NCAA? Retrieved June 19, 2017, from http://www.ncaa.org/about/resources/media-center/ncaa-101/what-ncaa

Nyad, D. (1989, May 28). View of sport: How illiteracy makes athletes run. *The New York Times*. Retrieved from http://www.nytimes.com/1989/05/28/sports/views-of-sport -how-illiteracy-makes-athletes-run.html?pagewanted=all&src=pm

*O'Bannon et al. v. NCAA et al.*, No. 09–3329, 2014 WL 3899815 (N.D. Cal. August 8, 2014).

*O'Bannon et al. v. NCAA*, Nos. 14–16601, 14–17068 (D.C. 4:09-cv-03329-CW) (9th Cir. 2015).

Oriard, M. (2009). *Bowled over: Big-time college football from the sixties to the BCS era*. Chapel Hill, NC: The University of North Carolina Press.

Qualter, T. H. (1962). *Propaganda and psychological warfare*. New York, NY: Random House.

Rascher, D. A., & Schwarz, A. D. (2000). Neither reasonable nor necessary: 'amateurism' in big-time college sports. *Antitrust Magazine, Special Sports Issue, Spring 2000*. Retrieved June 19, 2017, from http://ssrn.com/abstract=926339

Rein, I., Shields, B., & Grossman, A. (2015). *The sports strategist: Developing leaders for a high-performance industry*. New York, NY: Oxford University Press.

Renfro, W. (2012, September 6). *Amateurism, professionalism, commercial activity and intercollegiate athletics: Ambivalence about principles*. Proceedings of the Santa Clara Sports Law Symposium, Santa Clara, CA (pp. 32–45).

*Ross v. Creighton University*, 957 F.2d 410 (7th Cir. 1992).

Rovell, D. (2010, December 8). NCAA prez: We won't pay student athletes, give jersey royalties. *cnbc.com: Sports Biz with Darren Rovell*. Retrieved June 19, 2017, from http://www .cnbc.com/id/40570628

Sack, A. L. (2008). *Counterfeit amateurs: An athlete's journey through the sixties to the age of academic capitalism*. University Park, PA: The Pennsylvania State University Press.

Sack, A. L., & Staurowsky, E. J. (1998). *College athletes for hire: The evolution and legacy of the NCAA amateur myth*. Westport, CT: Praeger Press.

Schwarb, A. W. (2015, November 17). Emmert: Colleges must continue to support student-athletes—NCAA president tells higher education leaders that much progress has been made but more is needed. Retrieved June 19, 2017, from http://www.ncaa.org/about /resources/media-center/news/emmert-colleges-must-continue-support-student -athletes

Selingo, J. (2012, March 2). The rise and fall of the graduation rate. *The Chronicle of Higher Education*. Retrieved June 19, 2017, from http://chronicle.com/article/The-RiseFall-of -the/131036/

Snidal, D. (1985). The limits of hegemonic stability theory. *International Organization, 39*, 579–614.

Southall, R. M. (2014, July 9). *Extended written remarks to the United States Senate Committee on Commerce, Science and Transportation*. Retrieved June 19, 2017, from http:// www.commerce.senate.gov/public/index.cfm?p=Hearings&ContentRecord _id=48f489fd-720f-44d7-8a68–53efaecf8139&Statement_id=65653b17–819a-4c6b

-b114–1c9add6bb3b5&ContentType_id=14f995b9-dfa5–407a-9d35–56cc7152a7ed &Group_id=b06c39af-e033–4cba-9221-de668ca1978a&MonthDisplay=7&YearDisp lay=2014

Southall, R. M., Eckard, E. W., & Nagel, M. S. (2016, April 6). 2016 adjusted graduation gap report: NCAA division-I basketball "Lost in the *madness:* NCAA division-I basketball graduation gaps significantly larger since 2011." *College Sport Research Institute (CSRI).* Columbia, SC.

Southall, R. M., Nagel, M. S., Amis, J., & Southall, C. (2008). A method to March Madness: Institutional logics and the 2006 National Collegiate Athletic Association Division I men's basketball tournament. *Journal of Sport Management, 22*(6), 677–700.

Southall, R. M., & Staurowsky, E. J. (2013). Cheering on the collegiate model: Creating, disseminating, and imbedding the NCAA's redefinition of amateurism. *Journal of Sport & Social Issues, 37*(4), 403–429. doi: 10.1177/0193723513498606.

Southall, R. M., & Staurowsky, E. J. (2014, April 25). College sport reform or collegiate model re-branding? An analysis of CAP Act and other federal legislative proposals. *7th Annual CSRI Conference on College Sport.* Columbia, SC.

Sperber, M. (1990). *College sports inc.: The athletic department vs the university.* New York: Henry Holt and Company.

Sperber, M. (2000). *Beer and circus: How big-time college sports is crippling undergraduate education.* New York: Henry Holt and Company.

Stark, R. (2015, April 17). *Making it theirs: How three words are energizing Division II.* NCAA. Retrieved June 19, 2017, from http://www.ncaa.org/champion/making-it-theirs

Staurowsky, E. J., & Sack, A. L. (2005). Reconsidering the use of the term "student- athlete" by academic researchers. *Journal of Sport Management 19* (2), 103–117.

Telander, R. (1996). *The hundred yard lie: The corruption of college football and what we can do to stop it.* Champaign-Urbana, IL: University of Illinois Press.

Thelin, J. R. (1994). *Games colleges play: Scandal and reform in intercollegiate athletics.* Baltimore, MD: The Johns Hopkins University Press.

Yaeger, D. (1991). *Undue process: The NCAA's injustice for all.* Champaign, IL: Sagamore Publishing, Inc.

Yost, M. (2009). *Varsity green: A behind the scenes look at culture and corruption in college athletics.* Stanford University Press.

Zimbalist, A. (1999). *Unpaid professionals: Commercialism and conflict in big-time college sports.* Princeton, NJ: Princeton University Press.

# 7

# Is This the Beginning of the End?

## Small Colleges and Universities Are Questioning the Value of an NCAA Program for Their Student Body

OLIVER RICK

As this book describes in detail, there are numerous ways in which the world of collegiate sport and the NCAA system is in an extreme state of flux. While some laud its successes, others heavily criticize the professionalized nature of what "amateur" scholastic sports has become (Pope & Pope, 2009). Those who consider the current system to be problematic query the underlying economic contradictions of these programs, their inability to return meaningful capital to the university, the lack of evidence supporting ongoing positive indirect returns on investment, the general growth in university spending on collegiate sports programs, as well as how they have become detached from the amateur ideals of the NCAA's core mission (Davis, 2010; Hoffer et al., 2015; Hogshead-Makar, 2010; Humphreys & Mondello, 2007; Kelly & Dixon, 2011; Knight Commission, 2009; Singer, 2008; Van Rheenen, 2012). Indeed, Pope & Pope (2009) suggest that these concerns have only intensified "as a result of widely publicized scandals involving student athletes and coaches, and because of the increasing amount of resources schools must invest to remain competitive in today's intercollegiate athletic environment" (p. 750). This situation has informed a broad pushback against the current system, centering on one particular concern: Who is served by the ongoing maintenance of a relationship between an organization that oversees a multimillion-dollar sports business (NCAA), and not-for-profit intuitions of higher education?

Much of the research that addresses this fundamental question is directed towards the world of "big-time sports," and although the scale and scope of collegiate sport at this end of the system, alongside its "uniqueness, ought to provoke reflection" (Getz & Siegfried, 2010, p. 1), this chapter looks to go beyond the big universities, the world of massive revenues, and even bigger operating budgets. This is a discussion of where the small universities and colleges with Division II and III NCAA programs, fit within the broader interrogation of the current collegiate sports system. With little revenue generated by these programs and significant costs to operate them, the economic logics being debated around Division I sports were never in question in the lower divisions of the NCAA. The potential of these programs to generate direct revenue through media rights and merchandizing is minimal. So what are the other benefits these schools see in maintaining an NCAA program? Indeed, are some colleges and universities finding it increasingly difficult to answer that question?

One school that seems to no longer see the logic in maintaining an NCAA athletics program is Spelman College, which decided to disband its program beginning with the 2013–2014 school year. Instead, "Spelman is choosing to move $1 million a year previously budgeted for varsity sports into what leaders call a 'Wellness Revolution' for all students—pouring resources into exercise classes and nutrition counseling and intramurals" (Cyphers, 2013, ¶2). Indeed, it seems that a discourse of student health has won out over the usually loud chorus of positive sentiments that exists behind the idea of college sports. Now, three years after the decision, few other colleges or universities operating NCAA athletics at this level have followed Spelman's lead. Through its actions, however, Spelman provides a useful point of entry into a discussion about the value of NCAA sports programs, and whether the health-related discursive framing employed around this decision could be the first step down an alternative path for small colleges and universities in particular or what Cyphers (2013) described as "a different Road to Atlanta than the one CBS hypes" (¶9). Spelman certainly occupies a unique position in higher education—as many small niche schools attempt to do—yet various points of commonality for these types of institution do exist and could lead other colleges and universities to find some value in the model Spelman has developed.

Building on a brief assessment of the current broader terrain of collegiate sports today, what follows considers the current challenges that exist around the maintenance of an NCAA program for small schools, and how these can be addressed through taking a similar path to that chosen by the Spelman College administration. It is a consideration of whether the discourse of health that comes with a "wellness revolution" is what gives legitimacy to a decision to move away from collegiate sports, in a time of massive popular support for the NCAA sports system. In many ways, it is a question of whether the dominance of a discourse of health today legitimizes—or potentially necessitates—a shift in focus that provides an alternative to the assumptions that further entrench patterns of significant investment in NCAA sports programs.

## The Contemporary Economic Terrain of NCAA Collegiate Sports

The interconnection between higher-education institutions in the United States and NCAA sports programs has long been a prevalent and yet simultaneously contentious part of the American collegiate landscape (Pope & Pope, 2009). NCAA sports—primarily football and men's basketball—generate revenue that rivals the economic performance of many American professional sports leagues (Kelly & Dixon, 2011). Additionally, it is important to recognize that—in no uncertain terms—collegiate sport also has become a social and cultural force. Its presence stretches across numerous media platforms and outlets, being the focus of television schedules, journalistic column inches, social media trends, and e-gaming formats. Yet, at the same time, the money rarely trickles down beyond a small number of super-achieving schools, thus calling into question the actual profitability that NCAA sports bring to most colleges and universities (Zimbalist, 2010). Even small-scale programs can cost institutions millions of dollars, and the positive effects that can accrue for the student body as a whole could be limited.

At the top end of the NCAA collegiate sports system, "big-time" sports programs dominate the media landscape, as well as annual spending and revenues. Large public universities such as Alabama, Ohio State, Florida, and many others can generate greater television rights, sponsorship, and merchandizing revenues than some professional teams, while filling larger-capacity stadiums. As Hoffer et al. (2015) suggest, bowl appearance revenues alone can be substantial.

> For example, the top five football bowl payouts in the 2011–2012 season included US$22.3 million to Louisiana State University (LSU), Ohio State, Oregon, Clemson, West Virginia, and Wisconsin; US$6.1 million to Alabama, Stanford, Virginia Tech, and Michigan; US$4.55 million to Nebraska and South Carolina; US$3.625 million to Arkansas and Kansas State; and US$3.5 million to Georgia and Michigan State (p. 577).

Indeed, these revenues only represent a small portion of gross yearly revenues and only a few of a limited rotating list of schools able to access this money.

Demanding massive media rights fees, developing superstar players, and constructing cutting-edge facilities—institutions of higher education have become part of a billion-dollar industry. This is a system unrivalled on a global scale and mimicked nowhere else (Getz & Siegfried, 2010). Indeed, this is a moment when "substantial resources are invested in paying coaches and maintaining high-quality intercollegiate programs at universities throughout the United States" (Hoffer et al., 2015, p. 577). Institutional support is strong, and the financial assistance that some programs receive can be substantial. Certainly, for athletic departments at the bottom end of Division I, and those in Division II and III—which generate little revenue—this investment from the university or college is essential.[1] Even at the top end of the sport, however, high revenue–generating athletic programs also have seen widespread cost increases that trend with revenues and have kept profits to a minimum. Instead of being able to feed direct funding into institutions, "The average Division I NCAA athletic department receives a subsidy of US$8.8 million annually" and "[e]ven schools in the six Automatic Qualifying (AQ) conferences receive an average annual subsidy of US$5.81 million" (Hoffer & Pincin, 2015, p. 3). The Knight Commission corroborates these numbers; its 2009 report suggested that "[a]ccording to 2007 NCAA financial data, half of all top-flight athletic programs rely on at least $9 million in institutional and governmental subsidies to balance their budgets" and that "[e]ven in the most prosperous conference, its members received a median subsidy of $3.4 million" (p. 14).

Clearly, when considered collectively college sport has drifted far away from any amateur idealism, growing into a financial behemoth today that paradoxically is still a monetary burden for most institutions (Tsitsos & Nixon, 2012). In the United States, we have collectively stood by and watched the development of a collegiate sport system that generates massive amounts of money on the back of projecting an idealized image of the amateur student-athlete, which exists seemingly only as a technicality. The NCAA, however, is a broad, complex, and multifaceted system of sports governance functioning across colleges and universities that differ in a number of ways. Once beyond the big stadiums, media presence, and money of the big programs the picture changes. The idea of direct revenue generation all but disappears past the top 50–60 institutions, and the amount of money "raised" by low-level Division I schools and beyond is laughable given administrative emphasis.

On the surface, at least, Division II and III programs appear to more faithfully adhere to a popular vision of amateur athletics and the pursuit of competition, distanced from the big business of "bowl season" or "March Madness" (Cyphers, 2013). Division II and III represent a larger population of student-athletes and coaches[2]—and there are few or no athletic scholarships and television coverage is limited to NCAA Championship contests. There are coach-teachers, committing time both in the classroom and on the field or court; minimalist facilities; and budgets that are relatively small. This is not to say that budgets for athletic departments are negligible, indeed they can still be significant in the overall spending at a small college or university, but they certainly do not rival the situation of some universities where they are spending millions of dollars on coaching salaries alone.[3]

Investments in programs are not made in pursuit of direct revenue streams, but are often positioned as essential in creating a high standard of student experience; increasing admissions derived revenues from non-athletes and athletes alike. For those athletes, very few will see a professional career in their chosen sport, and purer attempts to augment or enhance the educational experience might be more at the forefront of administrative thinking. Also, the programs that are supported in these divisions are much more varied, as they are detached from the necessity to generate revenue. This is not to say that Division II and III schools are unconnected from the dynamics of Division I sports, as they are part of how the NCAA is defining itself within a contemporary context of higher education. Yet, at the same time, the logics that underpin the ways these athletic departments are managed and exist as part of that system of higher education have some key differences.

A major impact of these differences is how the relevance of NCAA sport to the contemporary institution is understood. At the highest level, questions are raised about continuing to conjoin a billion-dollar sports industry with institutions of higher education—many of which are state entities. Conversely, for many smaller schools growing concerns center on whether an NCAA program is the best way to offer students a high standard of college experience and make the institution attractive to potential students. With limited budgets and greater reliance on tuition dollars driving a focus on admissions, small private universities and colleges must make heavily constrained choices about where they make and spend money to maintain competitiveness in the higher-education market. The investments in NCAA sports programs are not only stacked up against direct revenues, but are more broadly measured against a complex array of indirect metrics. Resultantly considerations of un-earmarked donations, admissions, and regional or national branding, are all taken into account by institutions that currently have Division II or III programs.

The cost of running an NCAA sports program can be high for a small college or university. Even a program with a modest number of sports can easily run costs into the millions of dollars. As such, research that demonstrates a lack of positive indirect returns derived from sports programs can be particularly worrying. As an example Humphreys and Mondello (2007) suggest in their study "results indicate that only restricted giving changes in response to athletic success" (p. 265). Therefore, athletic departments can generate increased funding through donations, but the money generated is regularly earmarked for use by athletic departments only, restricting the accrued benefits to student-athletes, athletic department staff, and facilities. Resultantly the authors go on to suggest that, "athletic success does not appear to induce donors to increase their unrestricted contributions in the following year" (Humphreys and Mondello, 2007, p. 265). As such, while athletic programs might become more sustainable through this system of giving, the benefits of this system are limited by the restrictions placed on these contributions.

Again, although this might provide a means through which athletic programs can maintain themselves, any investment into programs by schools' general funds will show little return for the college or university at large. Further, Hoffer et al. (2015) suggest "intercollegiate athletic expenditure has increased substantially over time in inflation-adjusted terms," and as costs increase the gap between spending and giving might grow, demanding more investment with still-limited open donations to the institution. These trends not only present an undesirable situation presently in linking athletics to the actions of donors, but it shows that the impact NCAA programs can have in this area only will worsen if increases in costs continue to grow—a situation that has a high likelihood as the effects of an "arms race" at the top end of the NCAA system roll further down to other divisions (Cooper & Weight, 2011; Hoffer et al., 2015; Hogshead-Makar, 2010; Tsitsos & Nixon, 2012).

Additional research has shown that the benefits of athletic programs can formulate in other ways, specifically around application and attendance rates, but this also might not be a straightforward issue. In reviewing the literature, Hoffer et al. (2015) found that "evidence suggests that success on the playing field results in increased applications for admission to the university (Pope & Pope, 2009, 2014), increased state appropriations (Humphreys, 2006), and other indirect benefits (Getz & Siegfried, 2010)" (p. 577). However, this research has mainly addressed Division I institutions and sports programs. It would be difficult to suggest whether this same effect will translate into the lower NCAA divisions. Schools of all sizes certainly draw on the visibility provided by their athletic programs to bring students to the school and increase admissions numbers, but with little mediated coverage the effects might be limited, particularly in scale and geographical scope. Certainly, at present the limited existence of research that focuses on the impact of athletics for recruitment at Division II and III schools leaves this point open-ended.

These are just two of what might be a complex set of factors for schools to consider when analyzing the role of their sports programs. Debate about the indirect impacts of NCAA programs for small schools and colleges will continue. Aside from issues of television rights, million-dollar sponsorship deals, and massive state spending on coaches' salaries, most college administrators have to navigate these often smaller and intricately nuanced issues. Indeed, as the academic market becomes more precarious in its current form, many will come to ask themselves whether an NCAA sports program is worth the expanding cost, and will demand more evidence around each of these factors to make better-informed decisions. Until this information is developed, college and university administrators still must weigh the difficult-to-define outcomes of these investments, and do so in the face of an increasingly challenging economic climate for higher education as federal assistance wanes, tuition growth becomes unsustainable, and competition from for-profit entities expands. When the evidence for positive impacts is scarce and other viable routes are open, many at the helm of these schools may well think about other potential options for spending at their institutions.

## Is Spelman College Leading a Revolution?

When looking for examples of how to work outside of the typical NCAA-based collegiate sports model, Spelman College in Atlanta might be a model that other schools can consider. Spelman describes itself in its mission statement as:

a historically Black college and a global leader in the education of women of African descent, [Spelman] is dedicated to academic excellence in the liberal arts and sciences and the intellectual, creative, ethical, and leadership development of its students. Spelman empowers the whole person to engage the many cultures of the world and inspires a commitment to positive social change (Spelman College, 2016, ¶4).

Occupying a small niche in the higher-education landscape, the college still is a highly regarded place of higher learning, boasting among its alumni "former slaves and a Pulitzer Prize-winning author" (Tierney, 2013, ¶2). Spelman is regularly recognized highly within the country's system of Historically Black Colleges and Universities (HBCUs), and stands out within the region.

Today, one of the most significant ways Spelman stands apart from other schools is in its decision to place its investment in student physical activity elsewhere. Since dissolving its NCAA sports program, the college has "flipped, shredded and repurposed the script, creating a whole new version of sports on campus" (Cyphers, 2013, ¶53), turning its back on a traditional collegiate sports model, seemingly forever. As mentioned, those in leadership at Spelman made the announcement in late 2012 that it would be ceasing its NCAA sports program "choosing to move $1 million a year previously budgeted for varsity sports into what leaders call a 'Wellness Revolution' for all students—pouring resources into exercise classes and nutrition counseling and intramurals" (Cyphers, 2013, ¶2).

Responding to a recent shift in conference alignments and facing the prospect of required renovations to the college's athletic facilities, the opportunity was taken to cut the cost of the sports program and to spend the money elsewhere to better serve the college's community. In this case, addressing the health and wellness based needs of the college's students, faculty, staff, and alumni. As such, former President Beverly Tatum has been vocal about the need to address health issues for women of African descent who in the United States are so disproportionately impacted by "lifestyle"-related issues and diseases.

In an interview with *Inside Higher Education,* Tatum highlighted that the college was "trying to create a culture on our campus where people see themselves as part of a community of women who are concerned about health and wellness" (Grasgreen, 2012, ¶13). Indeed, this was a statement that includes a focus on women and the desire to craft a sense of community that would seem to run counter to the neoliberal, radically individualistic mentality that leaders at so many institutions in America now hold. As King-White describes in Chapter 10, fielding competitive athletics programs at vast expense of students is the norm, not the other way around. Yet, at Spelman the presence of an athletics program was not necessarily seen as a mandatory part of how the college attracted admissions or donations. Essentially, the shift moved nearly $1 million in spending away from the athletic pursuits of only approximately 80 student-athletes at the college, and put that money towards supporting the healthy lifestyle practices of the whole college. The decision also later spurred the building of a state-of-the-art wellness center (New, 2014).

This decision was one that, although not unprecedented, is certainly unusual, with Spelman being only "the second college in the last decade to leave the N.C.A.A. altogether, the other being the New York City College of Technology in Brooklyn" (Tierney, 2013, ¶2). It was a decision that was informed by a number of factors, and many that might not be directly applicable or transferable to other institutions. For instance, some small colleges have a more significant history and contemporary connection to their sports programs, potentially changing what the balance sheet of costs and benefits looks like. What the dissolution of the NCAA program at Spelman did do was demonstrate that another path could be pursued. Alongside the aforementioned New York City College of Technology and a small number of others, Spelman has become part of a trend that defies the apparently dominant understanding that NCAA sports programming is absolutely imperative for a college or university. What remains to be seen is whether these each represent unique cases, or if they are signs of the initial stages of what might become a growing number of schools unwilling to invest into a system with such deep-seated contradictions and fundamental issues (Southall & Staurowsky, 2013; Tsitsos & Nixon, 2012).

An important factor that has set Spelman apart from other institutions that have also closed all or parts of their NCAA programs was the way in which those at the college framed the decision. In justifying ceasing NCAA programming, other schools have cited tightening budgets, low revenues, and significant issues with the structure of the teams. In contrast, Spelman administrators have talked about an active decision to replace varsity sports with greater spending on health initiatives. Former President Tatum staked out the intentions that drove the closure of the NCAA program by repeating the mantra of a "Wellness revolution." As part of approach Tatum suggested, "One of the things colleges try to create with students are these habits of the mind. . . . But it's also a wonderful time to develop what I call habits of the body" (quoted in New, 2014, ¶4). Put differently, an administrative focus on developing hyper-competitive individual and team "achievement" supported by (supposedly) throngs of cheering but relatively docile classmates, is being replaced by the development of the student-bodies' health and overall well-being at Spelman.

The decision by those in leadership appears to demonstrate not a forced response to economic hardships, but an active choice to make a change in line with the shifting nature of the contemporary moment, and the challenges faced by their particular community. Therefore, this was not an unfortunate or unintended action forced by the hand of financial tightening, but rather it was a choice to reroute spending in a way that is believed will return more value to the institution, its students, staff, alumni, surrounding community, and faculty. The following section demonstrates why and how this could work at Spelman when in a variety of other institutional contexts the response from stakeholders likely would be far less welcoming.

## Contrasting Collegiate Sport and Discourses of Health

Spelman received national attention when it made the decision to increase spending on a "wellness revolution" at the college, and to cease its NCAA sports programming to provide increased financial support for this renewed focus. Indeed this was an almost unprecedented decision made in the face of increasingly diminishing operating budgets for smaller colleges and universities. Within the contemporary moment, however, it should come as no surprise that Spelman turned to a discourse of investing in health as a legitimate means through which to justify this redirection in spending. As Cheek (2008) states "the 2000s have seen the continued emergence and consolidation of health as one of the guiding mantras of both governments and individuals" (p. 974), and there continues to exist a dominant discourse of health in the United States today. Expectations to engage with practices of health are ever present, the health industry in its many facets is booming, communities and the way we interact socially are intimately connected to health, how we understand our bodies is through a health lens, health technologies develop exponentially, and our political systems also are tied into conceptions of health. We live in a moment dominated by a discourse of health; it is a powerful system of terms and meanings. Yet, these are not benign frameworks of knowledge, in many ways it would be best to understand that we do not engage with a discourse of health, but rather a "healthist" discourse. As Smith and Easterlow (2005) discuss "Being well is the Holy Grail of all societies; life takes place under the lens of a 'healthist' gaze" (p. 173). Put differently, the ideas of health, wellness, and other connected terms have become privileged within our society and the expectation to participate in achieving good health is increasingly present throughout our lives.

Often attributed to Robert Crawford and his writing on *Healthism and the Medicalization of Everyday Life* in 1980, the concept of healthism refers to "a particular way of viewing the health problem, and is characteristic of the new health consciousness and movements" (p. 365). Others have built on this initial work from Crawford and complicated the concept in some extremely effective manners. Investigation into how these discourses of health function as healthist—developed over the last three decades—all contribute to explicating the ways in which this discursive framework can individualize, moralize, and extend responsibilities for achieving good health.

Outworkings of 21st century healthism take various guises and forms but are underpinned by new understandings of old problems, such as how to avoid death, how to view and respond to risk, and how to remain in an ever-vigilant state—a new and transformed version of a "what if" approach to health, rather than a "what is." It is no longer enough to be without, or actively working to prevent, physical disease to be considered healthy. Health has become the new fountain of youth, the promise of "potential perfection" (Fitzgerald, 1994, p. 196), a new version of the eternal quest for immortality, and a new form of a badge of honor by which we can claim to be responsible and worthy both as citizens and individuals. Thus, in many Western contemporary societies health approaches sacred status: Healthism is to the fore (Cheek, 2008, p. 974).

Certainly, ideas of health, and doctrines on the pursuit of a particular conception of "healthy" are not new. In the 1980s, Crawford was naming a trend that was already taking hold, and it appears to have continued to intensify since then (Crawford, 1980). The further privatization of healthcare alongside the cost-driven nature of what is left of public healthcare options, has created a greater focus on shifting care responsibilities to the individual. Most recently, mobile tracking technologies—described by Lupton (2013) as "mHealth" (p. 393)—have facilitated an even greater intensification of the healthist framework, which looks only to accelerate as we move forward.

The current formulation of this healthist discourse, which dominates how we talk about our bodies and health, orients most prominently around the idea of "obesity." As Rich and Evans (2005) suggest, "Concerns over an 'obesity epidemic' are frequently repeated in the national media, in feature reports that focus on the serious effects of being 'overweight,' 'obese' and the ills of 'fat' " (p. 342). We are bombarded with information about the threats obesity proposes to our collective well-being, as well as the responsibility each of us has to respond. The realities or veracity of the potential threat an obesity "crisis" poses is certainly up for debate (e.g., Gard, 2009; King-White, Newman & Giardina, 2013), however the prevalence of the messaging we are all exposed to is evident. Indeed, the ability of a concept of obesity to extend the individualized and moralized nature of health, and therefore the expectation for each of us to respond has been highlighted by many. Yet, this is just the most visible tip of an iceberg of health-related expectations, as well as pressure to act in the name of the greater good and collective health of our society writ large (Evans et al., 2004; McDermott, 2007; Murray, 2008; Trainer et al., 2015; Zanker & Gard, 2008).

A culture of health and exercise is growing, with greater expectations for participation in practices for improving our health, and future generations of college students will have grown up deeply shaped by the current context.

Indeed, the ubiquity of a healthist discourse and the culture it engenders will drive a new appetite for participation in health and wellness programs, and higher education already has responded. College campuses now are regularly developing or have already invested heavily in state-of-the-art facilities, equipment, research, and support for a multitude of related health practices. Any school that fails to cater for this growing demand for healthy resources inevitably will fall behind national standards and a minimum expectation expressed by college students today. The role of colleges and universities as sites of physical activity and health practices is not new, but the expectation for resources only grows with a student body steeped in a healthist discourse.

Additionally, for colleges and universities that might want to also adopt a focus on health and wellness over sports, the growing legitimacy of a discourse of health helps maintain support from other important stakeholders beyond the student body. It potentially provides another means through which to maintain support from university board members, donors, various state entities, and others as the schools pursue another path. In the cotemporary pursuit of mind, body, and spirit that many institutions of higher learning focus upon, investments in a program of health might hold as much legitimacy as the much-lauded NCAA sports system. Attracting funding and donations connected to health and wellness programming can connect with alternative sources that might be just as significant as those who give to athletics. Both private- and public-health related institutions consistently furnish million-dollar grants to research and programs that focus on health issues.

Spelman College alone reportedly garnered close to $18 million dollars in funding to build its Wellness Center (New, 2014). A resource the college saw as particularly necessary in its focus on servicing a population that suffers disproportionately with lifestyle-disease risks and is often targeted by healthist discourses. With high rates of inactivity and obesity, women of African descent are heavily impelled by the imperative to be healthier (Rosenberg et al., 1999). Indeed, Tatum appeared to recognize these unique challenges her students might face, discussing that the college had "not only a special responsibility, but a special opportunity" (Grasgreen, 2012, ¶7) to address these concerns. Yet, whether Spelman College is driven by the realities of a health crisis that acutely impacts its community, or merely is attempting to take advantage of the prevalence of a moment shaped heavily by a healthist discourse, it is not necessarily a key distinction to make here. Either way a discourse of health has clearly changed how we can discuss spending in our colleges and universities, a change that diverts away from a focus on propping-up the NCAA system, and gives this alternative path legitimacy. In public press, Spelman College administrators—and Tatum in particular—have expounded on the need to address health and wellness within their institution, and have received wide-reaching support.

## Mapping the Future Direction of NCAA Sports Programs
## at Small Schools and Universities

As discussed, it is clear that the benefits of maintaining an NCAA sports program might be questionable. Growing costs, little direct economic return for a vast majority of schools, the limited impacts on admissions and unrestricted donations, the relatively small number of students the system can service, and the present legitimacy of focusing on wellness programs within a broad framework of health(ism) could all count against the NCAA in significant ways. As such, Spelman might be a "canary in a coal mine," signaling not the end of the collegiate sports system as we now know it, but certainly heralding a time in which having a sports program is not a given for colleges and universities across America. What Spelman also demonstrates is that this shift might have the greatest impact on smaller schools. Already-tight budgets, rising tuition costs, and a distance from the potential of multimillion-dollar media deals all contribute to the intensity of the challenge faced by these smaller institutions. Additionally, the more specific and unique nature of many of these schools might make a shift towards health and wellness make more sense.

This indeed is a particularly important consideration for Spelman, being both an HBCU and an institution focused on educating women. The realities of the disproportionate health challenges facing women of African descent, and the uneven nature of pressures deriving from healthist discourses along lines of race and gender, are significant (Antin & Hunt, 2013). So significant that "Black American women have been described as one of the most vulnerable population groups in relation to health status" (Pieterse & Carter, 2010, p. 335). A sentiment that resonates in the statements of former Spelman president Tatum, "I have been to funerals of young alums who were not taking care of themselves, and I believe we can change that pattern not only for them but for the broader community" (Tatum quoted in Halvorson, 2013). Thus, Spelman's mostly black and female student body exists as a context through which the opportunity to close intercollegiate sport programming in favor of improving health outcomes for the community could be pursued to a greater extent.

Certainly, few other schools might share this demographic, and with it the same factors to consider when making choices about where to spend their resources. As such, although many schools can learn from the actions Spelman has taken, the intersection of race and gender that much of the school community occupies might have made the pressure to pursue this approach more intense or, at the very least, diminished a wide-reaching resistance to this decision. In a way, the normalized racist and sexist discourse surrounding "African American women, who disproportionately are considered at risk for obesity" and that face "another form of stigmatization by virtue of their biomedically defined risk" (Antin & Hunt, 2013, p. 27) might have been key in framing the legitimacy of this decision. Therefore, unless other schools mimic its demographics, Spelman might be relatively unique rather than being the first in a wave of schools that will make similar changes. It is hard to come to a conclusive statement on whether these factors mean that Spelman represents a more common concern with the realities of NCAA sports programs, or is a particular response to the specific systems of racism and gender-based discrimination that its student population experiences. It does, however, show what detaching from the current collegiate sports system can look like. As such, other schools might consider following a similar path, even if the discursive framing of the decision is different, especially as the contradictions in collegiate sport become harder and harder to resolve. At the very least, it might push the NCAA to reform. As an entity, the NCAA is being squeezed at both ends, where "[i]nterscholastic sports [has become] a failed state" (Cyphers, 2013, ¶28). At the top end of Division I sports, the logic of requiring high-revenue teams and sports superstars to maintain some myth of amateurism seems archaic at best. At the same time, Division II and III programs seem to make more sense within the amateur idealisms of the institution, but equally are threatened by rising costs and changing student demands for on-campus resources.

The NCAA already has responded to these challenges with new media campaigns that extend the long-existing "imaginative and strategic manufacture of language [used by the NCAA] to create the impression that the business practices associated with the running of "big-time" college sport are educational and not exploitative in nature" (Southall & Staurowsky, 2015, p. 409). These productions mimic the intensification of statements on amateurism that have come from the top, including NCAA President Mark Emmert, and can be expected to be a continued part of the association's future public-relations campaigns.

The reality of the way forward for collegiate sport might be more of a hybrid model. Although big revenue-generating programs might continue with the "arms race" (Hoffer et al., 2015), many schools will look to do more to provide a widely accessible means for all students to be physically active through a focus on a health and wellness approach. Some schools already are doing just that—blending spending on NCAA sports programs with investments in wellness programs, exercise facilities, and intramural sports. This might mean more money for other programs, and diminishing funding for NCAA sports. In many ways, sport in American colleges might start to look less unique globally and more closely resemble university sports programs in other countries. Professional sports feeder-systems have not been connected with higher education in many other countries, and although intercollegiate competition still exists, funding tends to be distributed more evenly across all sports teams and other physical activity–health and wellness programs. Additionally, a broader and more varied number of sports being played might be possible within this shift. The NCAA has seen many schools cutting programs, often to divert greater funding to revenue-generating sports, but a system that more equally divides funds might be able to go in the other direction. The increasing popularity of exercise sports (e.g., CrossFit, Spartan Racing) might just one area where colleges look to spend more money.

## Conclusion

Recent reports have shown that the decision made by Spelman has resulted in a number of successes for the college's new health and wellness mission, with increases in program participation as just one indicator (New, 2014). Yet, this still might not be enough for many schools to pursue the same whole-sale change that Spelman made in closing its NCAA program. In many ways, it was an expression of the college's unique position (Associated Press, 2012), but more gradual shifts might be seen, if they have not already happened. Certainly, it appears that "few institutions seem to be able to resist the lure of intercollegiate sports, even as one scandal after another has tarnished the reputations of universities throughout the country" (Tierney, 2013, ¶5), but as Spelman took its initial steps in closing its NCAA program Cyphers (2013) suggests that "the little college [was] fielding other calls, from officials at other campuses . . . investigating whether they, too, can dump sports" (Cyphers, 2013, ¶9). Therefore, it might not be wide-reaching, but a mini-revolution of sorts in small schools that identify with what Spelman is trying to achieve could be possible.

Many smaller schools are private and rely heavily on admission numbers to make financial ends meet. Some are diversifying their revenue streams (e.g., creating what are pay-full-tuition-for-play football programs). For many, however, securing a bulk of their revenue dollars still centers on attracting students to the institution. As such, providing the highest standard of experience for every-one attending is critical, and all the money spent in service of these goals for the institution is increasingly under scrutiny. If the idea of investing in health and wellness resources better addresses funding targets than spending on an expensive NCAA sports program does, then broader changes might be coming.

In many ways, collegiate sport is in its heyday, but a growing expectation for us all to partake in achieving our good health might just tip the balance against a system that is on the edge in small colleges and universities. With middling attendances at events, little evidence to link sports with greater admission rates or non-earmarked donations, and a trend in expanding costs, the culture of health that the next generation of college students brings with them might be the catalyst needed for change. It might not be change that ever reaches to the "big-time" programs of Division I, but if a different model is coming for the sys-tem of collegiate sport, small colleges and universities such as Spelman might well be where it begins.

## Discussion

Is moving out of the NCAA a viable alternative for most schools? Are there other organizations that could help facilitate intercollegiate athletics in more productive ways or is the NCAA the best model?

### NOTES

1. In the most recent release of the USA Today (2015) database that summarizes NCAA finances, some smaller colleges and universities report receiving subsidies from student fees, direct and indirect institutional support, and state money that amounts to over 90% of program revenues. In total subsidy amounts this can reach over $35 million at certain institutions.
2. The NCAA (n.d.) states "More than 170,000 student-athletes at 444 institutions make up Division III, the largest NCAA division both in number of participants and number of schools" (¶7).
3. My alma mater, the University of Maryland, will be spending reportedly close to $5 million dollars on head coach salaries in 2016 as they hired DJ Durkin to lead the football team while buying out previous coach Randy Edsall's contract.

### REFERENCES

Antin, T. J., & Hunt, G. (2013). Embodying both stigma and satisfaction: An interview study of African American women. *Critical Public Health*, *23*(1), 17–31.

Associated Press. (2012, November 1). Spelman picks fitness over sports. Retrieved June 19, 2017, from http://espn.go.com/college-sports/story/_/id/8581578/spelman-college-cuts-all-sports-chooses-fitness

Cheek, J. (2008). Healthism: A new conservatism? *Qualitative Health Research*, 18, pp. 974.

Cooper, C. G., & Weight, E. A. (2011). An examination of administrators' nonrevenue, Olympic program values within NCAA athletic departments. *Journal of Intercollegiate Sport*, *4*(2), 247–260.

Crawford, R. (1980). Healthism and the medicalization of everyday life. *International Journal of Health Services*, 10(3), 365–388.

Cyphers, L. (2013, April 16). A different world: How one small college is quitting sports—and might lead a revolution. Retrieved June 19, 2017, from http://www.sbnation.com/longform/2013/4/16/4226848/colleges-leaving-ncaa-dropping-athletics

Davis, T. (2010). Reaction to "An economic look at the sustainability of FBS Athletic Departments": Implications for Reform. *Journal of Intercollegiate Sport*, *3*(1), 22–27.

Evans, J., Rich, E., & Davies, B. (2004). The emperor's new clothes: Fat, thin, and overweight. The social fabrication of risk and ill health. *Journal of Teaching in Physical Education*, 23(4), 372–391.

Gard, M. (2009). "Friends, enemies and the cultural politics of critical obesity research," in J Wright & V Harwood (eds.), Biopolitics and the 'obesity epidemic': governing bodies, Routledge, New York, pp. 31–44.

Getz, M., & Siegfried, J. J. (2010). What does intercollegiate athletics do to or for colleges and universities? (Vanderbilt University Department of Economics Working Papers, 1005). Nashville, TN: Vanderbilt University Department of Economics.

Grasgreen, A. (November 1, 2012). Beyond sports. Retrieved June 19, 2017, from https://www.insidehighered.com/news/2012/11/01/spelman-eliminates-athletics-favor-campus-wide-wellness-initiative

Halvorson, R. (2013). College cuts sports, focuses on fitness. *IDEA Fitness Journal, 10*(2), 16.

Hoffer, A., & Pincin, J. A. (2015). The effects of revenue changes on NCAA athletic departments' expenditures. *Journal of Sport and Social Issues, 40*(1), pp. 1–21.

Hoffer, A., Humphreys, B. R., Lacombe, D. J., & Ruseki, J. E. (2015). Trends in NCAA athletic spending: Arms race or rising tide? *Journal of Sports Economics,* 16(6), pp. 576–596.

Hogshead-Makar, N. (2010). Attitudes, platitudes and the collegiate sports arms race: Unsustainable spending and its consequences for Olympic and women's sports. *Journal of Intercollegiate Sport, 3*(1), 69–80.

Humphreys, B. R., & Mondello, M. (2007). Intercollegiate athletic success and donations at NCAA Division I institutions. *Journal of Sport Management,* 21, pp. 265–280.

Kelly, D., & Dixon, M. A. (2011). Becoming a "real university:" The strategic benefits of adding football for NCAA Division I institutions. *Journal of Intercollegiate Sport,* 4, pp. 283–303.

King-White, R., Newman, J. I. & Giardina, M. (2013). Articulating fatness: Obesity, neoliberalism, and the scientific tautologies of bodily accumulation. *The Review of Education, Pedagogy, and Cultural Studies* 35(2), 79–102.

Knight Commission on Intercollegiate Athletics (2009, October). College sports 101: A primer on money, athletics, and higher education in the 21st century, 1–29.

Lupton, D. (2013). Quantifying the body: Monitoring and measuring health in the age of health technologies. *Critical Public Health,* 23(4), pp. 393–403.

McDermott, L. (2007). A governmental analysis of children "at risk" in a world of physical inactivity and obesity epidemics. *Sociology of Sport Journal,* 24, pp. 302–324.

Murray, S. (2008). Pathologizing "fatness": Medical authority and popular culture. *Sociology of Sport Journal,* 25, pp. 7–21.

New, J. (2014, October 15). Fitness without athletics. Retrieved June 19, 2017, from https://www.insidehighered.com/news/2014/10/15/spelman-college-builds-student-health-initiative-years-after-leaving-ncaa

Pope, D. G., & Pope, J. C. (2009). The impact of college sports success on the quantity and quality of student applications. *Southern Economic Journal,* 75(3), pp. 750–780.

Pieterse, A. L. & Carter, R. T. (2010). An exploratory investigation of the relationship between racism, racial identity, perceptions of health, and health locus of control among black American women. *Journal of Health Care for the Poor and Underserved,* 21(1), pp. 334–348.

Rich, E., & Evans, J. (2005). "Fat ethics"—The obesity discourse and body politics. *Social Theory and Health,* 3, pp. 341–358.

Rosenberg, L., Palmer, J. R., Adams-Campbell, L. L., & Rao, R. S. (1999). Obesity and hypertension among college-educated black women in the United States. *Journal of Human Hypertension,* 13(4), 237–241.

Singer, J. N. (2008). Benefits and detriments of African American male athletes' participation in a big-time college football program. *International Review for the Sociology of Sport,* 43(4), pp. 399–408.

Smith, S. J., & Easterlow, D. (2005). The strange geography of health inequalities. *Transactions of the Institute of British Geographers,* 30, pp. 173–190.

Southall, R. M., & Staurowsky, E. J. (2013). Cheering on the collegiate model: Creating, disseminating, and imbedding the NCAA's redefinition of amateurism. *Journal of Sport and Social Issues,* 37(4), pp. 403–429.

Spelman College. (2016). About Spelman College. Retrieved June 19, 2017, from http://www
.spelman.edu/about-us

Tierney, M. (April 14, 2013). At a college, dropping sports in favor of fitness. Retrieved from
http://www.nytimes.com/2013/04/14/sports/at-spelman-dropping-sports-in-favor-of
-fitness.html?_r=0

Trainer, S., Brewis, A., Hruschka, D., & Williams, D. (2015). Translating obesity: Navigating
the front lines of the "war on fat." *American Journal of Human Biology, 27*(1), 61–68.

Tsitsos, W., & Nixon, H. L. (2012). The star wars arms race in college athletics: Coaches' pay
and athletic program status. *Journal of Sport and Social Issues,* 36(1), pp. 68–88.

USA Today. (2015). NCAA Finances. Retrieved June 19, 2017, from http://sports.usatoday
.com/ncaa/finances/

Van Rheenen, D. (2012). Exploitation in college sports: Race, revenue, and educational
reward *International Review for the Sociology of Sport, 48*(5): pp. 550–571.

Zanker, C., & Gard, M. (2008). Fatness, fitness and the moral universe of sport and physical
activity, *Sociology of Sport Journal,* 25, 48–65.

Zimbalist, A. (2010). Dollar dilemmas during the downturn: A financial crossroads for college sports. *Journal of Intercollegiate Sport 3*, 111–124.

# 8

## Confessions of a Human Trafficker

### Inside the Global Network (of International Student-Athletes in NCAA Football)

ADAM BEISSEL

The prominence and competitive success of international student-athletes (ISAs) is a growing trend in United States collegiate athletics (Love & Kim, 2011; Zonder, 2013). Over the past decade, there has been a nearly threefold increase in the number of ISAs coming to the United States to compete in National Collegiate Athletic Association (NCAA) athletics. The NCAA estimated that in 1999–2000, approximately 3,589 ISAs competed in NCAA-sponsored athletic competitions (Zgonc, 2010), but by 2009–2010, the number of ISAs participating in Division I, II, and III NCAA athletics had risen to 17,635, or more than 10% of the total student–athlete population (Jara, 2015). Although, as a percentage of the total student-athlete population this number is relatively low, certain sports in particular have a greater concentration of ISAs. Foreign-born athletes have a significant presence in "non-revenue sports" such as golf, skiing, swimming, and soccer (Hoffer, 1994; Weston, 2006), with ISAs dominating the NCAA national championships in tennis, as well as in track and field (Drape, 2006; Hall, 2015; Shannon, 2014). The proliferation and success of ISAs in collegiate sport and their profound domination of particular sports, has resulted in ISAs becoming the "new face of college sports" (Wilson & Wolverton, 2008).

Although the numbers are not as high, the number of ISAs is growing fast in revenue-sports such as football and basketball, as the "college football arms race" is on, and the increasing pressures for coaches to field competitive teams and "win-at-all-cost" philosophy leads them to fill their rosters with the most talented athletes they can find. International players, once a rarity in college football, are now commonplace. This, in part, is due to changes in NCAA rules, a simplified student visa process, and a growing international scouting network. In football, where the "collegiate sports–industrial complex" (Martin, Fasching-Varner, & Hartlep, 2017) and "billion-dollar ball" (Gaul, 2015) engender a big-money culture in college football with intense competitiveness, coaches—seeking to exploit a market inefficiency—have begun mining the globe for sources of untapped talent and undervalued athletic labor, and leaving no stone unturned (Beissel, 2015). The search for and recruitment of prospective student-athletes from around the world is so commonplace and important to maintaining program success, that you would be hard pressed to find at least one Top 25 DI NCAA collegiate football team without at least one ISA. The global recruitment of elite football talent is recurring; as college programs find more positive results with their international prospects, they devote more resources to keep their international-talent pipelines flowing. Perhaps no place in the world has been mined for elite collegiate football talent more so than the furtive American Samoan football fields.

This chapter presents an auto-ethnographic account regarding the author's complex and contradictory position from inside the global recruitment of ISAs as a volunteer assistant football coach with one of American Samoa's most talent-rich gridiron football programs—one that has consistently developed, produced, and exported dozens of elite athletic talent prospects for NCAA football programs. Based on firsthand fieldwork from "inside the trenches," the author critically interrogates and problematizes the global recruiting networks of NCAA football athlete prospects. These networks position athletes as commodities for capital accumulation, coaches as international marketers with portfolios of human capital for sale, and intercollegiate institutions as corporate firms scouring the globe for the next unexploited and underdeveloped talent market to outsource labor.

This chapter relies on a series of brief "confessions"—deeply personal, reflective, and introspective narratives gathered by the author while functioning in a dual role as researcher and football coach inside the global recruitment system of ISA football players. The chapter is a call to action for sincere reform, oversight, and greater transparency by the NCAA to resolve the—at times—highly secretive, immoral, unethical, and exploitative practices involved in ISA gridiron football player recruitment. It is hoped that research and future research like this—gathered from inside the global recruiting networks of ISAs—will encourage the NCAA and member institutions to implement a consistent global amateur standard that does not simply focus on academics and keeping players eligible. Rather, that it makes a policy and series of protections and reforms that protect the vulnerability of ISAs and promotes a more transparent, humane, and ethical system for recruiting ISAs.

## The Rise of the ISA (in American College Football)

Given the greatly increasing prominence and dominance of ISAs, the competitive recruitment of elite student-athlete prospects domestically, and the immense pressure to have winning intercollegiate athletics programs, the exponential growth of international student-athletes has increased drastically in recent years. Prospective student-athletes from all over the world come to the United States to earn the benefit of college education in exchange for their athletic labor. Each year an estimated 3,000 new ISAs join member institutions. The trend toward increasing internationalization of student-athletes has been historically concentrated in particular sports. In NCAA tennis, for example, "36.8 percent of women's tennis teams and 35.5 percent of men's tennis squads were comprised of athletes from outside of the U.S. in 2008–09" (Zgonc, 2010, p. 91), and "14 percent of female golfers, 13 percent of all skiers, and 10 percent of male soccer players in 2005–06 were foreign-born" (Wilson & Wolverton, 2008, ¶7). In addition to increasing participation rates, international athletes have dominated in individual sport competitions, leading teams and athletic programs to championship achievements in men and women's sports.

During the 2005–2006 NCAA season, 63 of the top 100 men's singles players and 47 of the top 100 women's players were ISAs, and they constituted more than 40% of the swimming field at the 2005 swimming championships (Weston, 2006). Perhaps no sport has been influenced by the increasing internationalization of student-athletes quite like track and field, where the "foreign invasion" (Smith, 2011) of ISAs in the sport has become a topic of concern in long-distance running competitions. After seven of the top eight finishers at the 2013 Division I indoor nationals were ISAs, proposals have been introduced to "cap" the number of "foreign mercenaries" or the age of an incoming athlete, to address what has been described as "an uneven playing field" and to preserve scholarship opportunities for American students (Lindaman, 2013). Recognizing the growing impact that foreign-born players have on the NCAA, the organization recently loosened some of the restrictions punishing international players who had trained with professional players overseas, making it easier for coaches to recruit foreign players without worrying about whether they are eligible to play in college (Kosmider, 2014). Now, NCAA student-athletes come from all over the world. Canada, Australia, Europe, and South America are the most common home countries, but it is hard to find a country that has not sent athletes to U.S. colleges and universities.

Though by no means the most likely place to find ISAs, college football's growth as an international spectacle has introduced the game to global markets and future student-athletes. NCAA peer institutions hold annual games in a broad array of locations outside of the United States, providing alumni and fans exotic travel locations and—more importantly—creating a set of conditions in which universities possess a brand identity necessary to extend their recruiting footprint. A few examples of these contests are California and Hawaii in Sydney, Australia (2016); Penn State and Central Florida in Dublin, Ireland (2012); Notre Dame and Navy (2012) in Dublin, Ireland; and an annual postseason "bowl game" held in the Bahamas. College football coaches and scouts taken advantage of this newfound global exposure by seeking those new consumers-turned-participants at the amateur level. Recruiting international amateur football talent is paying big dividends with several amateur college football players making it all the way to the National Football League (NFL) (e.g., Bjoern Werner, Germany; Ezekiel "Ziggy" Ansah, Ghana; Jay Ajayi, England; Jesse Williams and Brad Wing, Australia). Interestingly, the most visible and recognizable foreign-born footballers in the collegiate and professional ranks are American Samoans.

Indeed, the U.S. territory has developed from a largely ignored site for potential athletes into a fully developed global football labor market—supplying coaches and scouts with players via what has come to be known as the "Polynesian pipeline." Just how much elite football talent does American Samoa produce? It is estimated that a boy born to Samoan parents is as much as 56 times more likely to make it to the National Football League (NFL) than a boy born anywhere else in the United States (Pelley, 2010). At the collegiate level, *Sports Illustrated* estimated a few years ago that of the 800 boys who graduated from high school on the island between 2002 and 2003, an estimated 97 left to play football at a two- or four-year college in the United States—1 out of every 8 high school football players (Syken, 2003). It was estimated that there were more than 200 amateur football players of Samoan descent honing their talents at colleges and universities in college football by the 2015 season opener. These players were drawn from a pool of less than 500,000 self-identified Samoans around the world—only half of whom reside in locations where American football is accessible (Sager, 2015).

The over-representative volume of players coming directly from American Samoa (as opposed to the more accustomed paths that detour through the mainland or Hawai'i) has proliferated with the formulation of Field House 100 American Samoa (FH100); a nonprofit organization designed to help football players in American Samoa secure college scholarships through sports. By promoting the island's top athletic talent to interested college football talent scouts, the organization from 2011 to 2013 placed more than 100 American Samoan football players in colleges, amounting to an estimated US$4 million in scholarships (Hayner, 2012). More than a dozen of these are scholarships at the FBS level of Division I collegiate football, and include such universities as Oregon State, UNLV, Washington State, Hawai'i, Arizona, San Diego State, and Boise State. One football program—Washington State University—has established a Polynesian pipeline like no other, with 15 Polynesian players on the roster—or nearly 20% of the entire roster. Despite long odds, several American Samoans make the leap from college to professional, and the general public is beginning to notice. More to the point, 5 of the first 66 players selected in the NFL's 2015 draft are of Polynesian heritage, leading some to label American Samoa the "Dominican of the NFL" (Carter, 2004).

Although few coaches, fans, or athletic program administrators would dispute that recruiting ISA talent can bring greater success and, more importantly, increase the diversity of the collegiate-sports landscape, the competitive success of ISAs and the global recruitment of amateur athletes is gaining increasing attention and, in some cases, scrutiny from college coaches, players, parents, member institutions, fans, commentators, and scholars (Weston, 2006). The growing number of ISAs and in U.S. collegiate athletics and their particularly high concentration in certain sports presents several issues related to their adjustment, recruitment, and the applicability of a global academic standard. More specifically, because no global amateur standard exists, the increase in the number of ISAs presents complicated—and sometimes controversial—eligibility determinations. As Weston (2006) argues, "the different international education programs and athletic systems, coupled with language barriers, varied standards, and inconsistent record-keeping, can lead to uncertain assessments of an ISA's eligibility" (p. 832). The eligibility standard for a NCAA-sponsored intercollegiate athlete rests on two bedrock principles: athletes must be amateurs, and they must be students. According to NCAA bylaws, any individual who pursues sport as a vocation, even if the individuals fails at that pursuit, shall not be permitted in intercollegiate athletics.

In contrast, however, the European model of sport is sponsored through a club-based system, with a national sport federation as its governing body. The NCAA nation of amateurism is not a concept that is involved in the rules, regulations, or procedural aspects in these non-U.S. athletic federations. Complicating matters is the fact that most club systems are financed through membership fees, corporate sponsors, and government funding. Thus, there are inherent complexities and contradictions for countries where national sport policies and the European club model of sport is structured in such a way that young athletes are provided coaching, facility, and monetary resources from local and regional sport organizations to support their development (Pierce, 2007). This leads to many problems when attempting to apply the NCAAA amateurism bylaws to ISAs, and provided the impetus for some to call for reform.

The overarching theme for change is that "the NCAA, in conjunction with other sports organizations around the globe, ought to develop a global amateurism standard for the purposes of intercollegiate athletic competition" (Abbey-Pinegar, 2010, p. 344). Eligibility issues for ISAs are so complex that they remain the sole concern for the NCAA. In other words, despite the growing numbers and prominence of ISAs in college sport little focus has been on how these student-athletes end up in the United States, and what coaches and athletic departments do to recruit them.

## Literature on International Student-Athletes

Academic inquiry on the topic of the global migration and international recruitments of ISAs in collegiate sport in the United States is in its "relative infancy"

(Love & Kim, 2011, p. 91). One of the first major works focusing on the migration of athletes to elite U.S. colleges and universities was John Bale's (1991) book, *The Brawn Drain*. In this book, Bale examined the early emergence of foreign student-athletes finding their ways to U.S. colleges and universities as a form of talent migration. Through methods including surveys and interviews, Bale sought to provide insight into such questions as the number of international athletes attending American universities, where these individuals came from, and how they adjusted to American life. Bale (1991) identified what he called a "talent pipeline" producing a steady influx of foreign student-athletes to NCAA athletics, with some universities and coaches building connections with specific countries. He also suggests some ISAs are unsatisfied with the facilities and coaches available in their home countries, leading them to pursue opportunities elsewhere.

Contemporary research on ISAs has been mostly concerned with the possible motivations and selection process of the international student-athlete regarding this labor migration, and less concerned with ISA experiences and adjustment to U.S colleges and universities. Some of these studies examined the motivations of the international student-athlete in comparison to the domestic student-athlete (e.g., Popp, Hums, & Greenwell, 2009; Popp, Pierce, & Hums, 2011). Research also demonstrates that ISAs look at university sport participation from a different perspective than that of domestic student-athletes, placing a greater importance on academic achievement and a lesser emphasis on the competitive aspect of university competition (Popp, Hums, & Greenwell, 2009; Popp, Pierce, & Hums, 2011). In 2011, Love and Kim studied the motivations of migrant college athletes coming to the United States, adapting prior typologies of global athletic labor migration as a conceptual framework for understanding the increase of ISAs in college athletics. Common themes emerging from their analysis included: improved financial situations, desire to experience different cultures, and a preference to remain in the United States after their collegiate careers were over to pursue graduate coursework or employment.

Other studies have focused on the interpersonal motivation of ISAs to determine why ISAs choose to participate in intercollegiate sport within the United States (Garant-Jones et al., 2009). Berry (1999) determined that both male and female ISAs were motivated by athletic factors; however, motivational factors differed based on their region of origin. Garant-Jones et al. (2009) surveyed 212 ISAs and found that they were motivated by four factors, namely (1) attractiveness of intercollegiate athletics, (2) attractiveness of the school, (3) desire for independency, and (4) attractiveness of the environment. In conjunction, these two studies corroborated the notion that international student-athletes were motivated differently based on the sport they played and the global region of their respective native country.

The factors that influence ISA college selection differ from those that influence general student-athletes regarding college selection. Although numerous researchers have examined the factors in the college-selection process for domestic student-athletes (Kankey & Quarterman, 2007; Letawsky, Schneider, Pedersen, & Palmer, 2003), there is little research on the global recruitment and recruiting process of ISAs. Regarding the selection process of international student-athletes, scholarship has been shown to be a major motivation (Popp, Pierce, & Hums, 2011), as has the opportunity to obtain a degree from an American university, and the chance to stay in the United States after graduation (Love & Kim, 2011; Popp, Hums, & Greenwell, 2009). Some found academic factors, such as majors offered and academic reputation of the school, to be the most important variables for student-athletes (Goss et al., 2006; Kankey & Quarterman, 2007; Letawsky et al., 2003; Mathes & Gurney, 1985). Others found athletic components such as the amount of scholarship money offered (Doyle & Gaeth, 1990), the level of competition (Judson et al., 2004), and the coaches (Gabert et al., 1999; Klenosky et al., 2001) as the most influential elements during the recruiting process. Additional college selection factors rating highly in these studies included: (a) the college campus, (b) teammates, (c) school location, (d) social atmosphere, (e) potential playing time, (f) athletic facilities, and (g) support services available. Popp et al. (2011) has identified that the value of an athletic scholarship, the coach's personality, and academics are some of the most important items for ISAs when it comes to school choice. Remillard (2014) identified two primary student-athlete college selection factors: social and institutional. The former involves recruits selecting an athletic program based on personal and family relationships cultivated by coaches and scouts through persistent contact over the recruitment period. In terms of institutional factors, the academic status and program success have proven to be primary influences in selection process for ISAs (Remillard, 2014).

Although research on the motivations and selection process of ISAs is relatively substantial, there is an absence of scholarship on ISA experiences with the recruitment process and cross-cultural adjustment to U.S. campuses. Ridinger and Pastore (2000) analyzed the adjustment of ISAs to U.S. colleges by comparing them to those international non-student-athletes and domestic student-athletes. Building on this previous study, Popp et al. (2011) further refined the initial model of ISA development developed by Ridinger and Pastore's (2000), finding new dimensions including (a) a sense of adventure, (b) previous international travel experience, and (c) family influences. Zonder (2011) examined student-athlete perspectives on the internationalization of college athletics on both the domestic and international student-athlete experience and identified differences in the recruitment process. She found that ISAs are placed at a recruiting disadvantage with most coaches being risk averse in athlete recruitment, leading them to strongly preferring the certainty of domestic student-athletes over the potential of international ones. Moreover, Zonder found that ISAs place a stronger emphasis on academics and locations, whereas domestic student-athletes are primarily concerned with the personality of the coach, the program, and teammates.

More recently, Jara (2015) examined how and why coaches establish personal networks for ISA recruitment, success rates, and destinations of foreign recruitment. Although the recruiting success rate is consistent among domestic and international student-athletes (usually a 5-to 1-ratio), Jara found that the probability of recruiting ISAs improves to nearly a 1-to-1 ratio when players are recommended by the coach's personal network. Thus, international recruiting networks and personal contacts are believed to play a leading role in ISA, recruitment and Jara calls for more research examining the formation and effectiveness of international recruiting networks in creating successful athletic programs. Indeed, only 42% of all ISAs ever met the coach in person before attending their university, a number that is far greater in a place like American Samoa (Zonder, 2013).

Although these studies have provided some important insights, research still is necessary to improve our understanding of the establishment of international recruiting networks; the recruiting experiences of international student-athletes; and the role coaches, college recruiters, and international talent scouts play in the recruitment process. If we accept the premise that the recruitment of international football talent and prospects in the "college arms race" is more about the success of schools and programs, and less about serving personal and educational interests of ISAs, then what does this system of ISA recruitment look like from the inside? How do those people in positions of power within the global recruiting networks of ISAs control the right of movement of foreign-born athletic talent? How do they achieve consent for the recruitment and transfer from aspirant young footballers to enter freely into the NCAA's corrupt system of exploitation based on the lure of a "free" education? What rights and agency do these ISAs possess? To what degree do these coaches operate through coercion, deception, and prey on the vulnerabilities of young people? And how is the NCAA complicit in supporting this entire system of exploitation by focusing on global amateur standards and academic eligibility rather than the collective rights and interests of foreign-born athletes?

## Methods for Understanding the American Samoan
## Football Experience

In an attempt to answer these questions, this project used a qualitative inductive framework for collecting and analyzing empirical information to present an interpretive, naturalistic understanding the social world. The epistemological approach of qualitative researchers is to take seriously the narratives that individuals generate in order to understand the relationship between the researcher and respondent as reciprocal, in which both parties are involved in

a process of the co-creation of meaning (Denzin & Lincoln, 1994). The qualitative researcher questions the relationship between the nature of knowledge and scientific/observable evidence. Therefore, "reality" is understood to
be constructed through human interaction, a product of our experiences and
meanings we create, and social life is composed of multiple realities that have
multiple meanings and interpretations to different people. Qualitative research
is an interdisciplinary field of inquiry that cuts across several disciplines and
fields of research. Additionally, qualitative research is multi-paradigmatic in
nature and is sensitive to multiple practices for collecting empirical material to
make the world visible.

Unlike quantitative researchers—who often focus on artificially controlled
laboratory situations using deductive reasoning—qualitative researchers must
venture "out into the world" to interact directly with people and events to obtain
empirical material for their studies. In qualitative research, questions are not
determined in advance, and emphasis is placed on "the qualities of entities and
on processes and meanings that are not experimentally examined or measured"
(Denzin & Lincoln, 2005, p. 3). The qualitative researcher seeks information from
the phenomenon in question by asking people and observing actual situations
to understand the meanings and practices of the lived experience and must
"make sense of, or interpret, phenomena in terms of the meanings people bring
to them" (Denzin & Lincoln, 2005, p. 3). Thus, the qualitative researcher always
is a "situated observer" seeking information "directly," whose background and
social location influences the research process and shapes the research results.

To articulate the shared meanings, practices, and experiences of multiple
material realities for American Samoan footballers, I employ multiple qualitative approaches and practices to "situate" the phenomenon under investigation
within its context. I draw upon Denzin's (1997) interpretive ethnography framework as methodological practice to generate "thick descriptions and accounts"
of the networks of shared meanings and "interworked system of constructible
signs" (Gertz, 1973, p. 14) that constitute reality in a particular community, based
on voices heard and observations recorded in the field. As Denzin (1997) writes,
ethnography is a "form of inquiry and writing that produces descriptions and
accounts about the ways of life of the writer and those written about" (p. xi).
While recognizing the open, flexible, and permissible boundaries of interpretive ethnography, the goal is to map the social context.

Additionally, this project is informed by—and borrows from—Madison's
(2005) work on critical ethnography that applies critical theory to unsettle
"both neutrality and taken-for-granted assumptions by bringing to light underlying and obscure operations of power and control" (p. 5). Critical ethnography
"is political and pedagogical in its approach to examine people's cultural meanings and practices shape experiences of injustice, prejudice, and stereotyping in
people's daily lives" (p. xi). Critical ethnography incorporates reflexive inquiry

into its methodology by linking the situated researcher to those being studied and thus is inseparable from the social context. This allows for the qualitative researcher to not only capture articulation of meaning, but also for the situated observer to at times intervene into the asymmetric, iniquitous, and oppressive relations of power bound up in the networks of meaning in social reality.

To study the diffuse networks working to shape how American Samoan football prospects are recruited, I became a situated observer of the phenomenon to fully experience the interrelated political, social, cultural, and economic forces contributing to it. More specifically, Coach Paul, the head football coach of the Eastern High School Raiders (both pseudonyms), invited me to serve as a volunteer assistant high school football coach for the entire 2010 season after extensive conversations regarding my research. Coach Paul is a very influential figure in the American Samoa football community, and well-known as a very good football coach. As a participant-observer within the cultural production of the American Samoan football spectacle, I was provided unique and unprecedented access to interpret the lived experience within the community through multimethod approaches techniques for studying the naturalistic world.

Although specific responsibilities with the Eastern football program varied and evolved through the course of the study, they generally included—but were certainly not limited to—on-field coaching and athlete training; team tactics and strategy development; advanced scouting; game-day operations; film editing; multimedia publishing; academic advisement and tutoring; and managing purchasing and program financials. Throughout the duration of my fieldwork, I used a multimethod approach of collecting empirical materials: participant observation; structured/semi-structured interviews; detailed field notes; daily journal entries; photos/video/audio recordings; and informal dialogues and research collaborations with knowledgeable individuals. These manifold methods of empirical material collection allowed for a maximum variation sampling of texts that could cut across a vast array of experiences, performances, and subjectivities related to the American Samoan football. The wealth of empirical evidence (i.e., social relations, practices, and lived experiences) allowed for a new interpretive framework to emerge and make sense of the football phenomenon—including the international recruitment and relocation of players to U.S. colleges and universities.

This was not a passive and unobtrusive ethnographic observation. Rather, as an assistant football coach I could critically examine and interpret those subjugating forces (e.g., politics, power, praxis) acting upon the socially-constructed American Samoan footballing body from within the site of cultural production. At the same time, as a volunteer coach, my researcher co-presence was at once subjected to, and indeed (re)constitutive of, dominant power relations operating within the circuits of American Samoan football production. Given my complicated position and negotiation of roles in the field, and dealing with vulnerable human subjects (i.e., young people), I carefully considered the ethical conduct of my research, resting unequivocally on the following five principles: respect for dignity; free and informed consent; vulnerable persons; privacy and confidentiality; and justice and inclusiveness.

Throughout my ethnographic fieldwork, I experienced questionable, unethical, and immoral practices by people in positions of power within the circuits of football production. At times, I conscientiously objected to what I was asked to do, and intervened into various exertions of power and unethical behavior without compromising my researcher self. In other moments, I was complicit in the abuse of power and subjugation toward vulnerable young people by Coach Paul and others involved in the recruitment process, for fear of losing my insider status. Thus, I did the best I could to ameliorate these uncomfortable and undesired inheritances of power over the researcher subject—again, without exposing myself as a cultural outsider—by critically reflecting upon the moral and ethical concerns of the duties required by my position as assistant football coach through self-reflective writing.

In the end, and following King-White's (2013) framework for conducting a good physical cultural ethnography, I owed it to young aspirant young footballers to do best by and for them. In this case, most wanted nothing more than to "make it off the rock" and earn a college scholarship by playing football. The balance of this chapter provides a glimpse inside the ISAs recruiting networks from the author's season inside the American Samoan football spectacle. These insights are presented through a series of "confessions" adapted from my ethnographic field notes and journal entries where I discuss the unethical and immoral practices of ISA recruitment.

### Confession 1: The Act—I Was Pressured to Falsify Measurables and Manipulate Video Materials to Misrepresent Football Player Proficiencies

For an aspirant college football player, nothing is more critical to his personal and financial future than the highlight video. This video typically is a 4- to 5-minute composite of the selectively edited film demonstrating the player's sporting prowess, on-field accomplishments, and a fluidity of movement. College recruiters and scouts are sent thousands of individual players' films every year, and these are dissected, analyzed, and catalogued by coaching staffs. As one college football coach told me, "the film don't lie." Given the sheer volume of players and game films, coaches have precious little patience to watch an entire film. As one coach said, all they care about is "the first five plays." For nearly all footballers in American Samoa—which, again, is located some 5,000 miles from the west coast of California—they will never meet a college football coach and recruiter personally. The vast majority of football prospects have zero communication with college football coaches, minimal support networks in the United States, and little knowledge of a university's academic requirements, and even where it might be located. Their film is all they have. It is their currency in the global marketplace of international footballers.

My primary responsibility as a volunteer assistant coach with the Raiders football program was as a football analyst. In this role, I would use film-editing software to create advanced scouting reports and render player portfolios for multi-media marketing to college recruiters and talent scouts. Following each game, I would analyze digital film recordings by creating exhaustive logs of every play occurring during the game—both for our team and all others in the league—and identify tendencies of our opponents to be exploited in the next game plan. Throughout the week, Coach Paul would rely on my predictive modeling of player tendencies and coaching biases to implement cutting edge strategy to maximize the win expectancy for our team.

Once this weekly task was completed, I was charged with selectively manipulating existing digital film on our own players for the purpose of creating "highlight videos" for international talent scouts and collegiate coaches. Using stylistic editing (e.g., music, lighting, text) I would cast highly mediated and selectively edited renderings of player's performances and abilities. Once finished, I would load all of the films onto a team-based YouTube channel, and Coach Paul would directly email links to his U.S. collegiate coaching contacts on the mainland. The players had little input or knowledge of the responsibilities demanded of me by Coach Paul. Indeed, as I have written elsewhere, the coach used the digital video camera as means of surveillance to further his own disciplinarily structures and apparatus with the team (Beissel, 2015). Athletes largely were kept in the dark about my methods of filmmaking, and had little contribution to their depiction as a talented footballer in the film. I was granted control over so much of their fate.

Under Coach Paul's guidance and careful observation, I was given explicit instructions to render favorable highlight videos to increase the marketability of football talent. I was directed to disclose personal and confidential information such as height-weight measurements, 40-yard dash times, and Scholastic Assessment Test (SAT) scores by posting them along with the highlight videos. More problematically, I was given explicit instructions to manipulate these figures to create favorable depictions for our players. Heights and weights were inflated; 40-yard dash times became faster; and students' SAT score were inflated beyond realistic levels. Video clips showing poor play were not included in a recruit's highlight video. Bad behavior and personal fouls were stricken from the record. In one instance I was instructed to use a video clip of one player's on-field performance and pass it off as that of a different player on the team. Coach Paul often would tell me, "anything to get these kids recruited."

Standardized testing is a major barrier for American Samoan football recruits to getting college scholarship offers, as many recruits immediately are rejected due to poor performance on the SAT. This, in many cases, is a byproduct of a system of injustice. Samoan is the most common language spoken in household and in everyday conversation in American Samoa, and students rightfully struggle on the SAT because they do not have a basic mastery of the English language, and cannot understand the instructions. Because the U.S. territory recognizes English as its official language, however, the NCAA will not accept the Test of English as a Foreign Language (TOEFL) to assess the knowledge of non-English speakers who want to enroll in English-speaking universities. This irregularity worked to penalize American Samoans applying to colleges and universities on the U.S. mainland, whether the student intends to play football or otherwise.

Feeling undermined by the system, Coach Paul would inflate SAT scores and speak to a football prospect's intellectual abilities in an effort to present a more accurate rendering of a prospect's academics. Was this justice for players undone by an unjust system? Perhaps, but it also was not the truth. Of course, standardized tests scores be later would be verified by the NCAA eligibility center. But as Coach Paul told me, once a college coach or talent evaluator becomes enamored with a football player's abilities, there suddenly would be many options for him. These fibs—though seemingly minor on their own—bred a culture of deception in the international recruitment of American Samoan football prospects.

Although I felt strongly that public disclosure of personal information violated player's privacy rights, and the unethical behavior of deceiving schools and football recruiters with the use of false player data and media representations put me in a precarious position. In my dual role as researcher and coach, I was placed in the uncomfortable situation of having power over these kids' footballing futures, and at the same time, was subject to the power and authority of the coach and a system of exploitation and deception. These types of research bargains are not unfamiliar to the qualitative researcher in the field. Yet, for me, I never grew comfortable being asked to be complicit in a system of deception and lies. Just how did I reconcile doing what I felt was right with the requirements of the job? In the end, I did what I determined was in the best interest of the players, their family, and the community. That was to comply with the directives of the Coach Paul and the system of exploitation because what was most important to football prospects was to secure a scholarship from U.S. mainland colleges and universities.

### Confession 2: The Means—I Witnessed Coercion, the Use of Force, and the Concealment of Information Needed to Make Informed Decisions in the College-Selection Process

As time progressed, and my analytical and editing skills received praised by Coach Paul, player parents, and the players themselves, I grew closely connected with the college coaches and talent scouts involved in the football recruiting process. On many occasions throughout my time in American Samoa, the Eastern football program would receive unsolicited mail and phone calls from college coaches and recruiting coordinators from obscure mainland college football programs seeking to establish a Polynesian pipeline of football recruits. On the surface, there is, nothing illegal or immoral with this practice. Mainland football programs are seeking undiscovered sources of football talent, and they are willing to provide an opportunity to prospective football players who would otherwise go undiscovered and unrecruited. This mutual exchange—the player gets an education in exchange for their football labor power—seemingly would benefit both constituencies; the football player looking to get off the rock, and the football coach or program looking to establish a foothold in American Samoa for future football capital.

Given that the most dominant and recognizable Division I NCAA football programs can recruit the mainland successfully without taking the risk on a raw talent from American Samoa, however, the majority of programs contacting the Eastern football program typically were not nationally reputable. These programs often were unrecognizable and marginally competitive DI universities, small regional colleges, and two-year junior colleges collectively operating on meager athletics budgets offering previous little athlete support to manage the academics and adjustment of recruits. Put simply, these were schools that nobody had ever heard of.

Coach Paul's success with getting his players recruited off the rock created a context where he had been granted unchecked power and responsibility to appraise all scholarship offers. If you wanted to recruit a player from the Eastern football program, you had to go through him. To this point, Coach Paul had been, without question, successful in sending his best players to mainland universities throughout the years, and the community was deeply indebted to him for the transformative opportunities he worked to provide for young men in American Samoa. Coach Paul received no personal or economic gains for the types of life-changing opportunities he provided for his players, rather his benefit was a form of social capital in the American Samoan community.

Although he possessed impressive experience dealing with collegiate coaches and recruiters, and possessed a vast personal network of college coaches of whom he trusted, I found that he had little understanding of the academic standards of U.S. universities, and scarce knowledge of the cultural adjustment for students once arriving on the U.S. mainland. More problematically, he alone communicated with college coaches and assessed college scholarship offers without the consent, knowledge, and input of parents and the players themselves.

It was easy to discern that Coach Paul had complete control over the entire recruiting process and withheld important information for the football prospect regarding the recruitment, transfer, and destination of these schools from various stakeholders (most notably from the players themselves). At times, I would witness him use these scholarship offers and his position of power in the recruitment process to threaten and coerce and players onto the playing field. If a player did not conform to his authority, then the player would be disciplined by losing a college scholarship. These recurrent abuses of power crystalized Coach Paul's position of influence in the wider international recruiting networks of football students-athletes.

Coach Paul's complicated position was such that he concealed crucial information for football players and parents to make informed decisions in the college selection-process. By way of example, I recount the story of one of Eastern's most decorated and accomplished footballers. At 6 '1" and 220 pounds, William (a pseudonym) was an 18-year-old defensive end whose unique blend of strength and athleticism had earned him recognition as one of American Samoa's most promising football prospects. He failed to meet the minimum entrance requirements set forth by the NCAA clearing house (SAT scores and GPA did not meet the standard), however, and therefore had limited opportunities for playing collegiate football. Despite this constraint, and without the consultation of William or his parents, Coach Paul consistently worked his vast networks of college football recruiters to find a scholarship offer for William. Coach Paul solicited offers aided by the recruiting video that I produced to showcase William's athletic ability and sporting prowess.

After months of negotiating a deal, one mainland football program agreed to sign the player to a letter of intent upon Coach Paul's personal recommendation. This school, heretofore called Southeastern University, was a four-year public university in the southeastern United States, that competed at the DI FCS level that had made the playoffs twice since 1987. For all its futility on the field, the university likewise struggled in delivering a superior education to its students, ranking just 102nd of universities located in the U.S. South in the latest *U.S. News & World Report* list of top regional universities. Throughout the entire recruitment process, William never met the college coaches recruiting him, was provided with no information about the football program, and did not discuss academics and potential majors of study. He was never even provided the name of the university with which he had agreed to sign a letter of intent. I recall a conversation with William after verbally committing:

WILLIAM: Coach told me I have committed to [Redacted].

ME: Have you heard of [Redacted] University?

WILLIAM: No. Where is it (located)?

ME: It's in [a southeastern US state].

WILLIAM: Is it cold there?

ME: No, it's very warm.

WILLIAM: Is that near Seattle?

ME: No, it's quite a long way from Seattle.

WILLIAM: I have family in Seattle.

ME: Let me show you where it is on a map. (I show him the distance from the university to Seattle.)

WILLIAM: Is that far?

ME: Yes, [southeastern U.S. state] to Seattle is very far.

In retelling this story, I do not aim to embarrass or condemn an 18-year-old kid for lacking knowledge of U.S geography. Rather, it is to bring to demonstrate the lack of knowledge an ISA can have in the recruitment process brought about by the concealment of critical information by his high school football coach. Although he had already made a verbal commitment to play for Southeastern University, William, quite literally, did not even know where it was located.

In bringing up his family, William is clearly implying a desire to attend school in a location where he has a support network. As he later expressed to me, however, William was never consulted about his preference to attend school near his family. Nor was he asked about his preference for a major or general field of study.

The story of William is not unlike countless others I encountered throughout my time in American Samoa, in which essential information often is concealed from international football talent in the college-selection process. Yet, unlike William, the fates of other promising football prospects did not rest with their high school football coach, but rather with the island's football buscones.

## Confession 3: The Purpose—I Was Complicit in the Exploitation of ISAs by Football Buscones for Personal and Financial Gain

The circulation and distribution of individual player highlight films was not exclusive to the Eastern football program. Confidential player information, digital records, and links to their publicly available YouTube pages were given to the local nonprofit organization, Locker Room 411, which was founded by two American brothers who served as Christian missionaries in American Samoa. Having come to the island in just a few years earlier, the brothers never intended to be involved in college-football recruiting. As the missionaries' time proselytizing the community to Christianity grew longer, they were granted increasing social capital in the American Samoan community. The missionaries quickly recognized the cultural significance of gridiron football to the American Samoan community and the opportunities conferred to football prospects. Eventually, they began using connections to churches and ministries in the U.S. South to connect talented football players to evangelical coaches at major U.S. colleges and universities.

Over time, the two Locker Room 411 executives accumulated significant social capital in the community through their religious teachings, and became important gatekeepers in the Polynesian pipeline of elite football talent prospects. How their system worked actually was quite simple. The older brother, Bill, collected video and highlight reels from the island's seven head football coaches, including the films I prepared for Coach Paul at Eastern High School. Because Bill also was the pastor of the largest church on the entire island, parents and local coaches entrusted him with the futures of children on the island. In most cases, he would take digital film and edit a highlight video using the aforementioned techniques of selective profile building and athlete rendering. In other cases, he would be given previously prepared highlight films and confidential personal information (e.g., SAT scores, 40-yard dash times, athletic measurables) from assistant coaches like myself.

Once in possession of player highlight videos, Bill would send them to his younger brother Barry back on the U.S. mainland. Barry—who held an advances degree in marketing—was an expert negotiator of football talent in the college-football market. As Barry explained to me, he quite literally would drive around the United States south in his car and arrive unannounced at the offices of college football coaches offering what he described to me in an interview as, "briefcases full of prospects." He continued, "Need a left tackle? I've got those. A nose guard that can drive the center into the backfield? I've got that too. Whatever a coach needs, I can get him that." Over time, the frequent marketing and distribution of American Samoan talent to specific programs led to establishment of talent pipelines from American Samoa to specific programs, predominantly in the U.S. South where strong evangelical Christianity gives the missionary-based system justification and validity. This process proved enormously efficient and effective, as college coaches who are inundated with continuous player highlight videos and game footage, preferred the humanistic approach of the football salesman coming to their door. It was the selling of athlete commodities with a personalized touch. Over a short period, these two brothers have become an integral part in creating a market for American Samoan football talent.

In their system, the pair had wide-ranging control over the personal, educational, and financial futures of talented American Samoan footballers, many of whom were generally unaware of the transfer negotiations occurring on the U.S. mainland with college coaches and football programs without their consent. The players, their parents, and their coaches had little knowledge of the coaches or the football programs involved in the recruiting negotiations. Similar to Coach Paul's recruiting techniques, many of the players never met the college coaches or talent evaluators doing the recruiting. They rarely, if ever, had a campus visit to observe the school firsthand. And, in general, they were granted little involvement in the college-selection process. Unlike with Coach Paul, however, the football players had little contact with the brokers of their footballing futures. Whereas Coach Paul was a valued community member of Samoan ethnicity, Locker Room 411 was an anonymous organization run by American expatriates with little commitment to the American Samoan community.

This secrecy was, it seemed, intentional. The more disempowered and desperate the college football recruit, the greater the potential for his exploitation. Although the term exploitation is difficult to define precisely, it has been suggested that in the world of college athletics it occurs when "the coach, the team, the athletic department, the school, or the governing associations use college athletes for their own purposes without providing for the need of the athletes" (Edwards, 1984, p. 7).

As radical sociologist Harry Edwards posited years ago, "the elite high school athlete is besieged by forceful, hypocritical recruiting that is not possible for him to choose intelligently between available alternatives" (p. 7). In this system, football recruits could not individually or collectively advocate for their rights and interests in the recruitment process, instead placing their trust in a powerful political organization. This granted college coaches, recruiters, and talent scouts the authority to fully dictate terms of financial-aid packages and scholarship agreements to improve their own financial situation. A successful football recruit could bring in millions of dollars of revenue for the school and enable college coaches to receive financially lucrative multi-year contracts while recruits received almost nothing in return. Unlike domestic student-athletes—who also generate more revenue than they are compensated for in terms of their scholarship and aid—American Samoan ISAs lack the fundamental human rights and protections to make informed decisions in scholarship-selection process.

I was never quite clear of the endgame for the executives of Locker Room 411. Recent developments have confirmed initial suspicions that there were deeper and darker motivations behind their charity. Last year, the executives of Locker Room 411 were certificated as official NFL sports agents to negotiate professional contracts for their amateur collegiate football players. By extension of logic, they can identify raw 17-year-old football prospects from the island, showcase their skills to college coaches and scouts to secure a four-year scholarship where they will mature and develop their football talent playing, and benefit financially once the athlete signs a professional contact with an NFL team. In the process, they have become an increasingly indispensable part of the global commodity chain of athletic labor.

Through their collective actions, the pair could be loosely considered what Alan Klein (2014) terms a buscone—those individuals deeply intertwined into the transnational mobility and international migration of talented athletes. Writing about baseball in the Dominican Republic, Klein (2014) discusses how buscones train boys, often providing food, shelter, and medical care as they mature, until they are eligible to sign with a major-league baseball club. Throughout the process, the buscone attempts to create a market for his prospect's services by showing off his talents to different organizations in hopes of driving up his signing bonus. Upon signing a professional contract, the buscone receives financial compensation for the years of development, mentoring, and marketing. The football buscones of American Samoa present a clear and present conflict of interest by blurring the boundaries between amateurism and professionalism. They prevent the athlete from making informed decisions between alternatives, market their football talent through covert networks of trade and commerce, and stand to benefit personally and financially from the establishment of global commodity chain of American Samoan footballers.

## Conclusion

In its resolution 55/25 of November 15, 2000, the United Nations (UN) General Assembly adopted the Convention against Transnational Organized Crime and the Protocol to Prevent, Suppress, and Punish Trafficking in vulnerable persons, especially women, young people, and children. Article 3, paragraph (a) of the protocol defines human trafficking as involving three constituent elements (General Assembly resolution, 2000). First, the act (what is done) is the recruitment, transportation, transfer, harboring, or receipt of persons. Next, the means (how it is done) involves the threat or use of force or other forms of coercion, of abduction, of fraud, of deception, of the abuse of power, or of a position of vulnerability. Lastly, the purpose (why it is done) is defined as the reason for exploitation, which involves the manifold purposes of trafficking including, among other things, the receiving of payments or benefits through the exploitation and control over another person. National legislators are asked to adopt this broad definition of trafficking prescribed in the Protocol to ascertain whether a particular circumstance constitutes trafficking in persons.

Applying the Protocol to the circumstances and experiences involved in the international recruitment of ISA football prospects seemingly fits the broad definition of human trafficking. The act involves the transnational recruitment and transfer of football prospects through fraud and deception by falsifying personal information including athletic qualities and academic achievements included in player highlight videos and digital player profiles. The means includes coercion and the threat of force when high school coaches in positions of power suppress relevant information necessary for ISAs to make informed decisions in the college-selection process. The purpose encompasses the exploitation of ISAs by football buscones who benefit personally and financially from the system. The system of international recruitment of ISA football prospects violates the fundamental human right of movement through fraud, coercion, deception, and their commercial exploitation. Thus, the international recruitment of American Samoan football prospects has become a spiraling "arms race" to establish exploitative "Polynesian pipelines" where young and vulnerable peoples are pressured, through covert networks of trade and commerce, to join the NCAA's exploitative system for which they receive compensation (a scholarship) less than the revenue they generate for colleges and universities. It is exploitation for the sake of further exploitation.

Although the title of the chapter gives a more sensational impression of my actual involvement in the recruiting system, and implies I had far greater involvement than I actually did, I question constantly my tacit consent to what I witnessed in American Samoa. Was it guilt by association? Was I complicit in a system of exploitation? Was I in a position of power to challenge and subvert the coercive and exploitative system without the fear of losing my job and alienating those in authority positions? Answers to these questions, and more like them, are perhaps not so easy to offer. After all, my contribution to the vast networks of international football recruitment, trade, and commerce was both brief (one season in length) and relatively inconsequential (making a few highlight videos). Only through thoughtful self-reflection and drafting candid confessionals from my time could I contextualize my ethnographic observations within the immoral, unethical, and arguably illegal system of ISA recruitment. Nonetheless, I was granted a deep, if ephemeral, glimpse into the politics and power of college coaches and recruiters, high school football coaches, and football buscones. With the limitations of this study in consideration, I plead for future research from people in leadership positions and positions of power inside the global recruitments of ISAs to come forward and share their stories.

This chapter is a call for sincere reform, oversight, and greater transparency by the NCAA to resolve the—at times—highly secretive, immoral, unethical, and exploitative practices in the recruitment of ISA football players. I encourage the NCAA to adopt policy reforms and protections for ISAs similar to those of domestic-student athletes that promote a more transparent, human, and ethnical system of migration for ISAs. This includes the development and adoption of an ISA bill of rights to ensure that all future athletic recruits possess the power to make informed choices in the college-selection process.

## Discussion

International student-athletes bring about a whole new set of issues that American athletes do not bring to the table. Is this something institutions should ignore, because if they were to put a renewed focus on ISAs from a critical perspective it would lead to a number of other issues that would bog down administrators?

REFERENCES

Abbey-Pinegar, E. (2010). The need for a global amateurism standard: international student-athlete issues and controversies. *Indiana Journal of Legal Studies*, 17(2), 341–365.

Bale, J. (1991). *The brawn drain: foreign student-athletes in American universities*. Urbana, IL: University of Illinois Press.

Beissel, A. S. (2015). *The corporeal economy of American Samoa gridiron football* (PhD Dissertation). University of Otago, Dunedin, Otago, New Zealand.

Berry, J. (1999). Foreign student-athletes and their motives for attending North Carolina NCAA Division I institutions: Unpublished master's thesis. University of North Carolina at Chapel Hill.

Carter, I. (2004, May 2). The Dominican of the NFL. *The Star Kansas City*, p. 10. Retrieved June 19, 2017, from http://www.jonentine.com/reviews/KC_Star_Dominican.htm

Doyle, C. A., & Gaeth, G. J. (1990). Assessing the institutional choice process of student-athletes. *Research Quarterly for Exercise and Sport*, 61 (1), 85–92.

Drape, J. (2006, April 11). Foreign pros in college tennis: on top and under scrutiny. *New York Times*. Retrieved June 19, 2017, from http://www.nytimes.com/2006/04/11/sports/tennis/foreign-pros-in-college-tennis-on-top-and-under-scrutiny.html

Denzin, N. K. (1997). *Interpretive ethnography: ethnographic practices for the 21st century*. Thousand Oaks, CA: Sage.

Denzin, N. K. & Lincoln, Y.S. (1994). Introduction: Entering the field of qualitative research. In Denzin, N.K. & Y.S. Lincoln (eds.), *Handbook of qualitative research* (pp. 1–17). Thousand Oaks, CA: Sage.

Denzin, N. K. & Lincoln, Y. S. (2005). Introduction: The discipline and practice of qualitative research. In Denzin, N. K. & Y. S. Lincoln (eds.), *The sage handbook of qualitative research* (3rd ed.) (pp. 1–28). Thousand Oaks, CA: Sage.

Edwards, H. (1984). The college athletics arms race: Origins and implications of the "Rule 84" controversy. *Journal of Sport and Social Issues*, 8(1).

Gabert, T., Hale, J., & Montvalo, G. (1999). Difference in college choice factors. *Journal of College Admission*, 164, 20–29.

Garant-Jones, S., Kim, G. Y., Andrew, D. P. S., & Hardin, R. (2009). Motivational factors influencing international student-athletes to participate in the National Collegiate Athletic Association. *Journal of Contemporary Athletics*, 3, 295–314.

General Assembly resolution 55/25. (2010). *Protocol to prevent, suppress and punish trafficking in persons*, A/3/P/a.

Gaul, G. (2015). *Billion-dollar ball: A journey through the big-money culture of college football*. New York: Penguin Books.

Gertz, C. (1973). Thick description: Toward an interpretive theory of culture. In Gertz, C. *The Interpretation of Cultures*. Pp. 3–33. New York: Basic Books.

Goss, B. D., Jubenville, C. B., & Orejan, J. (2006). An examination of influences and factors of the institutional selection processes of freshman student-athletes at small colleges and universities. *Journal of Marketing for Higher Education*, 16, 105–134.

Hall, C. (2015). NCAA should put quota on number of international students recruited for tennis. *The Red & Black*. Retrieved June 19, 2017, from http://www.redandblack.com/sports/column-ncaa-should-put-quota-on-number-of-international-students/article_651032aa-b3f0–11e4-bd12–5ff3acf0013c.html

Hayner, J. (2012, August 8). FH100 exceeds it goal for 2012–13 to find college homes for local student-athletes. *Samoa News*, p. S1.

Hoffer, R. (1994). Foreign legions. *Sports Illustrated*, 80(22), 46–49. Retrieved June 19, 2017, from http://www.si.com/vault/1994/06/06/131242/foreign-legions-us-colleges-are-recruiting-so-many-foreign-athletes-in-nonrevenue-sports-that-their-rosters-now-resemble-the-roll-at-the-united-nations

Jara, E. S. (2015) *U.S. collegiate athletics: International student athletes recruiting process*. Master's Thesis. University of South Carolina, Columbia, SC.

Judson, K. M., James, J. D., & Aurand, T. W. (2004). Marketing the university to student-athletes: Understanding university selection criteria. *Journal of Marketing for Higher Education*, 14, 23–40.

Kankey, K., & Quarterman, J. (2007). Factors influencing the university choice of NCAA Division I softball players. *The SMART Journal*, 3(2), 35–49.

Klein, A. (2014). Dominican baseball: New pride, old prejudice. Philadelphia, PA: Temple University Press.

Klenosky, D. B., Templin, T. J., & Troutman, J. A. (2001). Recruiting student athletes: A means-end investigation of school-choice decision making. *Journal of Sport Management*, 15, 95–106.

Kosmider, N. (2014). Foreign-born players making mark in college basketball. *The Denver Post*. Retrieved June 19, 2017, from http://www.denverpost.com/2014/12/27/foreign-born-players-making-mark-in-college-basketball/

Letawsky, N. R., Schneider, R. G., Pedersen, P. M., & Palmer, C. J. (2003). Factors influencing the college selection process of student-athletes: Are their factors similar to non-athletes? *College Student Journal*, 37(4), 604–610.

Lindaman, B. (2013). International track and field athletes taking over? *Track and Field News*. Retrieved June 19, 2017, from http://www.trackandfieldnews.com/index.php/display-article?arId=85152

Love, A. & Kim, S. (2011). Sport labor migration and collegiate sport in the United States: A typology of migrant athletes. *Journal of Issues in Intercollegiate Athletics*, 4, 90–104.

Madison, D. S. (2005). *Critical ethnography: method, ethics, and performance*. Thousand Oaks, CA.: Sage.

Martin, L. L., Fasching-Varner, K. J., & Hartlep, N. D. (2017). *Pay to play: Race and the perils of the college sports industrial complex*. Santa Barbara, CA: Praeger.

Mathes, S., & Gurney, G. (1985). Factors in student-athletes' choices of college. *Journal of College Student Personnel*, 26, 327–333.

Pierce, D. A. (2007). *Applying amateurism in the global sports arena: Analysis of NCAA student-athlete reinstatement cases involving amateurism violations* (PhD Dissertation). Indiana University.

Pelley, S. (2010). American Samoa: Football island. *60 Minutes*. WCBS.

Popp, N., Hums, M. A., & Greenwell, T. C. (2009). Do international student-athletes view the purpose of sport differently than Unites States student-athletes at NCAA Division I universities? *Journal of Issues in Intercollegiate Athletics*, 2, 93–110.

Popp, N., Pierce, D., & Hums, M. A. (2011). A comparison of the college selection process for international and domestic student-athletes at Division I universities. *Sport Management Review*, 14, 176–187.

Remillard, A. (2014). College athletics recruitment: A deeper analysis. *Sport Management Undergraduate*. Paper 77.

Ridinger, L., & Pastore, D. (2000). A proposed framework to identify factors associated with international student-athlete adjustment to college. *International Journal of Sport Management*, 1(1), 4–24.

Sager, M. (2015) The Samoan pipeline: How does a tiny island, 5,000 miles from the U.S. mainland produce so many professional football players. *The California Sunday Magazine*. Retrieved December 18, 2016, from https://story.californiasunday.com/samoan-football-pipeline.

Shannon, N. G. (2014). NCAA's fear of foreign athletes. *Runners World*. Retrieved June 19, 2017, from http://www.runnersworld.com/running-times-info/ncaas-fear-of-foreign-athletes

Smith, B. (2011). Is U.S. college tennis under foreign invasion? *The Sport Digest.* Retrieved June 19, 2017, from http://thesportdigest.com/2011/03/is-u-s-college-tennis-under-foreign-invasion/

Syken, B. (2003). Football in paradise. *Sports Illustrated, 99*(17), 73–76.

Weston, M. A. (2006). Internationalization in college sports: issues in recruiting, amateurism, and scope. *42 Willamette Law Review,* 829–860.

Wilson, R. & Wolverton, B. (2008). The new face of college sports. *The Chronicle of Higher Education, 54*(18), 27–32.

Zgonc, E. (2010) 1999–00–2008–09 NCAA student-athlete ethnicity report. Indianapolis, IN: *National Collegiate Athletic Association.* Retrieved December 6, 2010, from http://www.ncaapublications.com

Zonder, E. (2013). *Student-athlete perceptions of increased internationalization in college athletics* (Master's Thesis). Eastern Michigan University, Ypsilanti, Michigan.

# 9

# Welcome to the Factory

## College Athletics and Corporatized Recruiting

JACOB J. BUSTAD AND RONALD L. MOWER

Over the past 20 years, the process of recruitment has been especially impacted by organizations that are structured around the intersection of fee-based services and digital media, thus combining technological innovation with the application of a market-based model for athlete recruiting. In the authors's view, these organizations evince the further transformation of athlete recruiting as an industry, in that the process of engaging and enrolling potential college athletes has been reshaped according to the logics of marketization and entrepreneurial strategies. Many of the same economic rationales that increasingly are applied to sport in the neoliberal university—and which are discussed elsewhere in this volume—have been instrumental in restructuring the recruiting process, resulting in what is defined below as "corporatized recruiting."

Similar to the other chapters in this text, this chapter argues that these transformations within recruiting mean that an increasing number of college athletes are being introduced to the structures and experiences of college sport as a cultural and economic industry (Cummings & Lofaso, 2010)—even before they arrive on campus—through the emergent market of recruiting services. Corporatized recruiting emphasizes that these services follow an entrepreneurial and commercially based model for assisting athletes in being recruited, and assisting coaches via access to digital media and player statistics. The chapter concludes by exploring the implications that these types of recruiting services have for athletes and their families, as well for as coaches, recruiters, and universities. As described in this chapter, the experiences involved in college athletic recruiting—for recruiters, athletes, and their families alike—continue to be shaped by economic and technological forces.

The chapter first examines a recent development in the processes of collegiate athletic recruiting: The formation of organizations structured towards assisting athletes in gaining recognition and scholarship offers in their respective sports. The analysis recognizes that this network of fee-based websites, recruiting databases, and "showcase" events amount to what Feiner (2015) has called an "extra layer to the process—and cost—of getting recruited." The chapter aims to provide an analysis of both the larger trends within recruiting and recruiting assistance, and specific examples of the types of institutions and strategies that are involved in this developing cultural economy of college athletic recruiting. It focuses on how these organizations form an added dimension to the process of producing and recruiting athletes—one that has varying implications for the experiences of athletes within different sports and with different social backgrounds.

There are numerous studies that contribute to the applied management of recruiting in regard to identifying the most important factors for student-athletes in choosing a school (Klenosky & Troutman, 2001; Letawsky et al., 2003), and developing best practices for coaches and recruiters (Czekanski & Barnhill, 2015). There is a clear gap in this literature, however, regarding situating the recruiting process within broader political, cultural, and economic trends. This chapter therefore addresses an aspect of athletic recruiting that lacks scholarly attention, and yet is increasingly common for athletes and their families—the market-based network of organizations and individuals that often play an important role in the experience of being recruited into a collegiate athletic program.

## Technology, Entrepreneurialism, and the Business of Recruiting

Throughout, the chapter focuses primarily on organizations that operate in the U.S. Mid-Atlantic region as prominent examples of this shift in recruiting. The emergence of online-based recruiting services, however, has not been limited to certain regions or cities, as these organizations are increasing their presence in the recruiting landscape for athletes and coaches of a number of sports and in various locations. This includes many recruiting-assistance companies that have remained localized in their focus on particular sports and areas of operation. Virginia-based Recruit757 serves as one example of this type of recruiting service, in that the organization concentrates solely on high school football in the 757 area code. As with other locally based recruiting services, Recruit757 features "national news from a local perspective, updates on the recruitment of local athletes and about players you won't get enough of on a national recruiting site . . . additionally, Recruit757 provides a scouting and video service to the colleges that recruit in 'the 757' region" (PRWeb, 2014).

There also is a growing number of national recruiting services offering assistance to athletes and coaches for a variety of sports across the country. One such organization is beRecruited.com, based in Atlanta, Georgia. It started in 2000 as a service for swimming and diving athletes but grew to encompass different sports and a nationwide scope of operation. By 2008, BeRecruited featured more than 200,000 athlete profiles and 10,000 registered college coaches (Shell-nutt, 2008), and the site has continued to grow—in 2016, the company claimed to include more than 2 million athletes and 250,000 college coaches (BeRe-cruited, 2016). These figures illustrate that at the local, regional, and national level, recruiting services have become a ubiquitous aspect of the experience for both recruiters and athletes alike.

This transformation in the recruiting process has occurred at the same time that, for athletes and schools, athletic recruiting has become more competitive than ever. The NCAA reports that of the nearly 8 million current high school athletes, approximately 480,000 athletes will compete at the collegiate level. These levels vary by sport, as well. Approximately 7% of high school men's basketball players play collegiately, and approximately 12% of high school lacrosse players play in college (NCAA, 2016). These statistics include both scholarship and non-scholarship athletes—meaning that the competition for limited opportunities for scholarship support is even more intense. In 2012, CBS reported that the odds of receiving a college athletic scholarship was about 2%, with the average scholarship amount at less than $11,000 (O'Shaughnessy, 2012). Further, competition between schools has meant that many universities have continued to increase athletic-recruiting budgets—especially for football and men's basketball—as schools seek to build successful athletic programs. According to *USAToday*, spending on football recruiting at FBS (Football Bowl Subdivision) public schools increased by $8.9 million, or about 30%, between 2008–09 and 2012–13. Further, this increase was "slightly more than the rate at which all operational spending on athletics rose" (Brady, Kelly, & Berkowitz, 2015, ¶3). Together, these figures serve to emphasize the importance of recruiting within contemporary college sports, in which athletes compete against one another for scholarships, and schools compete against one another for athletes.

In broad terms, the changes within athlete recruiting express a specific relationship between high school and college sport and the contemporary American economy, in that the types of services offered to potential recruits follow similar trends in other industries. These include mobility services, accommodation services, or product-delivery services that are premised on the interaction between consumers and digital technology—a more recent development in the rise of the "service economy" as the defining sector of American economic growth (Buera & Kaboski 2012). In 2006, the *New York Times* reported on the increasing role of online recruiting services as a digital and Web-based alternative to previous recruiting practices, explaining that these organizations "do more than build interactive Internet sites. They conduct elaborate e-mail campaigns, lobby college coaches, produce and edit polished videos and counsel their clients on everything from curriculum to essays for college applications" (Pennington, 2006). In the same report, an executive for a particular service described the future of recruiting as centered on technological interaction, through online sites that "will allow a college football coach in Ohio to watch a prospect's Friday night game in Georgia via cellphone or iPod" (Pennington, 2006). Nearly 10 years later, these features have been fully realized by recruiting services that have continued to center on providing services via digital technology, including compiling databases of video and player data that can be accessed anywhere in the country.

The integration of technology into the recruiting experience for potential college athletes also has been accompanied by the use of digital media within recruiting for colleges and universities more generally, as schools seek to connect and communicate with a new generation of students (Lindbeck & Fodrey 2009). Following Hill, Burch-Ragan, and Yates (2001), this merging of technology and the university recruiting experience has extended to athletics.

> Closely linked to student athlete information management is the role of technology in recruiting prospective student athletes. Many collegiate settings offer virtual tours of campus and athletic departments. Such applications enhance a coach's ability to reach students even when coaches must limit recruiting visits. Information exchanges related to eligibility requirements and administrative forms are easily negotiated through the Internet as well. Prospective students can directly access and establish their eligibility status through the NCAA Initial-Eligibility Clearinghouse Web site. Also, the NCAA offers a list of approved core courses, a transfer guide, and international academic standards to assist in the recruitment process. (p. 72)

As Thruston (2015) explains, within college athletic departments this has meant that instead of traditional forms of recruiting using phone calls and mail, "coaches are now using newer communication methods such as web tours, web cameras, webcasts, social networking sites, scouting and recruiting services, instant messaging, and email" (p. 24).

In short, the contemporary recruiting industry is marked by the proliferation of different forms of communication and data sharing that have been made possible through digital technology and the Internet. For coaches and athletes, more information is available than ever before, and this information is accessible through an ever-increasing number of sources. As Feiner (2015) suggests, the sheer amount of data now available—to recruits regarding potential programs and opportunities, and to coaches and recruiters regarding potential athletes—in turn has led to the increase in recruiting services as the "middleman" in the recruiting process. Recruits and their families often can be "overwhelmed with information" about how recruiting works, and these services function as "advisors to help them narrow down schools that fit for them academically and athletically, connect them with college coaches, and sometimes provide videos and websites of their athletes" (Feiner 2015).

The recent expansion of recruiting services, however, also is evidence of more than the impacts of digital technologies within the recruiting process. Recruiting services also evince the renewed importance of particular models for economic development, in that these services most often initially are founded and operated by either a single individual or small group of individuals as "entrepreneurs." The pervasiveness of recruiting services therefore serves to demonstrate the further marketization of sport within neoliberalism, wherein sporting organizations and experiences are effectively organized and operated as profit-making institutions (Miller, 2012). As discussed by Peters (2016), the entrepreneur as a social and economic actor is a critical figure within the context of neoliberal policy and planning, as symbolized by the notion of *homo oeconomicus*, or "the economic man." This concept is based on the idea that humans are most often rationally and self-interested economic agents, and has been widely influential in the formation of neoliberal economic and social policy, in which the citizen is recast as an "entrepreneur of himself" (Peters, 2016, p. 298)—responsible for his or her economic decisions and the implications of these decisions. Accordingly, profiles of the individuals who are responsible for different recruiting services often focus on entrepreneurial qualities, in that these services were developed to create revenue sources within the process of assisting athletes in being recruited.

For example, a 1998 *Baltimore Sun* profile focused on Steve Sclafani, founder and CEO of The Baseball Factory, a recruiting service in the mid-Atlantic United States—this profile serves to emphasize the significance of entrepreneurialism within the transformation of recruiting.

> The Baseball Factory's first tryout drew three people. By 1996, Sclafani had moved the company into an office the size of a walk-in closet and had 150 clients. The following year, the client list swelled to 1,100. This year, working from new offices in Ellicott City and making a profit for the first time, Sclafani is projecting 4,000 clients—each paying a $422 fee—and gross revenue of $1.5 to $1.6 million. "I never even had second doubts at all," Sclafani said. "It had to work. There was a need." (Rice, 1998, ¶21–22)

This recognition of the economic motivations and rationales for recruiting services emphasizes that these organizations have emerged alongside the ascent of the entrepreneur as a key actor within the contemporary American economy. These "heroic entrepreneurs" often have been represented as an integral part of economic development, and at the same time they reassert the primacy of entrepreneurialism as a key aspect of neoliberal policy (Hancock, 2016).

A 2014 update on The Baseball Factory—since expanded and rebranded as "Factory Athletics," with services in sports other than baseball—again serves to illustrate the importance of entrepreneurs within the process of recruiting.

Now known as Factory Athletics, the company has helped develop some 50,000 young baseball players, including more than 300 who have made it all the way to the Major Leagues. Among those major leaguers are such all-stars as Justin Verlander, C.C. Sabathia, Prince Fielder and Mark Teixeira. Along the way, the business that was launched on a shoestring in Sclafani's apartment has blossomed into a $14 million-a-year company, with a 23,000-square-foot office on Berger Road in Columbia and a national reputation for providing a service that is rare in the baseball world. (Pichaske, 2014, ¶4)

The example of The Baseball Factory/Factory Athletics serves to demonstrate that a merging of technology and entrepreneurialism has served to transform the collegiate-athlete recruiting process, through the proliferation of profit-based organizations and services. This chapter next discusses the changes within the recruiting process in relation to contemporary college sport as a cultural and economic industry that is situated within the context of the neoliberal university, and then further examines how recruiting services are structured and operate.

## College Sport as Culture Industry

Collegiate athletics initially emerged as part of a supporting role to the broader educational mission of universities, which sought to address both the intellectual and physical aspects of human development. Contemporary college sport is marked by a thoroughly antiquated—and increasingly inequitable—model of collegiate amateurism that is neither true by definition or spirit (Nixon, 2014; Sperber, 1990). Many public universities face a problematic paradox, as these nonprofit, tax-exempt institutions whose primary role is to educate and prepare future generations now spend significantly on achieving athletic success, in many cases prioritizing athletics over academic success (Nixon, 2014; Zimbalist, 1999, 2016). As Zimbalist (2016) has recently argued, "college sport leads a schizophrenic existence, encompassing both amateur and professional elements. The courts, the IRS, and sometimes the universities themselves cannot seem to decide whether to treat intercollegiate athletics as part of the educational process or as a business" (2016, p. 5). The line between "amateur" and "professional" sport therefore has been blurred by the production of "big-time" college sports, extending from the tremendous impact of television revenues, which have thoroughly amplified the processes of institutional brand marketization, commercial sponsorship, and inordinate spending on coaches, administrators, facilities, and recruiting (Nixon, 2014; Sperber, 1990; Zimbalist, 2016).

Seeking to remain competitive in what has been called the "athletic arms race," universities increasingly have sought consistently successful athletic programs, allowing the perceived value of institutional exposure and commercial profit to outweigh the vital functions and purpose of higher education (Giroux, 2013). The neoliberal university is characterized by a context in which college sport is inextricably linked to broader processes of commercialization, consumerism, commodification, and administrative entrepreneurialism rather than a space for critical thinking, dialogue, and civic engagement (Giroux, 2013). According to this logic, the university becomes a profit-driven corporation, providing educational, athletic, and social services to meet market demand. Universities therefore increasingly seek to retain and subsidize the most popular, trending, and fiscally productive athletic programs concomitant to their market value and economic impact (Hill et al., 2001). The prioritization of free-market principles in this restructured university governance means that funding for academics has become increasingly devalued, often in the interests of building and maintaining athletic programs that mirror professional sport in every way except the payment of a wage to its principal laborers (*see, e.g.,* Southall & Nagel, 2016; Zimbalist, 1999).

Universities and the NCAA have sustained this paradox by carefully mobilizing language that promotes understandings of the "student-athlete" and "amateurism" within the American public sphere (Giroux, 2013; Southall & Staurowsky, 2013). In this mode, the college sport industry has increasingly been conflated with the business of selling the university—it's brand identity, location, sporting (and by extension academic) prestige, and associated cultural economies that frame the twenty-first-century "college experience" for "consumers" of higher education:

> the circulation of money and power on university campuses mimics its circulation in the corporate world, saturating public spaces and the forms of sociality they encourage with the imperatives of the market. Money from big sports programs also has an enormous influence on shaping agendas within the university that play to their advantage, from the neoliberalized, corporatized commitments of an increasingly ideologically incestuous central administration to the allocation of university funds to support the athletic complex and the transfer of scholarship money to athletes rather than academically qualified, but financially disadvantaged students (Giroux, 2013, p. 4).

Indeed, the corporatizing of the university is representative of broader neoliberal processes that prioritize profit margins and market logics ahead of humanistic ideals, critical pedagogy, and a democratic public sphere (Sperber, 1990; Giroux, 2013). Increasingly pulled into the "athletic trap" of exorbitant spending to attract new recruits, pay coaches, and build new facilities (Nixon, 2014), NCAA member schools' negotiate multimillion-dollar contracts with private corporations for arena naming rights, exclusive signage, and apparel licenses (Cummings & Lofaso, 2010).

As universities travel further down the path of commercialism, it becomes increasingly difficult to rationalize the educational mission of a nonprofit, tax-exempt entity that invests significantly more in unapologetically commercialized athletic spectacle than it does in academic success (Nixon, 2014; Sperber, 1990; Zimbalist, 1999). Nevertheless, "big-time" college sport remains firmly embedded within a university structure that has itself become commodified, branded, and increasingly indistinguishable from other corporate entities providing educational services, knowledge, and training. This means that the transformation of collegiate athletic recruiting is inextricable from the process in which younger generations of athletes are likewise recruited to become "unpaid professionals" (Zimbalist, 1999) or "indentured servants" (Rhoden, 2006) within the contemporary college-sport industry. Recruiting services therefore both reflect the themes of commercialization and marketization evident within college sport, and simultaneously serve as an introduction to this industry for athletes and their families.

## Corporatized Recruiting

Recruiting sites and firms often feature their own particular design for structuring and delivering services, and each has unique aspects of their history and development. However, the following analysis emphasizes that these organizations also most often share a common interest in comprising an added dimension to the recruiting process that assists athletes and coaches, and a common strategy predicated on fee-based assistance for potential recruits. The following outlines the three facets of recruiting services that constitute what this chapter defines as *corporatized recruiting*: online databases and athlete profiles; recruiting assistance via personal and group consultation; and "showcase" events and competitions that bring together recruiters and potential recruits. Nearly all recruiting organizations—whether local, regional, or national in scale and scope—incorporate these different aspects of their services into the recruiting process, and these features are therefore an increasingly common part of the recruiting experience.

### Databases and Athlete Profiles

A key aspect of many recruiting services is developing and managing online databases comprising profiles for potential recruits, enabling both athletes and coaches to share a greater amount of information across a larger area. Athlete profiles often include basic personal data such as height, weight, wingspan, and other physical stats, as well as performance measures (such as 40-yard dash times, vertical jump, and broad jump) that are relevant to the particular sport. The ability to organize and input data by athletes and their families has meant that recruits can further personalize their profiles by adding statistics and media coverage of outstanding performances and awards. Moreover, the ubiquity of cameras for both photos and video has meant that an increasing number of recruits have access to these types of media, which can be used to further augment the athlete's profile. At the same time, coaches are able to review profiles and data for numerous potential recruits, through a platform that organizes this information into a digital interface premised on bringing recruits and recruiters together.

For many larger, nationally based recruiting organizations, the management of databases and athlete profiles has been the most important aspect of growing their sector of the recruiting-services market. As one example, NCSA (Next College Sports Athlete) reflects how recruiting, technology, and entrepreneurialism have merged in recent years. Started by a former collegiate athlete, this organization began "in a basement office" and has since grown to operate across the United States—with offices in San Francisco, Boston, and Chicago—primarily by using the online database and athlete profile service to build an "online community" of nearly 1 million athletes by 2015 (Dewey, 2015). Next College Sports Athlete provides athletes the opportunity to "get noticed" by recruiters within its network of 35,000 college coaches across a variety of sports, and claims to have "helped more than 83,000 student-athletes commit to colleges" since 2000 (NCSASports, 2016). Further, NCSA—along with several other national organizations—has worked to extend the online database and profile service to an increasing number of devices and formats, including the design and development of a mobile app for different phones, and enhanced online content and features (Dewey, 2015).

### Recruiting Assistance

Along with the maintenance and development of online databases and profiles, programs based on providing athletes and their families with recruiting assistance are another important aspect of recruiting services. These include different types of aid and support that services market as necessary toward the goal of becoming a college athlete and, most often, to secure partial or full scholarship funding. Services typically offer support through two types of assistance: sharing information to educate athletes and families about NCAA rules and regulations regarding the recruiting process, and both direct and indirect help in being identified and recruited by potential coaches and programs. The former type of support is based on ensuring that athletes are aware of the rules that they should follow with regard to contacting or being contacted by coaches and recruiters, as well as any regulations about being eligible as a student-athlete.

The second type of assistance—in terms of support in being recruited, culminating with the athlete joining a college athletic program—is how most recruiting services establish their market share and create revenue. These services can vary widely in terms of what is offered and the associated costs—ranging from lower costs for an athlete profile and communication with recruiters, to greater costs for more individualized and personal consultation. Feiner (2015) explains that this means that recruiting consultants can (and do) charge between $2,500 and $3,000 for a year of unlimited and direct consultation, with the rationale that "the alternative of making a mistake in the process could end up costing more in both money and heartache." A growing number of smaller local and regional organizations have emerged within the recruiting assistance market, however, meaning that there are different options available for the type of support rendered and cost involved. Recruiting-assistance organizations often offer a lower price—typically between $200 and $500—for a combination of both the database profile and education, and personal attention for recruits. This combination can include services including gathering data and producing media such as highlight tapes for prospective coaches to review (Hiro, 2010).

### Showcase Events

The final corporatized recruiting form is "showcase" events and competitions that are organized as an opportunity for athletes to perform in front of coaches and recruiters. These events—often including "elite," "all-star," or "all-America" in the event title—have become ubiquitous in the recruiting process, and are now available for nearly every high school athlete across a wide variety of sports. Moreover, these events demonstrate the relationship between recruiting organizations and corporate sponsors, as showcases often provide an opportunity for athletes to be noticed by coaches and for coaches to identify potential recruits, but also enable corporate sponsors to align brand identity with particular consumer markets. Under Armour, for example, has taken on a role as a primary corporate sponsor for a series of "All-America" showcases, ranging from regional competitions to nationally televised "all-star" events. This sponsorship role has included a partnership with the aforementioned Factory Athletics and Baseball Factory, leading to the creation of the Under Armour All-America Baseball Game in 2008.

Although the previous Baseball Factory showcase had been held at a smaller venue in Massachusetts, the partnership with Under Armour enabled the event to move to a Major League Baseball stadium and feature national television coverage.

> With the help of a top-tier sponsor and access to a major league stadium, Baseball Factory kicked off its inaugural Under Armour All-American Game at Wrigley Field Sunday afternoon . . . Sunday's game in Chicago was a huge step-up in terms of hype, publicity and national television exposure (Blood, 2008, ¶1).

Therefore, although most top-level prospects are recognized and contacted by coaches, most high school athletes rely on a variety of resources to enhance their opportunities to participate in intercollegiate athletics.

Along with databases, profiles, and recruiting assistance and consulting, showcase events are touted as a chance for these mid-level prospects to gain recognition from coaches, and are therefore part of the growing "do-it-yourself" approach to recruiting that is demonstrated through the growth of recruiting services (Futterman, 2008). The transformation of recruiting therefore reflects the neoliberal ideology of individualism, as the athlete and his or her family are responsible for seeking out—and paying for—the opportunity to "showcase" that athlete's talents and abilities. These events are structured in a model similar recruiting assistance and consulting fees, in that showcase participation fees can range from $100 for local events to between $500 and $1,000 for regional or national multi-day events, most of which also require travel costs (Feiner, 2015). These types of competitions thus again demonstrate that recruiting has been effectively transformed through the prevalence of recruiting services that collectively are recognized as "corporatized recruiting."

## Conclusion: Welcome to the Factory

As analyzed in this chapter, for an increasing number of high school athletes, an introduction to college sport as an economic industry no longer takes place during the first game, the first practice, or the first day on campus. Instead, athletes and their families are experiencing the intercollegiate sport marketplace during the recruiting process, whereby a growing number of organizations and actors have inserted themselves into the middle ground between the athlete and a potential college commitment and scholarship. Consider, for a moment, the implications that recruiting services have within the context of current and future trends of collegiate athletic recruiting. On one hand, we can recognize that, in theory, recruiting services inevitably lead to more exposure for athletes, more interaction between coaches and athletes, and more opportunities for athletes to gain a college commitment and possible scholarship funding. This arguably is true for athletes within certain sports, for example "minor" and "non-revenue" sports for which recruiting budgets typically are much smaller than those of major sports such as football and basketball (Futterman, 2008). These sports also most often include women's sports, as these teams and programs have continued to grow following Title IX legislation that has resulted in an increased number of scholarships for female athletes (Hiro, 2010).

This argument, however, often emphasizes increased opportunity, but concurrently avoids the implications of a system that is premised on fee-based services and is populated by organizations that seek to profit from the recruiting process. In this model, the merging of technology, entrepreneurialism, and athletic recruiting might provide further opportunities, but only for those athletes that have the adequate resources to afford and access these services. This includes the ability and aptitude to use new forms of technology—including mobile phones, tablets, and applications—that are at the center of the transformed recruiting experience. Hill, Burch-Ragan, and Yates (2001) argue that technological development within higher education often is a "double-edged sword" in that it can both increase efficiency and cause rising costs for universities and athletic departments that are characterized by budget constraints. Moreover, the differences in athletes' and families' affordability and accessibility with regard to recruiting services points to the broader issue of technology and information literacy in contemporary America. This has created a form of social inequality—termed the "digital divide"—between those who can access and develop knowledges related to new technologies, and those without access to these technologies and knowledges (Norris, 2001).

More importantly, access to technology comprises only a part of the larger issue that surrounds for-profit recruiting services and the implications of corporatized recruiting: the inequity between athletes and families that can pay for these services and those who cannot. Therefore, although many recruiting services would like to expand the opportunity to play college sports to include more athletes, this system has a double-edge; fee-based models most often provide access only for those that have the requisite financial resources. As Feiner (2015) explains, many potential college athletes need to use fee-based recruiting organizations, meaning that recruiting is being transformed into a "pay-to-play" situation in which those athletes that have financial resources have an advantage in garnering recognition from coaches and recruiters.

Within particular sports, the impact of recruiting organizations already has been recognized with regard to financial resources and which athletes and families can benefit from fee-based services. As one example, the prevalence of recruiting services for baseball has meant that the sport is increasingly seen as an "upper-class sport" by athletes, families, and coaches (Feiner 2015). Finally, even for those athletes that do have the technological and economic resources required for access to recruiting services, there is an ongoing debate about the relative value of these organizations. This has included a recognition of the "good, bad, and ugly" within the recruiting services industry—in which, "like any industry, there are good recruiting services and there are companies that are just trying to separate you from your money" (Bastie, 2016, ¶2).

Regardless, the process of participating in college athletics has been marked by an "extra layer" of engaging with recruiting organizations—these organizations have developed through the integration of technology and entrepreneurialism, and continue to transform the recruiting experience through a growing system of fee-based services. These services include online databases and athlete profiles, recruiting assistance and consultation, and showcase events and competitions, that can be referred to collectively as corporatized recruiting. As demonstrated throughout this chapter, corporatized recruiting therefore signals that athletes—and their families—are being introduced to the industry of intercollegiate athletics before enrolling as a college athlete.

## Discussion

Should we be concerned about the rise in privatized recruiting? It seems to be a more efficient way to help prospective athletes be "seen" by coaches. Is it really all that bad if people use money to help their children "get ahead"?

### REFERENCES

Bastie, F. (2016). Recruiting column: Recruiting services: The good, the bad and the ugly. *USAToday*. Retrieved June 19, 2017, from http://usatodayhss.com/2016/recruiting-column-recruiting-services-the-good-the-bad-and-the-ugly

BeRecruited.com (2016). About us. Retrieved June 19, 2017, from https://berecruited.com/resources/about

Blood, M. (2008). Under Armour game steps up. *Baseball America*. Retrieved June 19, 2017, from https://www.baseballfactory.com/PDFs/BaseballAmericaAAGameArticleReprint2008.pdf

Brady, E., Kelly, J., & Berkowitz, S. (2015). Schools in power conferences spending more on recruiting. *USAToday*. Retrieved June 19, 2017, from http://www.usatoday.com/story/sports/ncaaf/recruiting/2015/02/03/college-football-recruiting-signing-day-sec-power-conferences/22813887/

Buera, F., & Kaboski, J. (2012). The rise of the service economy. *The American Economic Review*, 102(6), 2540–2569.

Cummings, P. & Lofaso, A. (2010). Commercialization: the recruiting and selling of the modern athlete: overview. In *Reversing field: Examining commercialization, labor, gender, and race in 21st century sports law*. Morgantown: West Virginia University Press.

Czekanski, W. & Barnhill, C. (2015). Recruiting the student-athlete: An examination of the college decision process. *Journal for the Study of Sports and Athletes in Education*, 9(3), p. 133–144.

Dewey, S. (2015). How NCSA became the go-to tool for college athletic recruiting. *BuiltInChicago*. Retrieved June 19, 2017, from http://www.builtinchicago.org/2015/12/15/how-ncsa-helps-make-everyday-cinderella-stories-including-their-own-tech-version

Feiner, L. (2015). Pay-to-Play: The Business of College Athletic Recruitment. *Forbes*. Retrieved June 19, 2017, from http://www.forbes.com/forbes/welcome/?toURL=http://www.forbes.com/sites/laurenfeiner/2015/06/23/pay-to-play-the-business-of-college-athletic-recruitment

Futterman, M. (2008). The do-it-yourself athletic scholarship. *The Wall Street Journal*. Retrieved from http://www.wsj.com/articles/SB122955741002616195

Giroux, H. A. (2013, October 29). Public intellectuals against the neoliberal university. *Truthout*. Retrieved June 19, 2017, from http://www.truth-out.org/news/item/19654-public-intellectuals-against-the-neoliberal-university

Hancock, D. (2016). Neoconservatism, bohemia and the moral economy of neoliberalism. *Journal for Cultural Research*, 20 (2), p. 101–121.

Hill, K., Burch-Ragan, K., & Yates, D. (2001). Current and future issues and trends facing student athletes and athletic programs. *New Directions for Student Services*, 93, 65–83.

Hiro, B. (2010, September 27). PREPS: College recruiting services offer assistance to high school athletes seeking scholarship money. *San Diego Union-Tribune.* Retrieved June 19, 2017, from http://www.sandiegouniontribune.com/sdut-preps-college-recruiting -services-offer-2010sep27-story.html

Klenosky, D. & Troutman, J. (2001). Recruiting student athletes: A means-end investigation of school-choice decision making. *Journal of Sport Management,* 15 (2), p. 95–107.

Letawsky, N., Schneider, R., Pedersen, P., & Palmer, C. (2003). Factors influencing the college selection process of student-athletes: are their factors similar to non-athletes. *College Student Journal,* 37 (4), p. 604–616.

Lindbeck, R. & Fodrey, B. (2009). Using technology in undergraduate admission: Current practices and future plans. *Journal of College Admission,* 204, 25–30.

Miller, T. (2012). A distorted playing field: Neoliberalism and sport through the lens of economic citizenship. In D. Andrews & M. Silk (eds.), *Sport and Neoliberalism: Politics, Consumption, and Culture.* 23–37. Temple University Press.

Nixon, (2014). *The athletic trap: How college sports corrupted the academy.* Johns Hopkins University Press, Baltimore: MD.

Norris, P. (2001). *Digital divide: Civic engagement, information poverty, and the Internet worldwide* (Communication, Society and Politics Series). Cambridge, UK: Cambridge University Press.

NCAA. (2016). Probability of competing beyond high school. Retrieved June 19, 2017, from http://www.ncaa.org/about/resources/research/probability-competing-beyond-high -school

NCSASports. (2016). How we do it. Retrieved June 19, 2017, from http://www.ncsasports.org /how-ncsa-works

O'Shaughnessy, L. (2012). 8 things you should know about sports scholarships. *CBS Money-Watch.* Retrieved June 19, 2017, from http://www.cbsnews.com/news/8-things-you -should-know-about-sports-scholarships/

Peters, M. (2016). Education, neoliberalism, and human capital. In S. Springer, K. Birch, & J. Macleavy (eds.), *The Handbook of Neoliberalism.* London: Routledge International.

Pennington, B. (2006, January 29). College hopefuls reach out to recruiting services. *The New York Times.* Retrieved June 19, 2017, from http://www.nytimes.com/2006/01/29 /sports/ncaafootball/ college-hopefuls-reach-out-to-recruiting-services.html

Pichaske, P. (2014, June 10). Columbia's Factory Athletics celebrates 20 years of building better athletes. *Baltimore Sun.* Retrieved June 19, 2017, from http://articles .baltimoresun.com/2014-06-10/news/bs-exho-columbia-business-builds-better -athlete-20140604_1_baseball-factory-all-county-baseball-player-american-legion -baseball

PRWeb. (2014). Recruit757 to host inaugural uncommitted senior showcase for high school football players to get last chance exposure with college coaches. Retrieved June 19, 2017, from http://www.prweb.com/releases/2014/01/prweb11499585.htm

Rhoden, W. C. (2006). *Forty million dollar slaves: The rise, fall, and redemption of the black athlete.* Three Rivers Press, New York, NY.

Rice, M. (1998, April 5). Firm goes to bat for players—Baseball Factory matches skills with scholarships. *Baltimore Sun.* Retrieved June 19, 2017, from http://articles.baltimoresun .com/1998–04–05/news/1998095143_1_baseball-factory-sclafani-baseball-scholarship

Shellnutt, S. (2008, June 29). Recruits make online pitch—Athletes post profiles for coaches to see. *Atlanta Journal-Constitution,* p. H10.

Southall, R. & Nagal, M. (2016). *Big-time College Sport's Contested Terrain: Jock Capitalism, Educational Values, and Social Good.* Article submitted online for Sport Management News.

Retrieved September 26, 2016, from http://www.humankinetics.com/news-and
-excerpts/news-and-excerpts/big-time-college-sports-contested-terrain-jock
-capitalism-educational-values-and-social-good

Southall R. & Staurowsky, E. (2013). Cheering on the collegiate model: Creating, disseminating, and imbedding the NCAA's redefinition of amateurism. *Journal of Sport & Social Issues, 37*, 403–429.

Sperber, M. (1990). *College Sports, Inc.: The Athletic Department vs. the University.* Holt: New York, NY.

Thruston, K. (2015). *Recruiting without borders: The rise of technology in collegiate athletics* (honors thesis). Appalachian State University, Boone, NC.

Zimbalist, A. (1999). *Unpaid professionals: Commercialism and conflict in big-time college sports.* Princeton University Press: Princeton, NJ.

Zimbalist, A. (2016). Reforming college sports and a constrained, conditional antitrust exemption. *Managerial and Decision Economics.* Published online in Wiley Online Library, http://onlinelibrary.wiley.com/doi/10.1002/mde.2789/full

# 10

# "Some Kind of Joke"

## Consultancy Firms and College Athletics

### RYAN KING-WHITE

As the preceding chapters have outlined, the changes in intercollegiate athletics brought about by the twinned forces of late capitalism and neoliberal ideology have produced myriad unintended and unexpected outcomes in the ways that college sport is organized, expressed, and experienced. One interesting— and relatively new—enterprise in intercollegiate athletics is executive search and consultation firms. Much like coaches outsourcing recruiting to companies such as Factory Athletics, Elite Sports Recruiting, and Victory Recruiting to enable coaches to have access to more on-field talent (discussed in Chapter 8 by Beissel, and in Chapter 9 by Bustad and Mower), academic and athletic administrators have asked for help from private consultants who can provide access, lead the hiring process for administrators and coaches, and produce reports to help guide the athletic department within the institutional vision (e.g., Schrotenboer, 2013; Schrotenboer & Axon, 2013; Smith, 2012).

Throughout the past 30, years a number of prominent consultation firms including Parker Executive Search, DHR International, Korn/Ferry International, and CarrSports, have worked in the background to dramatically influence who is hired in key positions, and often the decisions that these hires make moving forward (Bonner, 2010; Mull, 2010; Schwarz, 2014a; WNST Staff, 2013). Far from the days of one person, such as former Big-8 Commissioner Chuck Neinas (who still conducts searches for Parker), helping a university, these corporations offer entire teams of individuals to assist in the decision-making processes. On the surface this seems to be beneficial to most stakeholders, the consultant group makes a profit by helping the university get the best possible candidate and make the most logical choice based on the firm's seemingly independent findings (Schrotenboer & Axon, 2013).

This chapter aims to more deeply examine the taken-for-granted assumption that consultant firms' connection with an academic institution is so unquestionably beneficial for all stakeholders. More to the point, it focuses on and provides a brief history of the development of one consulting firm, CarrSports, then traces their recent work performed at Towson University, University of North Carolina–Wilmington (UNC-W), and University of Alabama–Birmingham (UAB) regarding their sport programming from 2010–2015 (all three cases ended in public controversy). The author then theorizes what the rise of consultancy has meant for (athletic) administrators at higher-education institutions more broadly.

## Who Is CarrSports, and Are They Beneficial to Universities?

CarrSports Consulting LLC. began in 1997 as CarrSports Associates under the direction of Bill Carr, former athletic director for the University of Florida (1979–1987) and for University of Houston (1993–1997). Prior to his foray into athletic administration, Carr was an All-American football player for the University of Florida, played one season with the New Orleans Saints, and then returned to become an assistant coach at his alma mater. Between his stints at Florida and Houston, Carr began consulting for athletic administrators as the president of Sports Resources Group, Inc. All told, Carr has spent the better part of the past 50 years involved in intercollegiate sports, and certainly has been able to make key connections with coaches, administrators, and agents during that time (c.f. Solomon, 2012).

Throughout the past 20 years, Carr has assembled a team of 7 experts in intercollegiate athletics to help universities make decisions based on their programming needs. Generally, CarrSports consults for what are popularly referred to as "mid-major" universities (Mull, 2010), and has become an important power broker—shaping who coaches and administrates and how, as well as shaping (re-)alignment within those conferences. Given CarrSports' considerable influence in particular, and among all consultancy firms in general, questions have begun to arise about why these firms exist in the first place, particularly because they appear to be doing the "most important job for an athletics director" (Solomon, 2012, ¶3) for them, and at a considerable cost to the institution.

Administrators praise consultancy firms such as CarrSports because they offer a "stealth option" (Smith, 2012, ¶8) featuring extreme discretion (McCarthy, 2006), and "secrecy and plausible deniability, for the schools and the coaches" (Solomon, 2012, ¶13) involved in the search. They also note that consultants can work 24/7 with coaches' agents, sift through resumes, and better align coaches with institutional needs. Dan Parker, head of the most powerful college athletics consulting firm, Parker Executive Search, furthers this argument, stating that "a search expert will conduct as many searches in a year as an athletic director might in his or her career" (Smith, 2012, ¶12). Thus, there are many (good) *reasons* why a university administrator would use consulting firms.

Critics such as sport economist, Andrew Zimbalist, however, respond that hiring consulting firms "is a waste of money. Any Athletics Director should know who's hot and who's available in the coaching fraternity" (McCarthy, 2006, ¶10). Speaking solely on Chuck Neinas, although it could further apply to all consulting firms, Zimbalist further states, "I don't see what information Neinas brings to the table that an AD can't get themselves. . . . But if they don't hire him, and they make a mistake, somebody will say, 'You blew it, everybody else in the conference used Neinas.' So he has this self-perpetuating monopoly" (McCarthy, 2006, ¶11).

Thus, the broader critique is that consultants operate in the shadows, hold oligarchic control over access to jobs, publish weakly researched studies that simply affirm the desires of athletics administrators, are rarely held accountable for their work, and essentially assume the athletics directors' most important duties outside of fundraising (i.e., hiring, strategic planning, and reporting a programmatic vision to the university president). The following section uses these competing visions of athletic consultancy as a framework to evaluate the role CarrSports has played in shaping the athletics departments at Towson University, UNC-W, and UAB. More specifically, CarrSports was hired by each institution to aid in the hire of key personnel, and to later provide direction for how the institution would move forward regarding athletics. As mentioned, decisions at all three schools based on the reports that CarrSports submitted to athletic directors were met with strong resistance by a variety of stakeholders (often all the way up to state government officials), and ultimately led to (partial) overturns of original decisions. I believe this exercise will help provide the empirical evidence needed to articulate why and to what ends consultancy firms are becoming so popular in contemporary college sports.

## Getting the "Right Person" or Setting the Table for Future Work?

A Freedom of Information Act (FOIA) request sent to each institution revealed that CarrSports was hired by Towson University and UNC-W in 2010 to assist in a search for a new athletics director. With Carr's aid, the two schools selected Mike Waddell and Jimmy Bass, respectively, to lead their athletics departments at a cost of $25,0000 each (Dunn, 2010. Meanwhile, UAB's athletics director, Brian Mackin, who had been head of athletics since 2007, hired CarrSports to consult on a search for a head football coach in 2011 (UAB Athletics, 2011), and for a men's basketball coach in 2012 (Jerod Haase was hired) (Solomon, 2012) for $43,000 plus expenses.

In the grand scheme of things, spending $95,000 on four different coach and administrator searches does not seem all that egregious when it comes to using university finances. Certainly, it would not take much digging to find instances where administrators allocated funds to far more troubling ends. Famed feminist sport sociologist, Mary Jo Kane, once served on the University of Minnesota's athletic director (AD) search, and praised the use of a consultancy firm by suggesting that they were more prepared to find qualified candidates than she was, and that using one makes fiscal sense (Schrotenboer & Axon, 2013). The relationship between CarrSports (and other consultancy firms at other schools) and these universities and athletics administrations, however, often does not end with the hire of a few coaches for "revenue" sports and as ADs.

Indeed, the Towson (Waddell), UNC-W (Bass), and UAB (Mackin) triumvirate would rehire CarrSports to consult on how each athletic department should move forward. When viewed critically, it could be suggested that two of these men hired the people (partially) responsible for getting them their jobs in the first place. Despite these seemingly "incestuous" (Schrotenboer & Axon, 2013) hiring practices, they are remarkably commonplace. North Carolina State Athletics Director, Debbie Yow, argues "once you've been in a business relationship with an entity that provides a service and it's [sic] gone well, why would you not return to a service provider if there was a need?" (Schrotenboer & Axon, 2013, ¶41). The key qualifier in the statement is "gone well." Curiously, Yow never specifically delineates who determines that and to what ends.

Certainly, one would think that Waddell and Bass believe that their initial experience(s) with CarrSports had "gone well" because the firm helped guide institutions to choose them as athletics directors. Mackin had to have faith that CarrSports' work helping him hire a football coach had "gone well" if he rehired the firm a year later to assist in basketball. Further, administrators at Towson University, UNC-W, and UAB likely would suggest that their experiences with CarrSports had "gone well" simply because if they did not think so then it would be an admission that hiring a consultant was a waste of money. With everything "going well" it must have come as a shock to everyone involved when the consultancy reports that CarrSports would subsequently provide to each athletics director faced such public scrutiny.

Specifically, on October 2, 2012, Mike Waddell announced that Towson's Athletics Department was going to discontinue men's soccer and baseball, and add men's tennis. In a *Baltimore Sun* interview Towson said:

> Through the process, we found the program at Towson would not be financially viable for the long term. Our three main charges are to be competitive, financially stable and compliant with federal law. This is a very difficult decision and it came after examining a wide range of criteria (Markus & Karpovich, 2012, ¶5).

Waddell cited the lack of competitiveness in football and men's basketball as meaning that money needed to be funneled to those sports, that the school would save approximately $800,000 by making the cuts to be reinvested in those sports, and that:

> TU recently underwent both an internal and external review of its Title IX compliance and, as a result of both internal and external counsel, made the decision to switch to Prong 1 compliance (i.e. substantial proportionality). Achieving substantial proportionality under Prong 1 will be a multi-year effort but will ensure long-term compliance (University System of Maryland Board of Regents, 2013, p. 27).

Thus, based on CarrSports reporting, the institution made the decision to make the suggested changes.

On May 23, 2013, Athletics Director Jimmy Bass announced that UNC-W men's indoor track, men's cross country, men's and women's swimming and diving, and softball would be cut. In a report submitted to the university community, Bass suggested that the cuts were needed so that the Athletics Department could save $800,000. The plan would be to use those funds to reinvest in men's basketball. Finally, the report argued, the discontinuation of those specific sports and addition of sand volleyball would help UNC-W become Title IX compliant (UNCW, 2013).

Slightly more than a year later, on December 2, 2014, Athletic Director Brian Mackin announced that UAB would be discontinuing football, men's bowling, and men's rifle. When pressed for reasons why the UAB decided to move in that direction,

> [u]niversity officials cited the results of a review conducted by CarrSports Consulting that found that "in order to more effectively invest in the success of priority programs" the final seasons for UAB football, bowling and rifle need to be in the 2014–2015 academic year (Gray, 2014, ¶2).

President Ray Watts suggested that the bowling and rifle teams were being cut to offset Title IX issues, and assured university athletic supporters that "we are not looking to reduce the athletic budget, but instead to reallocate our resources to remaining athletic programs" (Gray, 2014, ¶13). Additionally, Mackin stepped down from his role as athletics director to become the special assistant to athletics (Solomon, 2014a).

As mentioned, in all three cases a well-organized public response against these decisions came to fruition, and in each situation the institution's stated goals were altered. The following section outlines what happened at Towson, UNC-W, and UAB with regard to the difficult contexts that each school's athletics department must operate within, and what became of the upheaval. Then the chapter discusses why—if there have been such consistent difficulties posed for schools using consulting firms—firms continue to be utilized in higher education.

## Fiscal Constraints to Winning and Gender Equity in Intercollegiate Athletics

Although there are specific differences in each school's decision making (such as which teams to cut), the reasons given for making the cuts are strikingly similar—*fiscal responsibility, competitiveness,* and *Title IX compliance.* From a public-relations perspective, these seem to be perfectly reasonable solutions to the seemingly difficult balancing act between trying to budget and attempting to have on-field success. By digging into the substance of each of the claims made by athletics and university administrators based on CarrSports advice, however, the veracity of each school's reports and claims become much less defendable. The following provides a slightly deeper look into each claim.

### Fiscal Responsibility

Currently 231 Division I institutions open their books annually for *USA Today* to report on their athletics departments' finances. In 2014–15, 151 of the institutions had budgets that were more than 50% subsidized by student tuition and fees. As mid-major institutions, it makes sense that Towson, UNC-W, and UAB would have athletics programs that students heavily subsidize because their greater stakeholder communities rarely support them (c.f. King-White et al., 2014). Indeed, Towson University (80.4% budget subsidy), UNC-W (73.21% budget subsidy), and UAB (61.47% budget subsidy) fit the profile (Berkowitz et al., 2015). Student fees at these schools that are earmarked to fund intercollegiate athletics have skyrocketed in the past 30 years[1] (c.f. King-White & Beissel, 2015; King-White, Beissel, & Newman, [forthcoming]). With the rising costs of higher education threatening to outweigh the economic benefits of attending college (Mumper & Freeman, 2005) and the associated decline in the quality of (higher) education (Giroux, 2014; Hersh & Merrow, 2005) this call to action for fiscal responsibility would seem to fit in lockstep with reform.

Indeed, it would be fiscally responsible to remove teams from the intercollegiate athletics roster as a means of "saving money." Yet, that is not what the administrators at any of the schools actually intended to do. The money Towson, UNCW, and UAB were allegedly going to save by cutting athletics programming was *never* expected to be returned to the students or to the university. More specifically, in all three cases, Mike Waddell, Jimmy Bass, and Ray Watts (UAB's president who announced the cuts after Brian Mackin stepped down) explained that they were going to reinvest those funds in other sports programming. Thus, the belief here is that by spending that money on fewer teams the surviving teams would be more successful. This belief leads to the second prong of the CarrSport consultation.

## Competitiveness

Having an athletics program that fields competitive teams year after year is an (athletics) administrator's dream scenario. Common sense dictates that successful sport programs (particularly men's basketball and football) drive up the number of donations and applications to, as well as the quality of students at, an institution (see Chapter 3 this volume); this is backed by *some* research. Harvard economist, Doug Chung, for instance has published articles in *Marketing Science* (Chung, 2013) and *Management Science* (Chung, 2015) that suggests winning in football or men's basketball does benefit successful institutions. Additionally, George Mason Sport Management Professor Robert Baker's, unpublished work[2] was included in a press release distributed by the university and claimed that George Mason realized "$677,474,659 in free media (exposure)" during its run to the Final Four in 2006 (George Mason University, 2008, ¶11).

Therefore, the logic associated with the CarrSports report is not to be "fiscally responsible" by slashing the athletics budget, but rather to (re)invest in "revenue-producing" programs at Towson University, UNC-W, and UAB—specifically men's basketball. Yet, there is no guarantee that spending hundreds of thousands or even millions of dollars on college athletics programs equates to the success needed to actualize those benefits (e.g., Getz & Siegfried, 2012) or even if the associated benefits of winning teams ever really happen at all (Peterson-Horner & Eckstein, 2015). Thus, what CarrSports advised these schools to do was—quite literally—to gamble public funds on 18-to-24-year-old men to win on the basketball court for the potential future benefit of the university—to bet on something that academic research is unsure is actualized even when there is "success." Worse, the (athletic) administrators actually attempted to do it, and partially banked on the general public's ignorance about Title IX to do so.

## Title IX Compliance

The third prong of the CarrSports strategy was to help all three institutions become Title IX compliant. As Ellen Staurowsky pointed out in Chapter 5 and, really, throughout her entire career (c.f. Staurowsky, 2000, 2003a, 2003b, 2005, 2010, 2011, 2012), however, administrators often only concern themselves with Title IX issues when it benefits their vision for how to move their athletics department forward. In all three cases the Waddell, Bass, and Watts triumvirate claimed that the teams they wanted to cut from the roster had to be the ones to eliminate to remain Title IX compliant.

The Office of Civil Rights (OCR), however, specifically states that cutting male opportunities to the direct benefit of female opportunities (in sport or otherwise) is a "disfavored practice" (Reynolds, 2003, ¶11). Yet, as Staurowsky (2011) outlines, not even coaches and administrators are aware of Title IX language, much less the general public. What happens then is that administrators claim to have their "hands tied" by the law and that they must cut the teams at that time to prevent lawsuits. This also defies logic in that the OCR openly states that they will work with noncompliant programs (again, sport or otherwise) to go through the process of becoming compliant (Reynolds, 2003).

## The Aftermath

Towson University did end up cutting men's soccer from its roster, but was able to "save" baseball with a two-year $300,000 grant from the state of Maryland, $2 million in state funds to upgrade the softball complex,[3] and a private fundraising campaign that netted the athletic department $500,000 to go towards the baseball team's operating budget (Cox & Wells, 2013). Despite public furor over how she handled the situation (Wells & Calvert, 2013), university President Maravene Loeshke remained in her position until she had to step down for health reasons and subsequently succumbed to adrenal cancer in the summer of 2015 (Kelly, 2015). Athletic Director Mike Waddell, who was making $122,000 at Towson University, took a job as senior associate athletic director at Arkansas University (Markus, 2013), then left that position a year later to become senior associate athletic director for external operations at the University of Illinois, earning $180,000 in salary.[4] The university hired Tim Leonard from Southern Methodist University as its new athletics director at a salary of $200,000. "*Bill Carr* of CarrSports Consulting, LLC assisted (Donald) Fry and the advisory committee with the university's athletic director search" (WNST Staff, 2013, ¶14; emphasis in original).

At UNC-W, Chancellor Gary Miller resigned from his position at the end of the 2014 school year, taking a $50,000 pay cut when accepting a similar position at the University of Wisconsin–Green Bay (Detweiler, 2014), and was replaced by interim President William Sederberg. In December 2014, during a press conference with Jimmy Bass, Sederberg claimed that cutting the track and field and cross-country programs was a "99 percent done deal" (Catenacci, 2014, ¶5). After an unprecedented fundraising effort that netted the athletics department $255,781.56, however, the track and field and cross-country teams were "saved" through the 2015–16 school year, and the department added sand volleyball to its roster (Detweiler, 2015). New Chancellor, Jose Sartarelli, announced through an official press release that the teams would remain on the roster long term in August 2015 (Sartarelli, 2015). Jimmy Bass remained the athletics director at a salary of $223,640—up from $220,000 at the time of his hiring.

During that same period, President Ray Watts survived votes of "no confidence" from the undergraduate, graduate, and faculty senate (Merrill, 2015), a report from OSKR's (a consultant firm that was hired by UAB but never used) Andy Schwarz (2014b) eviscerated the economic logic of the CarrSports report. Carr then released a more extensive report (Solomon, 2014b) that Schwarz (2015) *again* took apart point by point. Finally, a third firm, College Sports Solutions, found that football *could* work at UAB (Talty, 2015a). Watts—utilizing the thoroughly debunked CarrSports report in conjunction with the College Sports Solutions report—sat down with the owners that represented "forty percent of Birmingham's largest privately-held companies" (Talty, 2015b, ¶6) and convinced them donate $4 million to "save" UAB football. Plans then were unveiled to begin construction on a $12- to $15-million football operations facility (Champlin, 2015a), as well as a new track and field complex, clubhouse for baseball and softball, improvement to Wallace Gym for volleyball and basketball, a new beach volleyball stadium, a short-game golf facility, improvements for Olympic sports, and tennis facilities (Champlin, 2015a). Watts remains president, and the students voted in record numbers to accept a mandatory $50/year fee increase for athletics (Champlin, 2015c), Mackin took a job as a vice president at PNC Bank (Champlin, 2015b), and the university hired Mark Ingram from Temple University to lead university athletics moving forward.

In review, none of CarrSports recommendations to Towson, UNCW, and UAB hold up to critique and all were borderline illegal. To wit: Each school claimed that they needed to be fiscally responsible by cutting teams but were never actually cutting the athletics budget, and instead planning to reallocate funds to other teams to help them become more "competitive"—without providing any concrete numbers for what athletic success would mean. Finally, playing on the general public's ignorance about how Title IX works (e.g., Staurowsky, 2010), schools suggested that coming into compliance by making the cuts was necessary. This begs the question of why an institution ever would employ a consultancy firm that has consistently provided poorly researched reports and defended documents to guide their decision making.

## Conclusion: Consulting Firms as the Perfect Solution for the Modern University

The short answer to the question of why institutions would use firms such as those described above is that university (athletic) administrators have little to lose by hiring a consulting firm to produce these studies. All the controversy and negative publicity that these institutions received might raise questions including: How could this be? Is it not an administrator's goal to avoid these types of things at all costs? Is there no accountability?

Yet, when viewed through a critical lens, I assert that it was ultimately to the benefit of the university and its administrators to behave in the way(s) that they did. Though some might speculate as to why Waddell, Miller, and Mackin left their institutions, they landed in more prestigious and (for some) higher-paying positions (this is confirmed in Waddell's case). None of the other upper-administrators involved in these decisions were forced to resign, and many enjoy higher salaries today. CarrSports has continued to consult for Towson

University on the hiring of the new athletic director as well as helping prepare his vision going forward. Thus, although CarrSports helped create these issues in athletics at each institution, nearly every key decision maker ended up in the same place or a better one.

Further, when viewed through a more sinister lens, I argue that it is Carr-Sports apparent ineptitude that makes it so valuable to universities. At a time when administrators complain that the state has rolled-back funding to institutions of higher education (c.f. Weissman, 2015) thereby creating difficult fiscal realities[5] CarrSports' poor work actually has led to an increase in revenue at Towson University, UNC-W, and UAB. The threat of cuts for Towson baseball, UNC-W track, and UAB football produced the most successful fundraisers in the history of each institution's athletic departments.

As intercollegiate athletics become ever more privatized, administrators pushing for schools to behave with wanton disregard for student well-being (those that enter the athletics "arms race") is of no consequence. What this means is that in a perfectly neoliberal way, if a school using a poorly constructed consultation firm's report can threaten to cut teams based on the need to save money then—when push comes to shove—the only surviving programs are those that can generate revenue and donations; those that cannot do not survive (e.g., Towson Men's Soccer). Thus, what CarrSports and the (athletics) administrators at these schools have created are highly complex extortion rings, and it has "gone well" for them thus far.

## Discussion

Consultation firms help provide an institution with some protection when things go wrong with hires and decision-making mishaps generally. In athletics, why would this be considered a bad thing? Should there be restrictions on rehiring a consulting firm that serves on a search for an administrator? If the firm was good enough to help in the hiring process, should it also help that newly hired person lead the athletic program?

### NOTES

1. As of the 2016–17 academic year, Towson University charges students $846, UNC-W charges $682.55, and UAB charges $408 (annually). The UAB also receives a direct subsidy from the institution that is not reflected in the student fee schedule (Solomon, 2014b).
2. This author presumes that the work is unpublished because the evidence is spurious at best, and intellectually dishonest at worst. It served its purpose, however, because the university made it public "knowledge."
3. This project ended up costing $4 million.
4. CarrSports has consulted for both universities in the past, though no indication was made that they helped Waddell reach these positions.

5. Jordan Weissman (2015) cogently points out, however, that although this is true, so too is the fact that the number of college administrators has increased quite alarmingly, thereby leading to the allocation of funds to jobs that did not previously exist

## REFERENCES

Berkowitz, S., Schnaars, C., Upton, J., Hannan, M., Stern, M., Meyer, J., Carney, J., Glade, D., Gogola, F., Kennedy, E., Mackey III, D., Smith, J., Wagner, Z., Wardlaw, R., Yoder, J., Yu, J., Hubbard, J., Lewter, M. & Spencer, S. (2015). NCAA Finances. *USA Today*. Retrieved May 8, 2016, from: http://sports.usatoday.com/ncaa/finances/

Bonner, B. (2010). Search committee named at UNCW. *UNCW Press Release*. Retrieved May 1, 2016, from http://www.wect.com/story/13265587/search-committee-named-at-uncw?clienttype=printable

Catenacci, J. (2014). Chancellor: Athletic cuts "99 percent done deal." *PortCityDaily.com*. Retrieved June 7, 2016, from http://portcitydaily.com/2014/12/12/sports-uncw-athletic-cuts-99-percent-done-deal/

Champlin, D. (2015a). UAB presents plan for facility improvements at athletics campaign launch. *AL.com*. Retrieved June 7, 2016, from http://www.al.com/sports/index.ssf/2015/08/uab_presents_plan_for_facility.html

Champlin, D. (2015b). Former UAB athletics director Brian Mackin lands new job. *AL.com*. Retrieved June 7, 2016, from http://www.al.com/sports/index.ssf/2015/09/former_uab_athletics_director.html

Champlin, D. (2015c). UAB students vote yes to increase fees supporting return of football, rifle, and bowling. *AL.com*. Retrieved June 7, 2016, from http://www.al.com/sports/index.ssf/2015/09/uab_students_vote_football.html

Chung, D. (2013). The dynamic advertising effect of college athletics. *Marketing Science*, 32(5), 679–698.

Chung, D. (2015). How much is a win worth? An application to intercollegiate athletics. *Management Science*, published online December 9, 2015.

Cox, E. & Wells, C. (2013). Lawmakers reach compromise on Towson sports. *Baltimore Sun*. Retrieved June 7, 2016, from http://articles.baltimoresun.com/2013-04-05/news/bs-md-towson-sports-plan-20130404_1_towson-president-maravene-loeschke-towson-university-softball-field

Detweiler, E. (2014). Gary Miller named UW-GB chancellor. *StarNewsOnline*. Retrieved June 7, 2016, from http://dubhub.blogs.starnewsonline.com/21864/gary-miller-named-uw-green-bay-chancellor/

Detweiler, E. (2015). UNCW athletics: More money, same problems. *StarNewsOnline*. Retrieved June 7, 2016, from http://www.starnewsonline.com/article/20150729/ARTICLES/150729642

Dunn, A. (2010). UNCW looks for energy from new athletic director. *StarNewsOnline*. Retrieved May 1, 2016, from http://www.starnewsonline.com/article/20101019/ARTICLES/101019575/1177?p=2&tc=pg

George Mason University. (2008). The business of being Cinderella: Mason releases study on Final Four impact. *George Mason Press Release*. Retrieved May 7, 2016, from http://eagle.gmu.edu/newsroom/670/

Getz, M. & Siegfried, J. (2012). What does intercollegiate athletics do to or for colleges and universities. In L. Kahane & S. Schmanske (eds.), *The Oxford Handbook of Sports Economics* (pp. 349–372), Oxford University Press: New York.

Giroux, H. (2014). Higher education and the new brutalism. *Truthout.* Retrieved June 4, 2016, from http://www.truth-out.org/news/item/27082-henry-a-giroux-higher-education-and-the-new-brutalism

Gray, J. (2014). It's official: UAB kills football program. *Alabama.com.* Retrieved May 8, 2016, from http://www.al.com/sports/index.ssf/2014/12/uab_ends_football_program_rele.html

Hersh, R. & Merrow, J. (2005). *Declining by degrees: Higher education at risk.* Palgrave Macmillan: New York.

King-White, R. & Beissel, A. (2015). Show me the money: Student fees and the myth of athletics as a drain on the university. Delivered to the North American Society for the Sociology of Sport Conference, Santa Fe, NM.

King-White, R., Beissel, A., & Newman, J. (forthcoming). Sport in the corporate university: Towson University as neoliberal emblematic. *Sociology of Sport Journal.*

King-White, R., Newman, J., DeLuca, J., Friedman, M. & Beissel, A. (2014). Stakeholder becomings: An interdisciplinary, multi-method study of organizational politics and (de-)democratic decision making in intercollegiate financing. Delivered to the North American Society for Sport Management Conference, Pittsburgh, PA.

Kelly, J. (2015). Maravene Loeshke, former Towson U. president, dies. *Baltimore Sun.* Retrieved June 7, 2016, from http://www.baltimoresun.com/news/obituaries/bs-md-ob-maravene-loeschke-20150625-story.html

Markus, D. (2013). Mike Waddell leaving Towson for job in Arkansas athletic department. *Baltimore Sun.* Retrieved June 7, 2016, from http://articles.baltimoresun.com/2013-05-20/news/bal-mike-waddell-leaving-towson-for-job-in-arkansas-athletic-department-20130520_1_mike-waddell-tiger-arena-jeff-long

Markus, D. & Karpovich, T. (2012). Towson athletic department recommends cutting baseball and men's soccer. *Baltimore Sun.* Retrieved April 17, 2016, from http://articles.baltimoresun.com/2012-10-02/news/bal-towson-athletic-department-recommends-cutting-baseball-and-mens-soccer-20121002_1_mike-waddell-tennis-team-roster-spots

McCarthy, M. (2006). Big names is his game: Headhunter bags coaches. *USA Today.* Retrieved April 17, 2016, from http://usatoday30.usatoday.com/sports/college/football/2006–12–12-focus-neinas_x.htm

Merrill, A. (2015). Faculty senate agrees: No confidence in Watts. *KScope.* Retrieved June 7, 2016, from http://www.uab.edu/studentmedia/kaleidoscope/news/55-faculty-senate-agrees-no-confidence-in-watts

Mull, B. (2010). UNCW names committee, hires firm to search for new AD. *StarNews-Online.* Retrieved May 1, 2016, from http://www.starnewsonline.com/article/20101004/ARTICLES/101009839

Mumper, M. & Freeman, M. (2005). The causes and consequences of public college tuition inflation. In J.C. Smart (ed.), *Higher Education: Handbook of Theory and Research* (pp. 307–361), Springer Press: Great Britain.

Peterson-Horner, E. & Eckstein, R. (2015). Challenging the "Flutie Factor": Intercollegiate sports, undergraduate enrollments, and the neoliberal university. *Humanity & Society,* *39*(1), 64–85.

Reynolds, G. (2003). Further clarification of the intercollegiate athletics policy guidance regarding Title IX compliance. *Office of Civil Rights.* Retrieved June 7, 2016, from http://www2.ed.gov/about/offices/list/ocr/title9guidanceFinal.html

Sartarelli, J. (2015). UNCW statement regarding the track and field program. *UNCW Press Release.* Retrieved June 7, 2016, from http://uncw.edu/news/2015/08/uncw-statement-regarding-the-track-and-field-program.html

Schrotenboer, B. (2013). Chuck Neinas stays in executive search game at 81. *USA Today*. Retrieved April 17, 2016, from http://www.usatoday.com/story/sports/2013/06/06/search-firms-san-diego-state-colorado-chuck-neinas/2398733/

Schrotenboer, B., & Axon, R. (2013). Search firms come under fire after Rutgers flap. *USA Today*. Retrieved April 17, 2016, from http://www.usatoday.com/story/sports/ncaaf/2013/06/06/parker-executive-search-ncaa-rutgers/2398487/

Schwarz, A. (2014a). How athletic departments (and the media) fudge the cost of scholarships. *Deadspin*. Retrieved May 1, 2016, from http://regressing.deadspin.com/how-athletic-departments-and-the-media-fudge-the-cost-1570827027

Schwarz, A. (2014b). Screw the math: UAB can afford football, so why is it choosing otherwise? *Vice Sports*. Retrieved June 7, 2016, from https://sports.vice.com/en_us/article/screw-the-math-uab-can-afford-football-so-why-is-it-choosing-otherwise

Schwarz, A. (2015). UAB's tangled web of numbers don't add up. *Vice Sports*. Retrieved June 7, 2016, from https://sports.vice.com/en_us/article/uabs-tangled-web-of-numbers-doesnt-add-up

Smith, B. (2012). Hired guns: How search firms are changing the business of college coaching. *Forbes.com*. Retrieved April 18, 2016, from http://www.forbes.com/sites/chrissmith/2012/03/30/hired-guns-how-search-firms-are-changing-the-business-of-college-coaching/#3a8988936fdf

Solomon, J. (2012). Meet the outsider who helped shape UAB's future. *The Birmingham News*. Retrieved May 3, 2016, from http://www.al.com/sports/index.ssf/2012/05/meet_the_outsider_who_helped_s.html

Solomon, J. (2014a). The Day UAB football died a painful death. *CBSSports.com*. Retrieved May 8, 2016, from http://www.cbssports.com/college-football/news/the-day-uab-football-died-a-painful-death/

Solomon, J. (2014b). Death of UAB football: Anger remains, but study banks on healing. *CBSSports.com*. Retrieved June 7, 2016, from http://www.cbssports.com/college-football/news/death-of-uab-football-anger-remains-but-study-banks-on-healing/

Staurowsky, E. J. (2000, Spring). Beyond Title IX and separate but equal: Boys and girls playing & playing together. *PSAHPERD Journal*, *70* (1), 6–7.

Staurowsky, E. J. (2003a). Title IX and college sport: The long painful path to compliance and reform. *Marquette Sports Law Review 14* (3), 95–121.

Staurowsky, E.J. (2003b). Title IX in its third decade: The Commission on Opportunity in Athletics. *Entertainment and Sports Law Journal* 2(3), 70–93.

Staurowsky, E. J. (2005). Title IX manifesto: Reflections on the Commission on Opportunity in Athletics. In Simon, R. (ed.)., *Sporting equality: Title IX thirty years later* (pp. 165–182). New Brunswick, NJ: Transaction Press.

Staurowsky, E. J. (2010). Title IX literacy: What every citizen should know about Title IX, gender equity, and college sport. For inclusion in Lampman, B. (ed.). *Learning culture through sport: Exploring the role of sport in society* (2nd ed.) (pp. 107–123). Lanham, MD: Rowman & Littlefield.

Staurowsky, E. J. (2011). Title IX literacy: What coaches don't know and need to find out. *Journal of Intercollegiate Sport, 4*, 190–209.

Staurowsky, E. J. (2012). "A radical proposal": Title IX has no role in college pay for play. *Marquette Sport Law Review*, 22 (2), 557–595.

Talty, J. (2015a). UAB report reveals costs to reinstate football; decision now rests with Ray Watts. *AL.Com*. Retrieved June 7, 2016, from http://www.al.com/sports/index.ssf/2015/05/uab_report_reveals_how_much_it.html

Talty, J. (2015b). How a group of businessmen saved UAB football. *AL.com*. Retrieved June 7, 2016, from http://www.al.com/sports/index.ssf/2015/06/how_a_group_of_birmingham_powe.html

UAB Athletics. (2011). Garrick McGee introduced as head football coach. Retrieved May 8, 2016, from http://www.uabsports.com/sports/m-footbl/spec-rel/120511aac.html

UNCW. (2013). Intercollegiate athletic review committee report, p. 1–23.

University System of Maryland Board of Regents. (2013). Report on intercollegiate athletics FY–2013, p. 1–34.

Weissman, J. (2015). The *New York Times* offers one of the worst explanations you'll read of why college is so expensive. *Slate.com*. Retrieved May 23, 2016, from http://www.slate.com/blogs/moneybox/2015/04/06/why_is_college_so_expensive_the_new_york_times_offers_an_awful_explanation.html

Wells, C. & Calvert, S. (2013). Ire grows after Towson president cuts teams. *Baltimore Sun*. Retrieved June 7, 2016, from http://articles.baltimoresun.com/2013-03-24/news/bs-md-towson-sports-protest-20130323_1_loeschke-president-maravene-s-mike-gottlieb

WNST Staff. (2013). Towson names Leonard new athletic director. Retrieved May 3, 2016, from http://wnst.net/towson-tigers/towson-names-new-ad-to-lead-tigers-program/

# ACKNOWLEDGMENTS

I would like to thank all of my authors and my editor for their hard work in putting this volume together. In addition, I thank Dave Andrews for taking me on as a student and not giving up even if it would have been easy, Michael Silk for those early years at Maryland, and Stephen Mosher and Ellen Staurowsky for getting me to engage in sport critically at Ithaca College as an undergraduate. Josh Newman deserves special mention for serving as a guiding beacon, and Adam Beissel for the hours of phone conversations about this project and other things. I must also make space to thank Michael Giardina for all the unsolicited help and guidance he has offered over the past 15 years—from choice of graduate school, to serving on my dissertation committee, to how to submit a book manuscript proposal, to serving as an editorial guide on this project. You never had to do any of that, but you did, and I will not soon forget it.

I also thank my friends Frank, Richard, Matt, Mike, Ed, Ben, Todd, and Tejas for always being there. Finally, I must thank my parents, Ed and Cindy White; my in-laws, Bill and Kathy King; my brothers and sisters (both immediate and in the extended form) Jacquelyn, Steve, Megan, Michael, Kristin, Jessie, Dustin, Morgan, Michael, Lauren, Kathryn, Bridget, Brian, and Katie; and my nieces and nephews, Emma, Marcus, Charlotte, and Charlie. I hope you like the project.

# NOTES ON CONTRIBUTORS

**Lauren C. Anderson** is a PhD candidate in the school of communication at Florida State University. Her research interests are critical/cultural studies, feminist theory, sports communication, gender-based violence, media representations of gender and race, media literacy, and qualitative methods.

**Adam Beissel** is a graduate of Towson University earning a bachelor of science in sport management and a master of business administration (with a sport-management concentration. After completing his master's work at Towson, Beissel pursued his PhD in the School of Physical Education, Sport, and Exercise Science at the University of Otago in Dunedin, New Zealand. Recently completing his PhD dissertation: *Sons of Samoa—The Corporeal Economy of Samoan Football*, Adam is currently an assistant professor of Sport Management at the University of Miami (Ohio).

**Jacob J. Bustad** is an assistant professor in the Department of Kinesiology, Sport Management Program at Towson University. He is interested in the sociocultural study of sport and physical activity, and teaches and researches physical cultural studies, the sociology of sport, globalization and sport, and sport history. Dr. Bustad's primary research examines the intersections of contemporary urban governance and public-recreation policy and planning, and is concerned with the equitable provision of physical activity in urban environments.

**Jaime DeLuca** is an assistant professor of Sport Management at Towson University. She earned a PhD from the University of Maryland in physical cultural studies, a MA from the University of Connecticut in sport management and the sociology of sport, and a BS from the Pennsylvania State University in business administration. Dr. DeLuca's research and teaching interests focus on both the management and socio-cultural aspects of sport. She has recently published work in the *Journal of Sport, Exercise & Health*, and the *Journal of Sport & Social Issues*.

**Michael D. Giardina** is an associate professor of media, politics, and cultural studies in the Department of Sport Management at Florida State University. He is the author or editor of 17 books, including most notably *Sport, Spectacle, and*

*NASCAR Nation: Consumption and the Cultural Politics of Neoliberalism* (with Joshua Newman; PalgraveMacmillan, 2011), which received the 2012 Outstanding Book Award from the North American Society for the Sociology of Sport (NASSS) and was named to the 2012 *CHOICE* "Outstanding Academic Titles" list; *Sporting Pedagogies: Performing Culture & Identity in the Global Arena* (Peter Lang, 2005), which received the 2006 NASSS Outstanding Book Award; and *Qualitative Inquiry—Past, Present, & Future: A Critical Reader* (with Norman K. Denzin; Left Coast Press, 2015). He is the editor of the *Sociology of Sport Journal* and Special Issue Editor of *Cultural Studies–Critical Methodologies.*

**Henry Giroux** is known as the father of American critical pedagogy, and his research focuses on a variety of areas including cultural studies, youth, critical pedagogy, democratic theory, public education, communication theory, social theory, and the politics of higher education. He is the Global Television Network Chair in Communications at McMaster University.

**Susan Searls Giroux** is an associate professor of English and Cultural Studies at McMaster University in Hamilton, Ontario. She has published numerous articles on U.S. racial politics, the persistence of racism in the post–civil rights era, the history and politics of the university, and anti-racist pedagogy, which have appeared in *Third Text, Social Identities, The CLR James Journal, JAC, Works and Days, Cultural Critique, College Literature,* and *Tikkun.*

**Matthew G. Hawzen** is a first-year doctoral student in the Department of Sport Management, from Hillsborough, New Jersey. He is advised by Dr. Joshua Newman. Mr. Hawzen earned a BS in sport management from Towson University, and an MS in kinesiology and health studies from Queens University. His research interests include political economy, identity politics, physical culture, and the body.

**Ryan King-White** is an associate professor in the Kinesiology Department at Towson University. He received his PhD from the University of Maryland, and has conducted research on topics including youth sport, professional sport fan communities, obesity and health discourse, and ethnographic methods. Dr. King-White's research has appeared in, among other venues, the *Sociology of Sport Journal; Review of Education, Pedagogy, and Cultural Studies; Sport, Education, & Society;* and the *Routledge Handbook of Physical Cultural Studies.*

**Callie Batts Maddox** is an assistant professor in the Department of Kinesiology and Health at the University of Miami (Ohio). Her current research centers on the connections between the active body, operations of power, and gender. Specifically, she is conducting ethnographic work on the lived experiences of female baseball players from both a local and global perspective. Participation in a traditionally masculine sport not only can disrupt normative gender binaries, but it also can create space for personal and community empowerment.

Dr. Maddox is part of a collaborative research project investigating the cultural construction of "Momthletes" and "Iron Dads"—terms used to describe the corporeal aspirations of new parents as they navigate the triad of professional responsibilities, parenthood, and fitness/bodywork. She also is completing work on a research article exploring how the mediated narrative of Mary Kom—an Olympic boxer from India—represents an embodied nationalism that offers an intensely gendered, partial, and conflicted vision of the Indian nation.

**Ronald L. Mower** is an assistant professor in the Department of Kinesiology, Sport Studies, and Physical Education at The College at Brockport, SUNY. Professor Mower teaches courses in the sociology and history of sport, as well as qualitative research methods. Broadly defined, his research interests include qualitative examinations of physical culture and the (in)active body, social power and inequality, and disparities within health, physical activity, and sport.

**Joshua I. Newman** is an associate professor of media, politics, and cultural studies in the Department of Sport Management at Florida State University. Dr. Newman's research and teaching draw upon critical theory and co-present techniques to interrogate the cultural and political economies of sport and the active body. In addition to having published numerous journal articles and book chapters on issues pertaining to sport and body cultures of the U.S. South, Dr. Newman is the author of two books, *Embodying Dixie: Studies in the Body Pedagogics of Southern Whiteness* (Common Ground, 2010) and *Sport, Spectacle, and NASCAR Nation: Consumption and the Cultural Politics of Neoliberalism* (with Michael D. Giardina, Palgrave, 2011).

**Oliver Rick** is an accomplished researcher and assistant professor at Springfield College. He graduated from the University of Maryland with a PhD in physical cultural studies, and has gone on to develop research into global sport media and policy, and a number of other topics. Dr. Rick's research record includes "David's Too Posh: Kicking Beckham's Mercenary Celebrityhood Around the Globe" published in *Fallen Sports Heroes, Media, and Celebrity Culture*, and "Bound to the Nation: Pacific Islands Rugby and the IRB's New 'One Country for Life' Eligibility Rules," published in *Sport in Society: Cultures, Commerce, Media, Politics*.

**Crystal Southall** is currently an assistant professor of exercise and sport science (ESS) at Western State Colorado University (Western) in Gunnison, Colorado, where she teaches numerous ESS classes, primarily within the sport and fitness management emphasis. Dr. Southall earned a BA in history from the University of Colorado at Boulder, a MS in human movement science with an emphasis on sport and leisure commerce from the University of Memphis, and a PhD in exercise and sport science with an emphasis on sport administration from the University of Northern Colorado. Prior to her time at Western, Dr. Southall taught at the University of Southern Maine (Portland, ME) and Nebraska

Wesleyan University (Lincoln, NE). Her research focuses primarily on the socio-cultural aspects of sport, particularly within college sport.

**Richard M. Southall** teaches and researches in the areas of sport ethics, college sport, and research methods. His research has led to publications in journals such as the *Journal of Sport and Social Issues, Journal of Sport Management, Sport Marketing Quarterly, Ethnic and Racial Studies,* and the *Journal of Issues in Intercollegiate Athletics.* Dr. Southall is co-author of two sport-management textbooks: *Introduction to Sport Management: Theory and Practice,* and *Sport Facility Management: Organizing Events and Mitigating Risks* (2nd ed.). Additionally, Dr. Southall has made more than 100 national and international research presentations.

**Ellen J. Staurowsky** is a professor in the Department of Sport Management at Drexel University. Her work—which draws upon socio-historical, legal, political, gender, and racial frameworks—focuses on social justice issues in sport, which include college athlete advocacy and rights, gender equity and Title IX, pay equity and equal employment opportunity, the exploitation of athletes, representation of women in sport media, the misappropriation of American Indian imagery in sport (mascot "origin" stories, use and misuse of survey research in reinforcing support for American Indian sport imagery, most notably the *Sports Illustrated* poll and the Annenberg Survey; racial implications of resistance to change among supporters and obstacles to change).

**Neal C. Ternes** is a first-year doctoral student in the department of sport management, from Overland Park, Kansas. Dr. Michael Giardina serves as Mr. Ternes' advisor at Florida State University. Mr. Ternes earned a BS in health and sport studies/journalism and mass communication from the University of Iowa, and a MS in sport management from Florida State University. His research interests include sport and media, and college sports.

# INDEX